A practical guide to
A level So[ciology]

J.K.Lane

Nelson

Specimen A level examination questions in Chapter 1 are
reproduced by permission of the Associated Examining Board.
Answers and hints on answers are the sole responsibility of the
author and have not been provided or approved by the Board.

Thomas Nelson and Sons Ltd
Nelson House   Mayfield Road
Walton-on-Thames   Surrey
KT12 5PL   UK

51 York Place
Edinburgh
EH1 3JD   UK

Thomas Nelson (Hong Kong) Ltd
Toppan Building 10/F
22A Westlands Road
Quarry Bay   Hong Kong

Thomas Nelson Australia
102 Dodds Street
South Melbourne
Victoria 3205   Australia

Nelson Canada
1120 Birchmount Road
Scarborough   Ontario
M1K 5G4   Canada

© J K Lane 1985

First published by Thomas Nelson and Sons Ltd 1985

ISBN 0-17-448118-7
NPN 9 8

Printed in Hong Kong.

Contents

Foreword

This book is intended for use alongside an A level sociology textbook. Its main purpose is to help students write sociology more effectively, rather than to provide comprehensive coverage of topics in sociology. Each chapter begins with a general introductory section, organised around a particular theme. This is followed by three or four essays on more specific issues. After each essay there is a brief commentary in which points raised in the essay are developed further.

The general introductory sections handle themes in sociology that cut across substantive areas. They are dealt with in relation to particular issues, but are applicable across the syllabus. Here you will find an explanation of the problem of methodology in sociology (Chapters 1 and 2), of perspectives in sociology (Chapters 4, 6, 7, 8, 9 and 11), and of the ideas of the founders of the subject (Chapters 5 and 10).

In the second part of each chapter, each essay is a self-contained argument that expounds a possible point of view on an issue in sociology. Each could form the basis of a question in an A level examination. The main role of the commentaries is to pursue ideas raised in the essay in greater detail through textual analysis of primary sources in sociology.

Introduction

How to survive a sociology examination

Sociology is a subject that is changing rapidly. It is a discipline in which evidence is normally open to more than one interpretation and questions can be defined in a variety of ways, and this has stimulated the development of different perspectives. In terms of these perspectives the usefulness of any method of gathering data and the meaning of even the most basic concepts are now problematic.

Today the trend in sociology examinations is to require students to confront these ambiguities. In practice this means that increasingly one is being called upon not to comprehend and communicate an agreed body of knowledge but to analyse critically the issues that divide modern sociologists. No longer is it sufficient to be able to describe what sociologists think about a particular facet of life; you have to 'examine', 'discuss', 'explain' how and why they disagree.

This introduction contains practical advice and hints to help you write essays on issues in modern sociology. However, before any specific advice is given, there is a general point you should be aware of. The essays in this book are not a recipe for avoiding the need to think for yourself. In every case they are but *one* approach to the question and not *the* approach. What this means is that if you try to learn these essays off by heart and reproduce them in an examination as a substitute for doing the course work you will not benefit from the book. This is not just because they are a little too long for you to reproduce them under examination conditions and, in most cases, a little too complex to be easily paraphrased but because a memorised synthesis borrowed from somebody else usually fails to carry that sense of authenticity characteristic of the best students' work and, if only half remembered, may be just a garbled mess. Try to use this book intelligently, as an accompaniment to your textbook, and not as a substitute for your own study. Do not regard it as a solution to the problem of writing essays but as a solution to the problem of *how* to write essays. There is a subtle difference.

When you begin to prepare for an examination the first thing to be clear about is what you are being examined on. If you believe that sociology is the study of people, of groups, of society – then think again! At A level and beyond, sociology is not about people but about ideas, and you will be examined on your ability to understand and communicate ideas. This is why the most useful examination you have previously taken is English language. This is not because you will be marked on your English but because it is only if you are competent in English that you will be able to communicate your sociological knowledge effectively.

There are three things you must do if you are to pass a sociology examination – or any other examination for that matter. They are summarised below.

Learn

● However fluent you are in the English language and however talented you may be you cannot write a sociology answer unless you know some sociology. A common failing of sociology students is that all or part of what they write is written from a 'common sense' point of view. While it is very useful to illustrate your essays with examples from newspapers, literature, current affairs programmes and so forth they cannot provide the basis of an answer.

● Learning means first of all acquiring the language of sociology. Sociological concepts are not just jargon; they have a precise meaning (sometimes more than one) and will help you answer a question more effectively. Learning also means knowing something about the empirical basis of sociology, that is, about the research that contributes to sociological understanding. This is not just a matter of name dropping.

Finally, you should know the basic ideas of different perspectives and the standard criticisms sufficiently well to put them together in an argument.

Understand

● If you are articulate and if you have learned the material on the topics you have covered, you still cannot answer the question unless you understand what it means. If you do not know what it means you have no way of deciding what is relevant.

Another common failing of sociology students is that they write on the topic and not on the question. Sometimes part of what they write will be relevant because in writing on the topic they will unwittingly stumble on points of significance. However, if they cannot show why those points are significant and show the relationship between the question that is asked and the material they present their answer is at best marginally relevant and will be marked down as a consequence.

● Understanding a question involves first of all reading it carefully. This means that you should study every word. You should pay particular attention to any technical terms and be prepared to define them. If the title includes a statement which is itself problematic you must be able to explain why. Finally, if after reading the question you still have no clear idea as to what it means you are best advised to tackle a different one. Although you may not know your second choice topic as well, if you understand the question you are at least assured that what little you know is relevant.

Communicate

● A shapeless mass of unconnected ideas will not get high marks. A good answer must be logically constructed; it is not a random collection of the first throughts that come into your head. This means that you should try to organise your thoughts and impose a synthesis upon the material you include. Remember, if your answer does not make sense it will not deserve any marks. You will be assessed on what you write, not on what you meant to write.

● Communicating in a written essay means that your answer should be internally consistent. This will mean spending a few minutes working out a plan. If your essay is soundly planned, it will have a beginning, a middle and an end. An introduction and conclusion are not luxuries that you can dispense with, but integral parts of your answer.

The general formula then is:

LEARNING + UNDERSTANDING + COMMUNICATION = ANSWER

However, you may still feel unsure of yourself when it comes to applying this advice. If this is so, it will help you to look more closely at how to construct an answer.

The first thing to do, having already paid due attention to examination rules and directions to candidates, is to read the questions that you are faced with. In most examinations there is a choice and you will therefore need to decide which question to begin with. Proceed by elimination and begin by ruling out those questions which deal with topics or issues that you have no sociological knowledge of. This should leave you with a range of 'possibles' to study more carefully.

Do not just scan your eyes across the examination paper and pretend to yourself that you have read it thoroughly. Much will depend upon making the right choices and you can easily overlook a 'possible' if it is worded in an unfamiliar way. It is also very easy to see what you want to in a question rather than what is actually there. For example, 'account for' means *explain* and if you merely describe you do not answer the whole, or even the main part, of the question. Similarly, if the question says, for example, 'examine the contribution of' or 'evaluate recent assertions' it is not sufficient merely to describe the views mentioned. You also have to assess their validity. Whatever strategy is called for, and partly this is a matter of personal judgement, some description of studies, opinions, perspectives and methods may be necessary. However, descriptive material should never be introduced as mere padding. Where you feel it is appropriate to describe make sure you explain the significance of what you include.

Another favourite ploy of examiners is to place certain limits around a question. For example, you may be required to illustrate or explain your answer by reference to one particular area or period of time. If that is what the question says then that is what the question means and do not try to convince yourself that it says something different. If you ignore the limits of the question then part of what you write is not relevant and part of your time and effort is wasted.

Remember that all your essays should be logically divided into paragraphs. Each paragraph should make a separate point and you will need to organise your sentence structure to convey that point to the reader. However, when you first read a question it may well prompt all sorts of ideas and they can come to you in any order. So, when you decide to answer a given question in the examination, jot down your ideas as they occur to you in the first few minutes and go on to sort them out. You are then in a position to write your introduction.

The first thing to be clear about is that your introduction should be concise. If it rambles across a number of paragraphs you will find that you spend too much time explaining what the question means and leave yourself too little time to answer it.

The second thing is that you should never simply write the question out as a statement in your first sentence. What you could do instead is take key concepts from the question and define what they mean, or you could develop theoretical issues that the question raises, or you could put the question in historical context, or you could explain its empirical meaning. All the essays in this book begin in the first paragraph by doing one or more of the above.

The approaches mentioned above serve two main purposes. Firstly, you will gain marks by demonstrating that you know what the question means. For example, it will not be assumed that you know what social mobility is (Question 18), nor that you understand the role of the organic analogy in the development of the functionalist perspective (Question 39), nor that you are aware that equality was one of the goals of the French and Russian revolutions (Question 16), nor even that you know the difference between a face-to-face interview and a postal questionnaire (Question 4). By making points like these clearly and coherently in your opening paragraph you demonstrate that you know what it is that the question refers to.

Secondly, you establish on paper criteria of relevance. In other words, you have put a boundary around the question. A sound introduction will not only tell an examiner what you understand by the question, it will also have helped you clarify it to yourself and will have provided you with a foundation upon which to build.

In the middle of the essay, your task is to present evidence and argument that bear upon the issue you have defined in your introduction. This is the main body of the essay, and it is here that you need to be able to demonstrate skills of sociological analysis. Although you are not expected to cover the issue comprehensively, what is important is that you are able to show familiarity with *some* relevant material and that you understand its empirical and theoretical implications.

Your final, concluding paragraph should be balanced and sociological. In practice, what this means is that in your conclusion you should never write 'I think . . .' or 'My opinion is . . .'. This is not because you have not been thinking, nor because you do not have opinions, but because these expressions are unsociological. They make it appear that your case rests upon personal feelings, whereas a sociological conclusion would rest upon the strength of the evidence and the validity of the arguments put forward by sociologists and explained by you in the main body of your essay. You will find in every case that it is just such a technical evaluation that is given in the final paragraph of the essays in this volume.

However, there are various strategies that you can employ. One way of concluding an essay is to come down on one side of a controversy within sociology. Examples of this are supplied by the conclusions to Questions 10, 15 and 19 which, to some extent or other, all deal with the relative merits of conflict and consensus approaches. Another way is to explain the limitations of a sociological perspective (Questions 28 and 29) or a sociological method (Questions 4 and 5). If you are dealing with a question of social causation you might well make a general statement about the significance of the factors you have considered (Questions 11 and 18). A more daring conclusion is one which shows how ideology penetrates sociology itself (Questions 27 and 31).

Whatever strategy you adopt, one final rule should always be observed. Your conclusion should be consistent with the rest of your answer. This means that sometimes you may be led to reject a view which is given in the title of the question. For example, examiners often ask you to discuss a statement. It is perfectly legitimate for your discussion to lead to a conclusion in which that initial statement is rejected.

Finally, and very importantly, remember to plan your time intelligently so that you can answer each question reasonably. Some teachers and examiners recommend that you allocate yourself strict periods of time for your essays and proceed to the next question when that time is up. If you have not quite finished, you may be able to return to it later in the examination, however briefly. It is very tempting to spend a disproportionately long amount of time perfecting one answer. But remember, even if that essay receives very high marks you will get no marks at all for a question that you do not begin to answer.

Chapter 1

Stimulus questions on methodology

In the introduction it was pointed out that sociology is changing rapidly and that examinations in the subject are changing too. One development in the way students are examined at A level is the introduction of questions based on stimulus material.

When attempting stimulus questions there are three basic rules that you should follow:

1 Study the stimulus material carefully. Although stimulus questions are not normally comprehension tests and you should not expect to find 'the answers' in the material that is given it is there to guide you. Furthermore the material is part of the question and if you ignore it you are ignoring the context that the examiner has given to the issues you are required to explain or discuss. Checking over the information given therefore serves two purposes. The positive benefits are that it may either prompt further ideas that will help answer the questions that follow or reveal information of direct use to your answer. It is also a precaution against overlooking something important in the stimulus material or misinterpreting the question.
2 Give separate answers to all parts of the question and clearly indicate which part it is you are answering. If you write a connected account and it is not clear which part of your script refers to which part of the question you will lose marks. If you give, in your answer to one part of the question, information that is not required you will gain no extra marks. If you do not answer all parts of the question you will not be marked out of the maximum possible marks.
3 Divide the time available to you roughly in line with the marks available for each part of the question. Bear in mind that from an examinations point of view it is not your opinion about the relative importance of the different parts of a question that counts — it is the examiner's!

To apply these rules to questions on methodology, you need first to understand what the term methodology refers to. A common error of students is that they confuse methodology with methods.

Methods are simply techniques of data collection. However, methodology is not so much concerned with the techniques themselves as with the relationship between evidence and explanation in sociology. Methodology, in this sense, raises more abstract (even philosophical) questions to do with the logical structure of sociological knowledge. The most important practical implication of this is that it is insufficient merely to learn what the different methods used by sociologists are and what advantages and disadvantages they have. It is necessary, in addition, to understand the general issues raised by the use of empirical data in constructing and testing sociological theories. One way of introducing these issues is to pose the question, 'What do sociologists understand by a sociological explanation?'

As with so many other problems in sociology this is a question that is answered in more than one way but the most important differences stem from the distinction that is commonly made between positivist and interpretive (sometimes called phenomenological) sociology. This distinction is useful because it is related to practical differences in the way sociologists tackle the task of doing sociological research; differences that amount to two quite separate views as to the aims and purposes of sociology itself. These differences, outlined in a simplified fashion below, will provide you with the landmarks you need in order to think about issues in methodology in a constructive way.

Positivism and phenomenology

The most crucial fact about positivism is its emphasis upon the unity of the sciences. In terms of this assumption it is commonly argued that the relatively 'young' social sciences should seek to follow the path taken by the more 'mature', and successful, natural sciences. This, it is said, will enable sociologists to discover the laws that govern social phenomena in much the same way as the natural sciences have uncovered laws of nature. Although laws of social evolution may never be as precise as natural laws this is usually regarded as due to secondary factors like the practical difficulties involved in studying people or the greater complexity of social reality. The crucial point for positivists is that factors like this are subordinate to the fundamental principles of scientific knowledge which are thought to be the same everywhere.

In contrast interpretive sociologists emphasise the difference between nature and culture. Their point is that natural phenomena only obey laws because in the natural world objects and events are determined by external causes. However, human beings act from motives and consciously seek to realise some end or value through their actions. If one wishes to explain action one must therefore in addition to taking account of external factors also seek to understand its inner meaning. For interpretive sociologists this is seen to impose fundamentally different obligations on the social scientist and means that for them explanations in sociology have a different character to explanations of natural phenomena.

The difference in attitude between positivist and interpretive sociologists over what a sociological explanation involves is not a new development and is best illustrated by comparing the views of classical sociologists. For example, Emile Durkheim believed that social facts were just as 'real' and objective as natural phenomena. This led him to argue that the sociologist should take the same attitude towards society that the natural scientist takes towards the material world. He expressed this opinion in his recommendation to sociologists that they 'consider social facts as things'. This is clearly a positivist point of view. However, Max Weber, who defined sociology as a discipline that 'attempts the interpretive understanding of social action', would have disagreed with Durkheim. He regarded social facts as ways of acting to which individuals attach a subjective meaning. This led him to argue that the sociologist should not just observe action from the outside (in terms of its consequences or effects) but also try to understand the motives of the people involved. This is an interpretive point of view. It means taking a very different approach from the natural scientist because in the study of nature the question of meaning never arises.

Implications for research: positivism

As well as the attitudes themselves it is important to understand their implications for research. This is because it is not much use knowing the difference between positivist and interpretive sociology if you are unable to use that knowledge to help you make sense of sociological material.

Positivists emphasise the importance of quantitative data; that is information on the extent of a social characteristic and its association with other variables. They point out that progress in the natural sciences has been largely due to the techniques of observation, classification and measurement that natural scientists have developed. In the natural sciences these techniques are judged by their reliability. This refers to whether an investigation can be repeated by others under controlled conditions and using the same methods to obtain identical results. If this is the case and the results are confirmed then the information yielded by the investigation can be (provisionally) regarded as fact.

Getting at 'the facts' is what many positivists regard as important. Although sociology may not have such sophisticated techniques at its disposal as the natural sciences positivists believe that in order to make progress sociologists must develop ways of measuring social behaviour. In particular positivists favour social surveys. They argue that by taking more care over sampling procedures, the wording of questionnaires, the conduct of interviews and so on it will be possible to improve the reliability of sociological knowledge. With more data, and more reliable data, at their disposal positivists believe that sociologists will be able to make more precise generalisations, so enabling them to discover the causes of social behaviour and make predictions about future trends.

Implications for research: phenomenology

Although interpretive sociologists agree with positivists in thinking of sociology as an empirical discipline they tackle the problem of doing sociological research in a very different way. Their basic point is that no hard and fast distinction can be made between facts and values when it comes to studying social action. The reason is that individuals are conscious of their behaviour (and that of others) and they act in terms of the significance they attribute to the events around them. It is thus the beliefs of members of society about what is worthwhile and how to achieve it that are the most important facts for the sociologist. However, this implies that the study of social phenomena must begin with the subjective 'states of mind' of social actors. Rather than impose an external meaning upon action as positivists do in their attempts to define and measure social facts objectively, interpretive sociologists argue that the sociologist should start with the meaning an action already has for the social actors involved.

In practice this leads interpretive sociologists to see the issue as one of the validity of data. For them, validity refers to the degree to which an account is true to the essential characteristics of the reality under investigation. However, since the characteristics of social reality depend upon the meaningful actions of its members the validity of an account will depend upon the sociologist being able to understand their subjective point of view. To this end the preconceived categories of positivist sociology are regarded as an obstacle and not an aid to research. They inevitably distort social behaviour because in the attempt to measure social facts objectively positivism pre-empts the point of view of members of society and pictures them as passively responding to external forces rather than actively creating their own social world.

In the last analysis what the interpretive sociologists are saying is that values are the underlying facts upon which social life depends and however adept sociologists become at measuring social facts this does not help explain their meaning. They argue that real progress in sociology depends upon the sociologist being able to change points of view so as to interpret social events in the same way as members of society make sense of them. In particular interpretive sociologists emphasise the usefulness of qualitative methods such as informal interviews and participant observation studies since these methods help break down the barriers between sociologists and those they study. Although positivists criticise such methods for their lack of reliability interpretive sociologists claim that because they help sociologists understand the points of view of members of society they more than make up for this in validity.

As has already been indicated the above account of the differences between positivist and interpretive methodology is simplified. In reality there are further differences between the two approaches as well as variations within each perspective. However, if you start with a clear idea of the difference between objectivity and values, the reliability and validity of data, quantitative and qualitative methods, and positivist and interpretive sociology, this will provide you with a framework for tackling questions on methodology. This is illustrated by the answers to the questions that follow.

Question 1
Participant observation: advantages and disadvantages

Method of study

The main method adopted for the research on which this study is based was participant observation. Participant observation, because it deposits one inside the culture of the group studied and forces on one the role of involved actor and participant, affords the academic researcher a unique opportunity of getting the right leads and following through situations whereby he can replace superficial impressions with more accurate insights. By combining his outsider's perception with an insider's view of the way of life under consideration, the researcher can thus get behind the statistical shapes and patterns and explore at first hand the wide variety of adaptive responses he encounters, studying them from the value positon of the people themselves, in their own terms and on their own ground. All the time he does this through prolonged, intensive direct exposure to actual life-conditions over a relatively long period of time. Not only can the findings of this intensive approach supplement and add significance to data gathered by more quantitative techniques, they can generate fruitful hypotheses which quantitative research can later refine and test.

(Source: K. Pryce, *Endless Pressure*, Penguin 1979)

(a) What are the 'quantitative techniques' which the author of the above passage states are different from participant observation? (5 marks)

(b) With reference to one particular area of social life, examine the distinctive contribution afforded by participant observation as a research method. (10 marks)

(c) With reference to the same area of social life, discuss the limitations of participant observation as a research method. (10 marks)

(*AEB* specimen)

(a) Quantitative techniques are techniques used to measure the distribution and extent of a social characteristic. They are also used to measure the strength of an association between two variables, such as the relationship between social class and educational achievement. They provide numerical data, usually in the form of percentages, proportions, averages or correlations, and represent a statistical approach to sociological research. The source of the data is mainly official statistics or social surveys by sociologists, particularly those involving formal interviews and/or pre-coded questionnaires. Quantitative techniques are used particularly by positivist sociologists who see measurement as a crucial element in all sciences.

(b) The street corner gang formed by (mainly) teenage youths is particularly interesting to sociologists because it is a form of social organisation spontaneously evolved by the young. In the US there is a long history of studying street gangs through participant observation. The usefulness of this method is that it enables the sociologist to gain an 'insider's view' and helps explain how social needs experienced by the young are fulfilled within the gang. These studies have shown that street corner gangs have a very complex structure and though some of their activities like vandalism or violence may appear irrational from the outside, participant observation studies help explain why the activities make sense to the young people involved.

By winning the acceptance and trust of gang members the sociologist is able to get information that gang members would never divulge in a structured situation like a formal interview or questionnaire. William F. Whyte was able to join in conversations with members of the Norton Street Gang like any other gang member and explains that he was able to learn the answers to questions he would never have had the sense to ask had he been using more conventional methods. Lewis Yablonsky in his study of violent gangs got so close to 'The Balkans' that their leader Duke allowed him to read the diary he kept on gang activities. Both studies show how on sensitive topics, particularly those involving criminal behaviour, this method enables the sociologist to get information that would be impossible by other means.

If the sociologist can build a relationship with the gang leaders, they can be particularly useful informants. Yablonsky explains how Duke was almost a 'co-researcher' in his study and Whyte achieved a similar relationship with Doc, the leader of the Norton Street Gang. Whyte explains that not only was Doc able to sponsor him in his dealings with other gang members, he also advised him on how to conduct himself in social interaction with gang members.

That is crucial if the sociologist is to become assimilated into the gang so that the presence of an observer goes almost unnoticed. If the sociologist can adjust in this way to the gang the method provides a unique opportunity to observe young people at first hand in their own everyday environment without imposing an artificial framework for research. In this way a more faithful explanation of the behaviour and point of view of these marginal groups is possible than by any other method. This is why it is so popular with interpretive sociologists (phenomenologists) who study social relationships from an interactionist or ethnomethodological point of view. Their emphasis on small group interaction together with the importance they place on interpreting events from the standpoint of those involved make participant observation an ideal research method.

(c) The acceptance by gang members of a social researcher is always a problem and participant observation studies generally take a long time to complete. (Yablonsky's study took four years.) Acceptance is always relative (never complete or absolute) and the sociologist's age, lack of familiarity with local knowledge, and values can all serve to prevent social barriers being broken down completely.

Inevitably participant observation involves the sociologist in adopting a status and role within the gang. This will structure social relationships with gang members and condition what is observed. For example, as male researchers both Whyte and Yablonsky formed strong sympathetic relationships with male members of the gang and there is little in their work about relationships between the sexes. They also found some gang members more forthcoming than others, giving only a partial picture of the gang as a whole.

By taking up a position within the gang it is also likely that the researcher modifies the behaviour of those under observation. Both Whyte and Yablonsky explain how in response to their enquiries the gang leaders Doc and Duke tended to develop theories and explanations of their behaviour which they would not otherwise have done. Yablonsky, who was engaged upon a crime prevention programme, used his position deliberately to attempt to influence the gangs away from violent behaviour. Both examples show how interaction involving the sociologist directly in gang activities can bias the results of a study.

However, interaction is a two-way affair. Whyte describes the danger of moving from being a 'non-participating observer' to becoming a 'non-observing participator'. Through membership of the gang the sociologist becomes subject to its social influences and this can lead to an inability to remain detached when giving accounts of gang activities. Though empathy with those one studies is crucial to participant observation, if the sociologist becomes too sympathetic to the point of view of gang members there is a danger of accepting their rationalisations of their actions too uncritically.

For all these reasons participant observation accounts are always likely to be biased. The reports of Whyte, Yablonsky and others who have studied street corner gangs are inevitably selective and there is no obvious way of checking on their accuracy. Since the research is not carried out in a systematic manner and does not provide a sound basis for generalisation positivists tend to dismiss this kind of research as unscientific.

Commentary

In relation to parts (b) and (c) of this question first choose your particular area of social life. Alternative areas you could choose include poverty, drugtaking, and education. Participant observation studies of poverty include *La Vida* by Oscar Lewis and *Tally's Corner* by Elliot Liebow. In connection with drug use two British studies that you might refer to are *The Drugtakers* by Jock Young and *Drugtakers in an English Town* by Martin Plant. There is also a number of British studies of schools which use participant observation. These include *Hightown Grammar* by Colin Lacey, *Beachside Comprehensive* by Stephen Ball, and, best of all, *Social Relations in a Secondary School* by David Hargreaves.

Finally, the overall usefulness of participant observation is well illustrated by Lewis Yablonsky when in the preface to *The Violent Gang* he explains that

> My relationship to the boys and the neighbourhood was similar to that of an anthropologist engaged in fieldwork. During the four-year period I directed the project I lived and worked in the area. It was natural for gang boys to 'hang out' in my office and under certain conditions to visit my home. Phone calls at all hours from gang boys with special problems, youths in jail, citizen volunteers with emergency gang-war problems, or the police were daily routine. The research was carried out under circumstances where my daily operation involved a continuing relationship with the people and conditions I was studying.
>
> ...Much was learned on both sides about the world and our relation to it. More specifically, the essence and meaning of gang behaviour and its violence were often more clearly revealed in these discussions than on designed questionnaires. (p.9)

However, later on we learn that

> At times when Duke and his boys described various angles of their gang organisation to me, I had the uneasy feeling that I was inadvertently helping them to make more explicit a pattern that originally did not have much definition. (p.64)

These quotations highlight one of the basic dilemmas faced by sociologists who use participant observation to gather data. On the one hand the sociologist has to get involved if the information obtained is to be valid but on the other hand being involved can bias the study. Extreme cases, where the sociologist is completely won over to the point of view of those studied, are sometimes referred to as 'going native'.

Question 2
Secondary sources: advantages and disadvantages

Types of secondary data

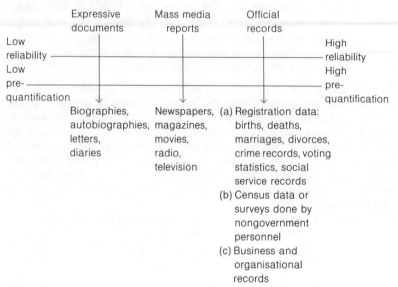

(Source: D.P. Forcese and S. Richer, *Social Research Methods*)

(a) Explain what sociologists mean by secondary data. (2 marks)

(b) Explain what is meant by reliability in this context. (2 marks)

(c) There are various ways in which expressive documents may be used by sociologists and some are more systematic than others. Explain one way in which sociologists could handle these documents systematically. (3 marks)

(d) Using one area of social life as an example, explore the advantages of using secondary data. (9 marks)

(e) Using one area of social life as an example, explore the possible disadvantages of using secondary data. (9 marks)

(*AEB* specimen)

(a) Data is evidence used in sociological studies. If the sociologist collects this material directly it is called primary data. If the material has been compiled for other purposes and is then taken over by the sociologist it is called secondary data. Secondary data can be either quantitative (for example, official statistics) or qualitative (for example, diaries).

(b) Reliability means the degree of trust the sociologist may place in the accuracy of types of secondary data. Expressive documents are regarded as fairly unreliable because they are often distorted by the personal motives of the author. Official records are regarded as more reliable because all officials are required to use standardised procedures when compiling factual information. It is therefore more likely that different officials will record information in the same way.

(c) One way of dealing systematically with expressive documents is content analysis. This involves constructing a series of categories and then examining documents and classifying the information they contain in terms of the categories. The categories themselves can be derived from commonsense (an ethnomethodological approach) or may be constructed analytically in terms of the data required to satisfy a hypothesis (a positivist approach). Content analysis gives a rough indication of the importance of certain themes by counting the number of times they reoccur.

(d) Secondary data has been widely used in the study of religion. It has the advantage of providing the sociologist at no cost with data that would be difficult, impossible, time consuming, or expensive to get by other means. In the study of primitive religion, for example, fieldwork is not always practical. Often the most interesting accounts come not from trained social scientists but from the explorers and missionaries who first contacted remote tribes. Their accounts have the advantage that the religious culture was then unmodified by the influence of western civilisation.

In his *Elementary Forms of the Religious Life*, Emile Durkheim used secondary data on the Australian aborigines. Though he never carried out fieldwork of his own Durkheim was able to analyse this material and develop a functionalist theory of religion. Peter Worsley also used secondary sources to study primitive religion in his book on cargo cults (*The Trumpet Shall Sound*). These cults arose in response to changes brought about by colonialism and records kept by administrators and the writings of missionaries provide much information on the circumstances that promote millenarian movements in third world countries.

Secondary data is often the only source when studying religions that are remote in time. Although, for example, sociologists have no direct means of studying the sixteenth century Reformation, Max Weber used the writings of Calvin and other early Protestants to analyse the essential characteristics of the Protestant ethic. He explains how the secondary sources show a change in Calvinist thinking. Initially Calvinists saw success in business as not without dangers but as their businesses grew and prospered this came to be interpreted as a sign of God's grace. In this way Weber developed his theory of how Protestantism was related to the early development of capitalism.

More recently secondary sources have played a major part in the secularisation debate. Although the 1851 census was the only census to include questions on religious observance it provides a useful marker against which to judge more recent trends. Thus, for example, the census showed that in 1851 36 per cent of the population attended church on the designated Sunday and, though there are no comparable census figures for later years, records of the various denominations allow an estimate in 1967 of an average attendance of 15 per cent (David Martin, *A Sociology of English Religion*, p.43).

(e) Secondary data has also been widely used in the study of crime because actions that break the law are usually difficult to observe at first hand and are often subjects that people will not tell the truth about in social surveys.

One frequently used secondary source is crime statistics but this data only gives information on the level of recorded crime and on the characteristics of convicted criminals. There are many reasons why not all crime is reported to the police. Rape victims may be embarrassed or frightened, victims of petty theft might not think it worthwhile, and offences committed by motorists are only usually reported when there is an accident. In addition there are many crimes without victims (like drugtaking) where there is nobody with a direct interest in informing the police, and other cases where the 'victim' is the public interest, the State or a bureaucratic organisation, in which few people bother to report minor crimes. Finally, there has in recent years been much social legislation relating to racial and sexual discrimination but though discrimination is widespread few prosecutions have been brought.

Because the nature and extent of hidden crime is unknown sociologists have no way of estimating the total amount of criminal deviance in society nor accurately measuring changes. In addition it is likely that information on criminals is also unrepresentative. This is because convicted criminals are failed criminals and the statistics give no information about the social characteristics of those who escape detection. Functionalist and subcultural theories that explain higher crime rates amongst the working classes in terms of their position in the social structure or their culture are therefore suspect because they rest upon biased samples.

Official statistics in any case only describe the extent of recorded crime and explanations about why people commit crime must be sought elsewhere. One qualitative source is evidence produced in court but here one must remember that what is said in court is said in the interests of the defence or prosecution and may be less than a complete or accurate account. Mass media reports on crime are even more unreliable because the media concentrate only on cases regarded as newsworthy. Finally, there are expressive documents that record the experiences and attitudes of those involved in crime or law enforcement. However, these nearly always contain serious distortions since much of what is said or written about crime by criminals, the police, judges, etc. is related to attempts to justify their actions.

Commentary

In relation to part (c) of this question, an alternative way of using expressive documents systematically is ideal type analysis. This is a qualitative method of enquiry since it involves constructing a model of all that is essential in a point of view so as to make explicit the subjective meaning of particular cultural facts. The best illustrations come from the work of Max Weber. For example, he used ideal type analysis in *The Protestant Ethic and the Spirit of Capitalism* and by systematically analysing the theological works of the early Calvinists (an expressive secondary source) was able to construct an ideal type that clarifies the essential doctrines of Protestantism.

In parts (d) and (e) you will have noticed that there is no stipulation that you should use the same area of social life. I have used two different areas because that makes it easier to highlight both the advantages and disadvantages of using secondary sources. However, if you did not want to use different areas a good topic for both sides of this question is suicide.

The key point about suicide is that because the victim is dead it is difficult to get first-hand information. Of course you could still try to interview potential suicides, or relatives and friends of suicides, or base your study on attempted suicides. However, there are difficulties with all three of these primary sources. Potential suicides are difficult to identify, relatives and friends are often reluctant to co-operate and the population of attempted (i.e. failed) suicides is markedly different from the population of actual suicides.

So, to some degree or other, the sociologist is likely to be forced back on secondary sources and this is reflected in the literature on this topic. However, if you were to choose suicide as your example you would need to be aware that the statistics on suicide are only part of the answer. Sociologists have also used second-hand case histories of suicides (for example, Jack Douglas, *The Social Meanings of Suicide*) and studied coroners' courts (for example, J. Maxwell Atkinson, *Societal Reactions to Suicide*). These sources of data also have advantages and disadvantages and an answer that showed no awareness of the relevance of qualitative secondary data would be marked down as incomplete.

Question 3
Sampling: representativeness and generalisation

In her book *The Captive Wife*, Hannah Gavron examines the position of women in society, in particular women with young children. The work was published initially in 1966 and derived in part from earlier work in patterns of family life such as *Family and Kinship in East London* (Young and Willmott, 1957). She attempts to assess the changes which took place in the intervening years and further to explore these problems with ordinary working and middle class people. She argues that many of the working class families discussed in previous studies were extreme rather than typical. Gavron selects a middle class sample and working class sample, 48 in each group. The working class sample was 'drawn from the practice lists of the Caversham Centre, a Group Practice in Kentish Town'. The middle class samples of wives were 'drawn (35) from a doctor's list in West Hampstead and (13) from the London lists of "Housebound Wives" register'.

(a) Given that Gavron only studied particular samples, to what extent would it be reasonable from her findings to generalise about all women with young children? (9 marks)

(b) How important is it that typical groups are chosen for studies of this kind? (8 marks)

(c) Is it ever desirable that nontypical groups are studied? Illustrate your answer with reference to other studies. (8 marks)

(*AEB* specimen)

(a) In order to generalise from particular samples to the population from which they are drawn it is necessary that the sample is representative of the total population. Samples can only yield statistically significant proportions, averages and correlations relating to the total population if the sample size is sufficiently large and if the sample is chosen in a random fashion.

Hannah Gavron's samples consisted of only 48 middle class and 48 working class families. This would be too small a sample to measure the extent of differences in the country as a whole. It is also significant that both the samples were drawn from different areas of London. In a national survey one would expect the samples to be drawn from all parts of the country and from a variety of housing areas (including mixed neighbourhoods) since there may well be regional differences in the problems faced by women with young children. For example, London is to some extent nontypical because, among other factors, it is the largest urban area in the country.

The sampling frames are also inadequate for the purposes of generalisation. A sampling frame should, as near as possible, be a complete list of all the individuals in a population so that each individual family has the same chance of being selected. However, in the case of Hannah Gavron's working class sample the frame used was the doctors' lists from one surgery in Kentish Town. There is no reason to suppose that a random sample of working class families in the catchment area of this one practice is typical of all working class families in London.

The middle class sample suffers from a similar weakness. However, in addition thirteen of the wives were drawn from the London lists of 'Housebound Wives' Register. These wives are almost certainly nontypical since by registering on the list they form part of a minority of women who define themselves as facing problems and who seek to do something about it by joining an organisation.

(b)   The kind of study carried out by Hannah Gavron was a qualitative study. It was not conducted in order to make reliable predictions about the extent of a social problem throughout the country but to make explicit the feelings of women facing difficulties caused by their family commitments.

In qualitative studies it is not so important that the group studied is strictly representative. Interpretive sociologists would argue that it is more important to understand the meanings and motives of social actors than to describe trends and make predictions. A study of women with young children, for example, can clarify what it means to be a housebound wife during times of social change. The results of such a study are more valid because they give a more authentic description of how women feel about their status and role.

So, although Gavron does not demonstrate that the women she studied were typical, or in her terms 'ordinary', this does not invalidate her research. On the contrary her very small samples have the advantage of allowing a more intensive and detailed study to take place. Although information gained in this way is not a valid basis for generalisation it does enable the researcher to probe more deeply into the point of view of women themselves. In this way it is possible to gain insight and understanding of the role conflict experienced by many wives and mothers. This insight can then be used to generate hypotheses that might be tested in a more rigorously positivist fashion by other studies.

(c)   Nontypical groups are groups that differ in some way from what is average or expected in a society. A complex society like modern Britain supports a wide range of life styles and in order to describe and explain this variety it is necessary to study all types of social groups including minority group behaviour.

Nontypical groups are often marginal and in Britain might include groups such as Rastafarians, gypsies, and ethnic minorities. Very often the behaviour of their members is portrayed in the mass media in terms of public stereotypes and dismissed as irrational or condemned as deviant. One of the benefits of studies of such groups is that they help to combat prejudice and enhance our understanding of social problems. For example, Martin Plant's study of drugtakers in Cheltenham (*Drugtakers in an English Town*), Ian Taylor's interpretation of soccer hooliganism (*Soccer Consciousness and Soccer Hooliganism*) and Dick Hebdige's analysis of punks (*Subculture: the Meaning of Style*) are all studies of minorities. Although, from the point of view of mainstream values, the behaviour of these nontypical groups makes no sense the authors in each case succeed in explaining its meaning to those involved and its relationship to other social facts.

In the study of social change it is often an advantage to study nontypical groups because, in so far as the group is extreme, it may illustrate the nature and significance of social changes more clearly. This is shown by a series of studies of affluent workers in Luton carried out principally by John H. Goldthorpe and David Lockwood. Their research was not into a typical section of the working class. Their sample of workers did not live in typical working class neighbourhoods and were more highly paid than average manual workers. However, precisely because the group was nontypical it could be used to test the embourgeoisement thesis. If this section of the working class was not becoming middle class, as Goldthorpe and Lockwood argued, it suggests that less advanced (and more typical) sections were unlikely to be evolving in this direction.

Commentary

From a methodological point of view Hannah Gavron's study is very similar to research conducted by Brian Jackson and Dennis Marsden and published in their book *Education and the Working Class*. In this book the authors were interested in finding out why so few working class children successfully completed a grammar school education. Their evidence came from a sample of 88 working class and ten middle class children who had passed through the grammar schools in Huddersfield in the late 1940s and early 1950s. Extensive informal interviews with these ex-pupils and their parents helped Jackson and Marsden vividly describe the problems that working class children faced in this type of school.

In connection with the value of this kind of research Jackson and Marsden explain that

> Where we can, we measure. But much of this survey is in the form of quotation, scene, incident. When we use this material we are not 'illustrating' the figures, or decorating a theme. The speaking voices are as basic as the tables. They *are* the theme. (p.18)

And

> This report is based on very small samples. They are not large enough for sophisticated numerical analysis. What we have done is try to go behind the numbers and feel a way into the various human situations they represent. (p.26)

It would be appropriate to take the same attitude towards Hannah Gavron's research (parts (a) and (b) of the question).

In connection with part (c) there are, of course, other studies you can draw upon. For example, the point about using nontypical samples to study social change could also be illustrated by reference to *The Symmetrical Family* by Michael Young and Peter Willmott. As part of their survey they interviewed 190 managing directors. This group was certainly not typical of most people in Britain in terms of their income, housing and life style. Young and Willmott also claim that they have a somewhat different family structure to the typical (or symmetrical) family. This leads the authors to suggest that there is evidence of a new type of family structure diffusing downwards from the top of the stratification system.

Chapter 2

Further questions on methodology

Before going on to look at particular issues in detail you will find it useful to begin by putting a boundary around this part of the syllabus. Of course you should not forget that boundaries in sociology are fluid and, for example, questions on methodology often can (and should) be illustrated by reference to examples drawn from research into substantive topics. Still, this does not alter the need to put your thoughts in order and one way of doing this is to ask why sociologists use a variety of methods of data collection. This will help you relate techniques of data collection (i.e. methods) to the purposes for which they are used (i.e. methodology).

As has already been said, one reason for the variety of methods used by sociologists is that there are various sources of information to draw on. This means that by using a combination of methods sociologists can compare different sources of data to check the reliability of their results. This, for example, is what Michael Young and Peter Willmott did in the course of the research for their influential community study *Family and Kinship in East London*. Their main source of information was a sample of 933 adults drawn from the electoral registers covering the London borough of Bethnal Green. However, Young and Willmott wanted to check that this group was representative and in order to do so they compared the social characteristics of the sample with census information for the borough as a whole.

The use of a combination of methods to make crosschecks or to give a more comprehensive account is not uncommon in sociology. However, not all methods are equally useful for all problems and as well as using more than one method in combination you also find that in their research projects different sociologists adopt different research strategies. The reasons for this can be divided into practical and theoretical.

Research strategies: practice

Practical reasons govern whether it is feasible to carry out a particular item of empirical research successfully. For example, all research is governed by limitations on time and money and whether a method is practical or not depends firstly on the availability of resources. Then there are the characteristics of the group being studied to be taken into account. For example, informal interviews have been successfully used in the study of small communities or a few households. However, if one wanted information on the demographic characteristics of an industrial nation like Britain it would be more convenient to turn to secondary sources like the census.

In addition to the size of the group being studied the sociologist also has to be aware of the importance of the way members of society evaluate the behaviour that is being studied. For example, it makes a great deal of difference whether this behaviour is approved of or not. In practice this is a major limitation on the usefulness of survey methods of investigation, since experience shows that on sensitive issues people often lie or refuse to answer. One type of behaviour where this problem is particularly acute is behaviour that breaks social norms and this is one reason for the extensive use of informal research techniques in the study of deviance.

However, at the start of a research project it is impossible to anticipate every contingency and it is usually advisable to test the feasibility of research before getting too involved. For example, in survey research a trial run or pilot survey is often carried out first. This has four main practical advantages. First, it helps the sociologist estimate how long interviewing will take and thus what resources will need to be allocated to the survey. Second, it helps iron out problems over the wording of questions. Third, it may provide a basis for estimating what the likely response rate will be. Finally, if the results are not encouraging the sociologist is not committed to the proposed survey and is still free to consider alternative techniques of data collection.

Research strategies: theory

In sociology, as in every science, it is always necessary to take a perspective because facts do not speak for themselves – they only 'speak' in answer to questions. Whether a technique of data collection is useful or not therefore depends also on the kind of question that the sociologist chooses to ask.

This is illustrated by the difference between longitudinal and cross-sectional surveys. A longitudinal survey involves repeated measurements of the attitudes and behaviour of a sample of people and is particularly useful when seeking answers to questions about social change. One of the most frequently quoted studies to use this technique is *The Home and the School* by J.W.B. Douglas. As the title suggests, Douglas was interested in the relationship between family background and educational attainment and, using the results of longitudinal research into the development of over 5000 children born in 1946, he was able to analyse the influence of factors like family size, gender, and position in the birth sequence on a child's progress over a period of time.

In contrast cross-sectional surveys rest on only a single measurement of the attitudes and behaviour of a sample, and are not nearly so useful in the interpretation of trends. So what type of method is chosen will also depend on whether the sociologist's interest is in explaining social processes or in describing the social structure.

However, this is not the only way in which the theoretical interest of the sociologist has implications for methods. In Chapter 1 a distinction was made between positivist and interpretive sociology. The general point to be borne in mind here is that whereas positivists are mainly interested in demonstrating causal relationships between social phenomena, interpretive sociologists are more concerned with the analysis of meaning. This is fundamental because the distinction between meaning and cause is the source of the difference between qualitative and quantitative methods.

Positivist approaches

The reason for this difference can be seen in an examination of the role of experiments. In the natural sciences most accepted facts have been established through experiments and such is the reliance of the natural sciences on this one method that they are sometimes referred to as experimental sciences. However, in sociology experiments are rarely used and you can see this as due to practical, theoretical, and moral reasons.

Experiments work by comparing either two groups of circumstances or two classes of phenomena that match each other in all significant respects except one. The factor that is different is known as a variable and the experiment consists in bringing the experimental group into contact with the variable so as to measure any changes by comparison with the control. In most cases this takes place in an artificial environment or laboratory because it is then possible to isolate control and experimental groups from the possible effects of other variables since one, or more than one, of these could also be the cause of any differences that are observed.

Clearly, then, the feasibility of carrying out experiments rests upon two conditions. First, one must be able to match the control and experimental group and, second, one must be able to isolate them from the possible effects of other variables. In practice both these conditions are virtually impossible to meet in sociology.

In order to match the control and the experimental group one needs to hold constant all potential causal variables except for the one that is being studied. However, whilst it is possible to find members of society who can be matched with others in terms of characteristics like age, gender, class of origin, educational level and occupation it is never possible to find pairs of individuals whose personal histories are alike in all respects. This means that there will always be more than one possible explanation for any differences in the behaviour of the control and the experimental group. When sociologists use experiments there is therefore always a residue of doubt over what causes any differences that are observed. In other words one can never be sure precisely what it is that one is measuring.

Even supposing that one started with perfectly matched groups there is still the problem of isolating them from the possible effects of other variables introduced in the course of experiment. Here the important point is that experience shows that people often respond differently because they are being experimented on. Any difference that is observed between the behaviour of the control and the experimental group may therefore not be due to the effects of the hypothetical causal variable that the experiment is designed to test. It could instead be due to the fact that if people know they are being used for the purpose of experiment they might choose not to act naturally.

Although there have been a number of ingenious attempts to get round these problems even positivist sociologists (who believe that sociology should model itself on the natural sciences) recognise that the kind of laboratory techniques developed by natural scientists are rarely practical in sociology. However, if physically experimenting with people in order to discover the causes of social events is not usually possible there is nonetheless one thing that you can do with them that you cannot do with natural phenomena. You can ask people questions. Then, presuming their replies are reliable, you can statistically measure the strength of the association between sociological variables like class and educational attainment, religion and voting behaviour, and gender and occupational status. For positivists this type of quantitative research is seen as a firm enough foundation for investigating the causes of social behaviour, and they regard survey methods of research as the sociological equivalent to experiments in the natural sciences.

Phenomenological approaches

The natural sciences rest upon the principle of determinism. According to this principle all events in the natural world are governed by invariable laws. The task of natural science is to discover those laws, and experiments provide scientists with the means to do so. However, interpretive sociologists stress that in the study of social action one cannot adopt a deterministic point of view. From this they draw the conclusion that it is not just impractical to apply the method of the natural sciences to the study of social action but also fundamentally misguided to attempt to do so.

The distinction which is often made here is between natural phenomena which react and individuals who act. In the language of interpretive sociology this means that what is distinctive about social actors is that they 'make choices' or 'decisions', they act 'from motives' or 'for reasons', and they 'interpret events' or 'define situations'. Through phrases like these interpretive sociologists make the point that social reality is not out there waiting to be discovered. On the contrary they see members of society as actively creating their own social world by making sense of experience and lending it significance.

This has far-reaching implications for methodology because a social world constructed out of the beliefs and actions of its members cannot be studied empirically without coming to terms with human subjectivity. However, this raises very different problems from those faced by the natural scientist, and interpretive sociologists argue that different problems require different solutions. In particular they reject the positivist view that sociology should seek to imitate the natural sciences by relying on quantitative methods of data collection. Their principal objection to this is that in trying to measure social phenomena scientifically positivists are committed to preconceived definitions, which ignore the empirical meaning of events to the social actors involved. What is needed, say interpretive sociologists, is an entirely different approach that is receptive to the actor's own perception of reality. From this follows the commitment to qualitative methods like participant observation or informal interviews, espoused by interpretive sociologists as an alternative to social surveys and official statistics.

The general point to emerge from this discussion of the limited role of experiments in sociology is that the reasons for preferring a particular technique of data collection ultimately include assumptions about the very nature of social reality and how it can or should be studied. So far these assumptions have been dealt with from the point of view of an interest in knowledge itself. However, research is also a social activity and as a member of society the sociologist is, like anybody else, bound by social norms. In practice this is yet another restriction on the use of experiments because attempts to experiment with people raise moral issues and are usually controversial.

Moral issues

An example of research which illustrates the problem is *Pygmalion in the Classroom* by Robert Rosenthal and Leonora Jacobson. They conducted an experiment on children attending an elementary school in California. The purpose of the experiment was to test the hypothesis that children who performed badly in school did so because teachers had low expectations of them. The experimental group was a random sample of twenty per cent of the children. The control group was the other 80 per cent. The variable introduced to test the hypothesis was that teachers at the school were falsely led to believe that the group of twenty per cent consisted of children that tests had shown would make rapid intellectual gains. To measure the effect of this teacher expectation all pupils sat a test at the beginning and end of the school year. The results of the tests showed that overall the twenty per cent who had been singled out as having more potential did in fact make greater advances than the rest.

The methodology of this study has been extensively criticised. However, the main question here is not whether it is technically feasible to carry out this kind of experiment but whether it is morally right to do so. In order to conduct their experiment the two sociologists deliberately misled teachers. Even more important, Rosenthal and Jacobson claim that the experiment demonstrated that teachers' expectations influence the performance of their pupils. If this is the case then the 80 per cent of children in the control group, whom teachers were not expecting to improve so rapidly, were put at a disadvantage.

Whether Rosenthal and Jacobson's experiment was justified or not is a matter of subjective judgement; of whether you feel the end justifies the means. However, most sociologists feel an obligation to the welfare of those who participate in their research. This means that in addition to practical and theoretical reasons yet another factor which influences the way data is collected (and presented) is the values of the sociologist.

Social values

When reading original research you should keep in mind the general issues in methodology mentioned in this introductory section. However, to use your reading to the best advantage you should also realise that research can be examined from more than one point of view. For example, values do not just affect the way research is carried out; they also affect which topics and issues receive the most attention. In subsequent chapters some of these topics and issues will be examined in greater detail. In anticipation of this it is worthwhile taking a preliminary look beyond methodology into the influence of the social context on the production of knowledge itself.

In relation to this you should bear in mind when reading sociological studies that the very decision to begin a research project presupposes that the sociologist views research in that particular area as interesting or important. However, in making that evaluation sociologists are influenced by their membership of an academic community and by the social and political climate of the times. Furthermore, these two related factors will also affect opportunities for doing sociological research and what, in practice, gets done or not done is partly a question of the attitude of powerful interest groups within society able to sponsor research they like and quash research they do not. Two final examples illustrate this.

Project Camelot was a social science research programme conceived and sponsored by the US Army in the 1960s. The aims of the research were ostensibly to identify the causes of revolution in underdeveloped countries and to predict the likelihood of revolution in specific third world, and even European, nations. However, the Army, who were prepared to pay up to six million dollars over the three to four years that the research would take, had rather different motives. Their main concern was not in understanding revolutions but in preventing left-wing revolutionary movements from seizing power in countries thought vital to the interests of the United States. In other words Project Camelot was a counterinsurgency programme with the underlying objective of helping the Department of Defence plan the US's global military strategy.

As things turned out Project Camelot never really got off the ground. Despite the amount of money available many social scientists approached by the directors of the project turned them down and when news of the proposed research leaked out it caused such a storm in the United States and Latin America that the US Defence Secretary stepped in and cancelled it. However, what the incident shows is that if bureaucratic organisations are permitted to use social scientists to manage events or manipulate people it can pose a threat to human freedom.

On the other hand sociologists are by no means always accomplices of the establishment. They can be a thorn in its side. This is illustrated by research into the psychological effects of long-term imprisonment carried out by Stanley Cohen and Laurie Taylor. Their main source of data was conversations they had over a four year period with inmates of the maximum security wing at Durham prison. In the course of the research friendly relations were established both with prisoners and with local prison officials. However, the Prison Department of the Home Office was opposed to any research that might be sympathetic to the point of view of prisoners and eventually it used its powers to close down the project. The researchers were refused permission to visit the men and even correspondence with them was curtailed.

The two examples quoted above show how sociology can have political implications. This is something which is all too easy to overlook when studying original research because in writing up their results the authors frequently leave out anything which might make their study appear less 'scientific'. However, sociological research projects that are actually carried out often involve false starts, personal rivalries and political rows. Laurie Taylor described the problems he faced in *Doing Sociological Research* (edited by Colin Bell and Howard Newby). This book also provides you with an alternative perspective to that of the sanitised appendices on research methods at the end of many published empirical studies. These never tell the whole story and more often than not leave out the most interesting parts.

Question 4
The social survey: face-to-face interview or postal questionnaire?

The face-to-face interview and the postal questionnaire are both data gathering techniques used in social surveys. The most obvious differences between them are that in one the researcher is present and the response is oral whereas in the other the researcher is absent and the response is written. However, these differences have practical and theoretical implications since they affect the scope and design of the survey and the type of hypothesis that can be tested.

Interviews are commonly divided into two types: structured and unstructured. In a structured interview the interview situation is standardised as far as possible. This is the source of similarities between structured interviews and postal questionnaires. In both cases replies are recorded on a questionnaire and the order and wording of questions, and sometimes the range of alternative answers, is preset by the sociologist. However, unstructured interviews are very different. They are normally preceded by a general conversation and the sociologist deliberately adopts an informal approach in an attempt to break down social barriers.

Unstructured interviews are most useful in qualitative research designed to analyse attitudes and values. Though rarely providing a valid basis for generalisation their main advantage is that they enable the sociologist to probe the subjective point of view of social actors. The value of this kind of interview for sociologists who adopt an interpretive perspective is clearly revealed by William Labov's enquiry into *The Logic of Non-Standard English*. In a series of interviews with Leon, a black child from Harlem, Labov showed that the interview situation was crucial to the interaction between the sociologist and the respondent. Leon appeared almost inarticulate when confronted by a formal interview situation but in an informal interview he felt confident enough to express his feelings.

An informal approach to interviewing has also been successfully used in research into roles within the nuclear family. This is illustrated in Elizabeth Bott's study *Family and Social Network*. She conducted interviews with only twenty families but because she used such a small sample Bott was able to get close enough to individual family members to analyse their relationships in depth. This led to new ideas about the connection between conjugal roles and types of social network and her work stimulated further research into this area.

However, face-to-face interviews also raise methodological problems. These stem from the fact that interviewers are themselves role players and their perceived status may influence the replies of the respondent. An example of how this can affect the reliability of data can be found in Hannah Gavron's book *The Captive Wife*. She conducted interviews with a sample of mothers and amongst the questions asked were enquiries into the disciplining of children. On three occasions Gavron reported seeing mothers using corporal punishment on their children when they had previously assured her that they did not.

This example is of general relevance because in cases where there is a perceived status disparity between the interviewer and the interviewee the results of interviews have to be interpreted with care. The inaccuracy of interviews on sensitive topics is confirmed by John and Elizabeth Newson's study *Patterns of Infant Care in an Urban Community*. They report a difference between the results of interviews carried out by their own team and the results obtained by health visitors. However, the direction and extent of interview bias is often difficult to estimate. For example, Michael Schofield used informal interviews in an attempt to measure the sexual experience of fifteen to nineteen year olds. In only six per cent of interviews did the interviewers feel completely sure of the validity of their results.

At first sight the postal questionnaire seems to offer the opportunity of getting round the problem of interview bias by reducing the personal involvement of the sociologist. Its other practical advantages are that it is cheaper than face-to-face interviews and can be used to contact a large number of respondents scattered over a wide area relatively quickly.

However, these advantages have to be weighed against the practical problems of conducting research by post. A lack of involvement by the sociologist means that there is little control over the information gathering process and one cannot even be sure that the questionnaire was completed by the person to whom it was addressed. That, of course, assumes there is a reply in the first place and one of the most intractable problems of mailed questionnaires is a low response rate. This diminishes the reliability of the data that is obtained and in *The Fishermen* Jeremy Tunstall reports little success with his postal questionnaire designed to gauge public opinion towards Hull trawlermen.

In addition questionnaires often rest upon dubious theoretical assumptions. This is particularly so with the pre-coded questionnaire where the respondent is required to choose an answer from a number of preset alternatives framed by the sociologist. In practice most postal questionnaires are pre-coded because they are easier to complete and the results can be quantified. However, despite these advantages the sociologist who uses this procedure is always open to the charge of putting ideas into people's heads.

A classic example which illustrates the problem comes from a Gallup poll conducted in the US in 1939. Asked to rate themselves as upper, middle, or lower class 88 per cent of the sample rated themselves middle class. However, soon after the survey was repeated with the term 'lower class' replaced by 'working class' and this yielded entirely different results. This example shows that the meaning individuals attach to labels can influence their reply and this is the basic problem of all questionnaires structured in this way.

Despite the weaknesses of interviews and questionnaires both methods of gathering data remain popular with sociologists. One reason is that they have such a wide variety of applications. At one extreme are unstructured interviews of small samples. Since this approach enables the sociologist to analyse people's motives and their definitions of a situation it is popular with interpretive sociologists. At the other extreme are pre-coded postal questionnaires sent to a large number of people. This is more likely to be favoured by positivist sociologists interested in measuring trends and making predictions.

Commentary

Here are two more examples of postal questionnaires.

First, Dorothy Wedderburn conducted a survey of the terms and conditions of employment of different categories of worker in manufacturing industry ('Workplace Inequality', *New Society*, 9 April 1970). The survey was based upon a postal questionnaire sent to 815 firms and achieved a response rate of 55 per cent. Wedderburn refers to this as 'encouraging' but it would be perfectly legitimate to take a more sceptical point of view. Since she received no data from almost half the firms she contacted it is difficult to judge the representativeness of the sample she did receive information from. This will affect the reliability of the results as an indication of differences in terms and conditions of employment throughout the country.

Second, in 1934 Richard La Piere published a paper entitled 'Attitudes vs. Actions' (*Social Forces*, No. 13: reprinted in Irwin Deutscher, *What We Say/What We Do*) which has since become a classic. La Piere's research was carried out over a two year period during which he travelled extensively in the US with a Chinese couple. In the course of their travels they stayed at 66 hotels, auto camps and tourist homes and were served at 184 restaurants and cafes. Only once were they refused on account of the race of the Chinese couple. Then, six months later, La Piere posted questionnaires to all the establishments they had visited. One of the questions in the questionnaire was 'Will you accept members of the Chinese race as guests in your establishment?' In all La Piere received 128 replies (a response rate of 51 per cent) and over 90 per cent of these replied 'No' to the relevant question.

This study clearly places a question mark over the validity of survey methods of investigation. The general point is made by La Piere himself when he states that

> Only a verbal reaction to an entirely symbolic situation can be secured by the questionnaire. It may indicate what the responder would actually do when confronted with the situation symbolised in the question, but there is no assurance that it will.

Question 5
Official statistics: what use are they in sociology?

Official statistics are a secondary source of data compiled by officials for practical reasons like the formulation of policy, government administration, and financial accountability. Social scientists need to be constantly reminded of this because, however objective the figures may appear to be, the collection of the information they contain is a social process. One consequence of this is that official statistics vary in their reliability. For example, although basic demographic information like birth and death rates is usually fairly accurate, figures on the extent of poverty or unemployment tend to distort the underlying nature and underestimate the severity of the problems they purport to describe.

These distortions do not necessarily, or even normally, arise out of deliberate malpractice by officials or politicians. Often they are caused by the way events are categorised for official purposes. In the case of unemployment, for example, the figures include only those who have registered as unemployed at unemployment benefit offices. Categories of people who do not qualify for benefit, such as some school leavers and married women, are not encouraged to register and are less likely to appear in the official statistics even though they may be looking for work.

This example shows how the status of individuals as recorded by officials may differ from their status as perceived from other points of view and there is no reason why the government's definition should be regarded as intrinsically more objective. Nowhere is this more clear than in the case of marriage and divorce. These are both legally defined in terms of the making or dissolving of a marriage contract and some sociologists have looked at variations in the figures for evidence of a deterioration in the health and stability of marriage. However, no such simple transference from the official statistics to the state of marriage is legitimate. This is because the marriage statistics do not include those cohabiting couples who have set themselves up as a separate household, perform conjugal roles, perhaps even have children, and who are, in every other sociological sense of the word, married even though they are not officially recorded as such. At the other extreme amongst the married population will be included many 'empty-shell' marriages and separated spouses who perform none of the social roles associated with the status of husband and wife.

Government figures on marriage and divorce show how official statistics sometimes only give a partial picture of the social facts they seem to describe. The reasons for this are brought into even sharper focus if one concentrates upon the consequences of statuses conferred upon the individual by the state. For example, committal to a mental hospital can involve financial loss, a sense of humiliation and stigma. This sometimes leads individuals to develop strategies to avoid being labelled. The degree of success of different social groups will depend upon a number of factors including their wealth and power and the official statistics will then systematically distort the extent of mental illness and its distribution between social groups.

This is a problem that is particularly acute in the case of the statistics on both crime and suicide. As phenomenologists have pointed out these statistics must be interpreted as the outcome of meaningful interaction between individuals and officials of the state. The basic error of many functionalist and positivist sociologists is that they neglect this fact. This is most clear in Emile Durkheim's book *Suicide*. The cardinal error that he made was to regard the suicide rate as a social fact which can be accepted at face value as an objective measure of the suicidal tendencies generated by a society. However, as Maxwell Atkinson has argued (*Societal Reactions to Suicide: the Role of Coroner's Definitions*), the social world is a world of meaning from which coroners themselves are not exempt. They construct a rate through a courts system charged with the responsibility for arriving at explanations that will make sense of death. In this sense the cause of death is a negotiated meaning rather than an objective reality.

The implications of this throw many doubts upon the use made of official statistics by positivist sociologists. At first sight the great advantage of the statistics is that they seem to provide a great mass of prequantified sociographic material that allows accurate measurement of the extent of types of social behaviour. However, closer inspection reveals that they are constructed out of the values of those involved in compiling the information. This means that where correlations are established, for example, between social class and educational attainment, one cannot directly assume a causal relationship. Max Weber was one of the few sociologists to have seen the importance of this clearly. In *The Protestant Ethic and the Spirit of Capitalism* he uses statistics to show an association between religious affiliation and business activity. However, the value of these statistics is seen by Weber to lie in their use as a guide to further enquiry and he recognises that by themselves they do not prove a causal relationship. This depends upon his qualitative analyses designed to demonstrate the meaningful correspondence between Protestantism and modern capitalism.

When explanation in sociology is seen to involve analysis of the subjective point of view of social actors the limitations of official statistics are revealed. Despite the claims of positivists the figures themselves explain nothing at all. All they can do is describe the extent of a social characteristic as measured by government officials. In some cases these measurements may suggest hypotheses for further study. However, further analysis is always necessary because the meaning of the figures cannot be taken for granted. This is particularly evident in relation to statistics on the extent of crime. Although at first sight they seem to supply information concerning the trend in crime and the social characteristics of criminals, in reality they are more likely to be useful as a source of information on law enforcement.

Commentary

Interpretive sociologists argue that what we call 'society' is not an independent reality but is rather the outcome of the meanings through which people make sense of experience. The most extreme exponents of this point of view are the ethnomethodologists. They seem to be arguing that the social world is nothing more than the interpretations of its members and that social phenomena like suicide and crime exist only in so far as people perceive them. This point of view has in recent years been employed in criticism of the use made of official statistics by mainstream sociologists.

One of the most outspoken of the ethnomethodologists is Jack Douglas and in his book *The Social Meanings of Suicide* there is a chapter on official statistics which is worth looking at for questions on both methodology and suicide. However, when you come to evaluate Douglas's ideas notice the self-contradiction into which he falls. Thus, on the one hand

it is a fundamental part of the argument throughout this work that there does not exist such a thing as a 'real' suicide rate. Suicides are not something of a set nature waiting to be correctly or incorrectly categorised by officials. The very nature of the 'thing' is itself problematic. (p.196)

On the other hand, later on Douglas tells us that he believes

studies of the organisations and social processes that produce official suicide rates . . . will show us that these official statistics are so greatly in error that they cannot be used in the scientific study of suicide. (p.230)

The flaw in the argument is that in order to know how 'greatly in error' the statistics are they would need to be compared with the 'real suicide rate' which, of course, Douglas has previously claimed does not exist.

In practice ethnomethodology is full of contradictions like this and when carried to its logical conclusion leads to the absurd and self-defeating position that no one can ever know anything at all. Barry Hindess puts this point in his book, *The Use of Official Statistics in Sociology*.

Question 6
Value freedom: is it possible? is it desirable?

The basis of Max Weber's methodology was his belief that sociology should be value free. By this he meant that sociologists should always endeavour to separate their research from any moral or political beliefs they might have concerning the unsatisfactory or satisfactory character of particular social phenomena. However, although Weber's view still remains an article of faith for many sociologists who think that sociology should aim to be scientific, his belief in the importance of value freedom has, in recent years, been increasingly criticised by sociologists who regard a value free sociology as both impossible and undesirable.

Very often the starting point for criticisms of the idea of value freedom lies with the observation that sociologists are members of a society and thus subject to the same social influences as those they study. For example, in his article 'Whose side are we on?' Howard Becker argues that because sociologists can never be genuinely detached or neutral in their attitude to research sociological interpretations of events are inevitably biased by the sympathies of their authors. Typically this point of view is supported by arguments designed to demonstrate relationships between knowledge and society. Thus critics of value freedom emphasise that new ideas are created within the institutional framework of an academic community and, if taken up by individuals or organisations, can have far-reaching social and political results.

However, the view that value freedom is impossible because sociologists are part of what they study is not a conclusive argument. It is equally true to say that humanity is part of nature, yet this does not prevent the natural scientist from achieving objectivity. Furthermore natural phenomena such as diseases are as much a focus of strong feelings as are social phenomena like war and revolution. The sociologist who has a value commitment to social justice is thus no different, in this respect, to the doctor committed to the health of a patient. Neither is necessarily prevented from conducting an objective investigation into the causes of social conflict or ill health by the mere fact of regarding the existence of such conditions as undesirable.

What these examples show is that value freedom is not a question of attitudes but of the ability of scientists to demonstrate the truth of their ideas empirically. Unlike value judgments which receive their assent from feeling scientific theories appeal to human reason. In practice this means that value freedom rests upon the willingness to subordinate sentiment to the objective analysis of experience. For the natural scientist this is usually achieved through experiment. However, because in sociology experiments are rarely possible some sociologists have argued that sociology lacks the means to avoid subjective judgements.

One representative of this point of view is Derek Phillips and in his book *Abandoning Method* Phillips puts forward the argument that because data collection is itself a social process, bias and invalidity will arise out of the effects of social interaction. His general point is that members of society act in terms of values and that one of the most important of these is their need for social approval. When they are faced with a questionnaire or an interviewer Phillips argues that respondents will act in ways they feel the sociologist will expect or agree with and that therefore the very act of gathering data will bias the results.

· Whilst Phillips is correct in pointing out the unreliability of survey methods this does not in principle invalidate the possibility of value freedom. For, as well as setting up artificial situations, sociologists can also gather data about actual behaviour patterns either through unobtrusive methods like participant observation or by way of secondary sources like historical documents. The importance of such data is well illustrated by its use in comparative studies. For example, Margaret Mead compared various tribal societies to demonstrate that sexual identity was socially constructed and Max Weber compared the economic ethics of various world religions to show how they were incompatible with modern capitalism. Though both these 'natural experiments' use qualitative techniques which give less precise results than laboratory methods, the basic principle of systematically comparing societies in order to identify the causes of different behaviour patterns follows the same logic as that of the natural sciences.

However, it is not only for methodological reasons that so many sociologists have rejected the concept of value freedom. In addition they have argued that because it is impossible for sociologists to be value free it is not desirable for them to pretend to be. This is Alvin Gouldner's opinion and in his essay 'Anti-Minotaur : The Myth of a Value Free Sociology' he proposes to study value freedom as part of the ideology of an occupational group.

From this standpoint Gouldner claims that the effects of the belief in value freedom have been variable. One of its satisfactory consequences was that it provided a theme around which all sociologists could unite and thus helped to establish sociology as a discipline. However, Gouldner maintains that it also had negative consequences in that through their adherence to the higher principle of value freedom sociologists were encouraged to neglect pressing moral problems. Increasingly therefore the conception of value freedom lost its relevance and since, for Gouldner, the influence of values is unavoidable anyway he argues that the time has now come for sociologists to be honest about their personal and political beliefs rather than seek to perpetuate a deceit.

Whether or not one agrees with Gouldner is, in the last analysis, a question of the value attributed to knowledge itself. Although allegedly a critic of value freedom it is significant that he avoids any examination of the logical issues involved and instead makes a direct appeal to sentiment. This is legitimate only if one believes that sociology should be openly propagandist. However, if sociology is to have intellectual value as a contribution to human understanding then sociologists must insist upon their intellectual obligations and defend the principle of value freedom.

Commentary

Sociologists are fairly evenly divided over the issue of whether or not sociology should be value free and you are free to argue either side of the case.

If you wish to argue in favour of value freedom then you should try to explain that there is a logical distinction between existential propositions (that is statements concerning what is) and normative propositions (that is statements concerning what ought to be). This was the basis of Weber's argument. Thus,

> What is really at issue is the intrinsically simple demand that the investigator and teacher should keep unconditionally separate the establishment of empirical facts . . . and his own practical evaluations . . . . These two things are logically different and to deal with them as though they were the same represents a confusion of entirely heterogeneous problems.

(*The Methodology of the Social Sciences*, p.11)

However, Weber's argument is not an easy one to follow and although the essay contains a simplified version of it you may prefer to argue the case against.

If you do this you should emphasise the fact that sociologists are members of society and cannot escape the influence of both its culture and its institutions. They derive their problems from the social and political climate of the times, they generally work for bureaucratic organisations, and their research can affect the lives of others. In terms of these relationships between knowledge and society you could then argue that in attempting to claim value freedom sociologists are acting in bad faith. This is Alvin Gouldner's theme. He argues that sociologists have a responsibility to make a useful contribution to society which they have evaded by hiding behind the idea of value freedom. However, Gouldner believes that

> Social science can never be fully accepted in a society, or by a part of it, without paying its way; this means it must manifest both its relevance and concern for the contemporary human predicament. Unless the value relevances of sociological inquiry are made plainly evident, unless there are at least some bridges between it and larger human hopes and purposes, it must inevitably be scorned by laymen as pretentious word-mongering.

(*For Sociology*, p.13)

Chapter 3

Work and organisations

The troubles and satisfactions that people experience at work depend to a large extent upon the institutions through which work is organised. An example of this is provided by the changes brought about by the development of the factory system of production. In England this originated in the early eighteenth century and, aided by developments in science and technology, it gradually spread to most branches of manufacturing. In the process it led to the decline of the domestic system. Under the domestic system production was centred on individual households. For example, in the textile industry before the development of factory methods of production contractors would typically put out their orders to independent artisans who worked either at home or in small workshops. However, with the coming of the factory system manufacturing was concentrated in one place, workers were brought together under one roof, and capital was concentrated in one pair of hands.

These changes in the organisation of manufacturing raise questions about the quality of life open to those who had to adjust to the new economic conditions. For example, how did the separation of work from domestic life affect family relationships? What were the effects of the growing division of labour on relationships at work? Why did the introduction of powered machinery destroy the expression of individuality at work? How was it that the dignity of labour was undermined and why were new forms of discipline and control necessary in the factories?

Analyses of industrial societies: Marx and Engels

You will find an answer to many questions like these in Frederick Engels' book *The Condition of the Working Class in England*. It remains one of the best descriptions of the harsh conditions and demoralising effects of the growth of the factory system in the early nineteenth century. Alternatively, you might look at Karl Marx's theory of alienation. This is a more abstract analysis of the psychological consequences of the factory system. However, what both authors shared was the realisation that the coming of a new economic order had fundamental implications for the lives of all those it touched.

Because Marx and Engels asked questions about the relationship between social structure and individual experience their early works are good examples of what it means to possess a sociological imagination. Furthermore, the dwindling legacy of the nineteenth century factory system remains with us today and there are still insights into modern industrial behaviour to be gleaned from these sources. However, the transformation of both work and society since Marx and Engels were writing is also something that you need to be aware of and this demands an understanding of the theory of bureaucracy.

Analyses of industrial societies: Weber

For Max Weber bureaucracy was the principal characteristic of modern industrial societies irrespective of whether production was organised along capitalist or socialist lines. In his view the factory system was but one example of bureaucratic means of administration that were also invading institutions like the church, the state, the army, political parties and other organisations. These other organisations include institutions that have developed rapidly since Weber was writing and you should bear in mind that schools, colleges, hospitals and the mass media are also bureaucratically organised. These are all further developments in what Weber interpreted as the rationalisation of all spheres of life.

By rationalisation Weber meant the increasing dominance of action that is calculated to achieve some practical advantage by the most technically efficient means. Although we all tend to think that we act rationally Weber distinguished four principal types of social action. Firstly, there is emotionally determined action. This is where our feelings get the better of us and we act without thinking of the consequences. Then there is traditional action. This is where a course of action has become routine and in acting we do what is customary in that situation. Thirdly, there is action orientated to the belief in an absolute value. This is where we disregard the consequences of our behaviour because of an overriding commitment to a 'higher' moral or religious principle.

All these types of action can be conceptually distinguished from action which is rationally orientated to a given practical end. This is where we not only try to anticipate the consequences of action but make a decision to act on the basis of the most effective means for achieving our objectives. This systematic approach to problem solving can also be pursued collectively and, for Weber, bureaucracy was the organised counterpart to this kind of rational action.

In Weber's work the principal feature that is used to distinguish bureaucracy from other types of organisation is the difference that its claim to legitimacy is founded upon. He argued that if a group is to work together effectively it requires from its membership a certain degree of voluntary submission to a higher authority. In order to guarantee its continuance the higher authority will therefore seek to cultivate a belief in the validity of the order that it has established. However, the claim to exercise authority over others does not always rest upon the same grounds and Weber distinguished charismatic, traditional, and legal authority.

By charismatic authority Weber meant the sense of duty that springs from what subordinates regard as the exceptional qualities of their leader. By traditional authority he meant the sense of duty that springs from customary obligations. Notice that in both cases obedience is a matter of personal loyalty based either on the supposed qualities that the leader possesses as an individual or on the traditionally sanctioned powers that go with the position. However, Weber argued that when authority rests on rational grounds it is impersonal because the sense of duty springs from an obligation to abide by rules. In this case obedience rests upon a belief in the legality of those rules and not on the purely personal authority or traditional rights of the leader.

Weber regarded this as crucial to an understanding of modern organisations and from the principle of an organisation that works according to rules he derived his ideal type of bureaucracy. The chief characteristic of bureaucracy is the existence of an explicitly formulated body of general rules governing the whole administrative process. Typically these rules are applied and enforced by a permanent, full-time, and specially trained staff of officials. They have their specific area of responsibility defined through the rules and their performance of official duties is co-ordinated by the organisation of official positions in a hierarchy. This means that lower officials are controlled and supervised by higher ones in a chain of command which extends throughout the organisation.

In describing the conduct of officials Weber referred to 'a spirit of formalistic impersonality'. By this he meant that officials are expected to treat clients, colleagues, superiors and subordinates without regard for personal likes and dislikes. Their task is to contribute to a rational system of administration based on the application of rules to particular cases. Anything that might interfere with or detract from this machine-like regularity is incompatible with the ideal type of bureaucracy. From this it follows that officials are appointed and not elected. Their appointment is on the basis of technical qualifications and not family connections. They are paid a salary and are not allowed to use their position for private gain.

In these ways bureaucracy enforces the segregation of private life from the performance of official duties. Since it does this to a greater extent than other forms of organisation Weber argued that it was potentially a more technically efficient means of administration than when submission was based on either charismatic or traditional authority. However, far from welcoming its growth Weber saw the spread of bureaucracy as a threat. Such was the power of this new instrument of social control that he foresaw a possible future in which modern technology would combine with bureaucratic organisation in a passion for order that would suppress all individuality.

This unresolved dilemma is important because Weber's belief that the spread of bureaucratic means of administration might well conflict with human freedom and self-fulfilment is the place to begin when trying to sort out the various strands in the contemporary debate. When you first look at issues in modern organisation theory it is easy to feel discouraged by the sheer variety and complexity of the ideas that you are expected to understand. However, recognise that what unites Weber's work with most other important contributions to the theory of organisations is an interest in the relationship between bureaucracy and human values. With this to guide you, you will see that the reason for the complexity is that there are many sides to this relationship and it can be explored or resolved from different points of view.

Theories of organisation: Merton, Blau and Gouldner

One influential contributor to the modern theory of organisations is R.K. Merton. In his article 'Bureaucratic Structure and Personality' Merton begins with a Weberian view of the structure of organisations. However, he goes on to explain that the emphasis on discipline within bureaucracies can lead to overconformity. In particular the obligation of officials to abide by rules is counterproductive when it leads to inflexibility, timidity, and an inability to deal with situations which are not anticipated in the regulations. These are dysfunctional aspects of bureaucracy. (For the full list see Merton's article.) Merton is therefore extending Weber's analysis by arguing that despite their rational structure bureaucracies often function in a very irrational way.

Peter Blau's research supplies an explanation of variations in bureaucratic efficiency. He criticises Weber for focusing on the formal structure of organisations, though it should be remembered that Weber's analysis was only concerned with the ideal type of bureaucracy. Nonetheless Blau is correct in emphasising that real bureaucracies have both a formal and an informal structure. Their formal structure is the way they are officially organised. However, within that formal structure there will arise an informal network of relationships. One consequence of this is that unofficial work practices will emerge as workers form their own groups and develop informal norms. To some extent these will govern the way tasks are performed and this means that in order to understand how bureaucracies actually operate one needs to look beyond their bureaucratic structure.

Another contributor is Alvin Gouldner. His point is that in real organisations characteristics of bureaucracy such as a hierarchy of authority, the division of labour, and the emphasis on rules can be more or less highly developed. Gouldner's interest lies in explaining the social processes which account for these differences. He explains that the degree of bureaucratisation will partly depend upon the extent to which it is possible to predict eventualities and devise rules and regulations to cover them (a point which is also crucial to Burns and Stalker's theory of mechanistic and organic systems of management). However, what also needs to be taken into account are the attitudes of managers towards the productivity of labour and the cohesiveness of workers who in certain circumstances may be able to resist the extension of bureaucratic control.

Merton, Blau, and Gouldner are all American sociologists who have, to some extent, been influenced by Weber. However, whereas Weber was interested in the idea of bureaucracy these modern sociologists have been more concerned with how actual organisations work. This means that unlike Weber they are also interested in studying what the attitudes of employees are towards the organisation for which they work, what specific rules exist to achieve the objectives of the organisation, and how in practice rules and regulations are enforced. These issues are all to do with how the efficiency of an actual organisation is affected by the values of those it employs. However, efficiency is not just a question theoretically related to values. It is also a matter of practical concern to management who in various ways have tried to reduce the uncertainty which stems from the fact that organisations employ people.

Theories of organisation: scientific management and the human relations school

The most visible effect of this has been the extension of managerial control in factories, offices, hospitals, schools and other work places. This is a characteristic feature of work in the twentieth century and the benefits that it would supposedly bring were first spelled out by Frederick W. Taylor. His *Principles of Scientific Management* was first published in 1911. Its importance does not lie in its theoretical contribution but in the impact that Taylorism had, and still has, on the way organisations are run.

Taylor believed that there was one way of performing any job of work that was the most efficient and it was the task of management to find that way and enforce appropriate work procedures. To this end he believed that the work of every employee should be planned in advance and rules should be devised detailing precisely how tasks were to be performed and what time was to be allocated to them. In making this part of management's role Taylor recommended numerous changes in work practices. Since then his ideas have been applied in many industries. This has generally led to control over the work process being progressively removed from the workers who do the job and transferred to time and motion experts.

Out of scientific management there grew the human relations school. Conventionally the two are separated because Taylor viewed workers as isolated individuals whereas the human relations school emphasises the way individuals are conditioned by their membership of groups. Also Taylor operated with a narrow economic view of the workers' motivation to work whereas human relations theory emphasises that people at work have social needs that cannot be met by purely economic incentives. However, what both approaches have in common is that their analysis of how work should be reorganised is structured in terms of the priorities of management. In the world of business and commerce these priorities are governed by the profit motive. The question then becomes one of how best to manipulate the wage-earning employees and though human relations theory gives a more sophisticated answer it is still guided by the same overall objective.

In practice the rationalisation of the work process has often led to increased productivity. This is why modern management techniques have spread from manufacturing industry to the service sector and state bureaucracies. However, whilst management tends to measure the benefits of rationalisation in terms of increased efficiency the costs often go unnoticed. This is because they are largely borne by the labour force. Although workers in western industrial nations have participated in a general rise in standards of living many would argue that this has not made the experience of work any more satisfying because it has gone hand in hand with the growth of an environment at work that allows less scope for self expression and autonomy.

Radical criticisms of rationalisation and bureaucracy

This view is particularly associated with the ideas put forward by radical critics of US society. A typical example is Harry Braverman's book *Labour and Monopoly Capital*. He emphasises that the overall purpose of administrative controls is to eliminate uncertainty. The modern corporation seeks to do this in a variety of ways. One way is by making the labour process less dependent on the skills of the labourer so that work can be more effectively controlled from above.

However, as well as extending their control over labour, large corporations are also engaged in developing ways of controlling prices and demand. This has led to the growth of cartels, price-fixing agreements and other means of superseding the market and to a massive investment in advertising and promotion as a way of manipulating consumers. In these ways monopoly capital seeks to guarantee future profits and growth. The critics argue that the whole process leads not only to the degradation of work but also to the manufacture of artificial needs and the corruption of values in the wider society.

The theme of American writers like Braverman is that modern organisations treat human beings in inhuman ways. The most extreme examples of this are found not in factories or offices but in what Erving Goffman has called total institutions. These include organisations like mental hospitals, prisons, and concentration camps. They are particularly repressive examples of bureaucracy because inmates of such institutions are largely cut off from the outside world and their lives are brought almost entirely under bureaucratic control. Officially this is regarded as necessary to the cure and rehabilitation of patients or offenders but Goffman's analysis of an American mental hospital shows that it often has the opposite effect. This is because incarceration is usually a degrading and mortifying experience which rarely helps the individual re-enter conventional society. However, it is not only the freedom of mental patients and other inmates of total institutions that is curtailed by bureaucratic means of administration. It may well be that the civil and political liberties of all of us are being undermined by the growth of bureaucracy.

Theories of organisation: bureaucracy and oligarchy

This is an argument which can be traced back to Robert Michels' book *Political Parties* which was first published in 1911. Michels was an Italian sociologist who took a particular interest in the growth of working class organisations committed to socialism. Although these organisations claimed to espouse democratic principles Michels argued that their very success led to bureaucratic, and therefore undemocratic, means of administration. In the process of organising the masses the rank and file were being largely excluded from effective participation in their own movement as power progressively passed to union bosses, professional politicians and full time organisers. According to Michels the result would be that the democratic ideals of working class politics would be subverted by the oligarchic structure of the organisations supposedly dedicated to their realisation.

Not all subsequent research supports Michels' view that the growth of oligarchy is inevitable. However, the suspicion remains that the organisations that are supposed to serve our needs are in fact becoming our masters. Nowhere does this danger seem greater than in relation to the State where the use of new technology as a means of surveillance and control outstrips the readiness of governments to devise new ways of protecting human rights. This potential threat to individual liberty has been dramatised by twentieth century novelists such as George Orwell and Franz Kafka. What the final outcome will be, no one can know for sure.

Question 7
The occupational structure: what are the changes? why are they significant?

At the turn of the century Britain was largely a working class society with over three quarters of the labour force classified as manual workers. Since then the proportion of manual workers has steadily declined and recent estimates are that they are now roughly half the labour force. However, this change has affected men and women differently. Amongst men the shift into non-manual work has been slower and a majority of male employees remain working class, but since the beginning of the century there has been a substantial increase in female employment. As a result women now make up approximately two fifths of the labour force and well over half of these are non-manual workers.

Changes in the proportion of workers in manual and non-manual occupations are related to changes in the size of different sectors of the economy. Employment in primary industries has declined most rapidly of all. For example, over nine per cent of the working population were employed in agriculture in 1900 but by 1970 this had fallen to one and a half per cent. In the secondary sector there has also been a decline in employment. During recent years this has been particularly marked in manufacturing industry. However, the service sector has continued to grow and by 1971 this employed over 50 per cent of the labour force.

Changes in the size and distribution of occupational groups are also related to changes in the organisation of economic activity. One of the main changes here has been the growth of the public sector which, if one includes the nationalised industries, now accounts for over a quarter of the labour force. However, even more important are developments in technology. These have led not only to a smaller but also a more heterogeneous working class. Increasingly manual workers have split into occupational groups separated by differences in skill, pay, and working conditions.

If anything the process of occupational differentiation has proceeded even further amongst non-manual groups where it is now possible to distinguish four main categories of worker. These are routine clerical and sales staff, technical and professional employees, managers and administrators, and owners of independent businesses. The first three of these occupational groups have expanded so rapidly that they are sometimes referred to as the new middle classes. Their growth has also modified the occupational hierarchy, and white-collar workers now occupy such a variety of work and market situations that the relative homogeneity of the middle class has been replaced by a fragmentary class structure.

The combined result of the above changes has been to alter the overall shape of the occupational structure. This used to be shaped like a pyramid but has changed because the hierarchy has shrunk at the base and expanded in the middle. One consequence of this is that there appears to be more upward than downward mobility. This is because the growth in the demand for non-manual workers has been met largely by recruiting people from working class backgrounds. As a result a sizeable proportion of the working class has been on the move and many sons and daughters of manual workers now perform white-collar work.

Most of this additional demand for white-collar workers has come from the expansion of the service sector, and women in particular have taken up the new employment opportunities. One effect of this is that many married women are no longer economically dependent on their husbands. In addition their earnings have contributed to the higher living standards enjoyed by affluent workers. Also, the fact that married women are concentrated in white-collar work has meant that the much smaller working class now has more ties with other occupational groups.

Some sociologists have claimed that the effect of these and other changes has been to widen the distribution of rewards and opportunities. According to this view social classes are tending to converge and the stratification system is being recast in a middle class mould. However, the significance of changes in the occupational structure should not be overestimated. Although they have contributed to some redistribution of income they have not materially affected inequalities of wealth.

It is this fact that is more significant than the shift into non-manual occupations. This is because the vast majority of white-collar workers are clerks. Most of these are engaged in routine office work, and pay, prospects and conditions of work are often no better, and sometimes worse, than those of manual workers. Furthermore, if one regards clerical and other low grade non-manual occupations as on a par with the manual occupations from which they are conventionally separated then the overwhelming majority of the labour force remain essentially wage earners.

The significance of changes further up the occupational hierarchy also requires careful interpretation. One of the most important of these is the emergence of a salaried managerial stratum with day-to-day responsibility for running modern business enterprises. This is alleged to have separated ownership and control of industry, a process Ralf Dahrendorf describes as the decomposition of capital. However, the consequences of this managerial revolution should not be overemphasised. There remains a basic identity of interest between owners and top managers who, in addition to direct financial links, often share a privileged way of life, a common culture, and family connections.

These facts show that despite changes in the jobs people do there is an essential continuity to the relationship between capital and labour. What has happened to that relationship is that social, economic, and political developments have combined to create a more complex occupational structure which has made class boundaries difficult to draw. However, as Frank Parkin has emphasised occupation remains the backbone of the reward system and this is underlined by the persistence of occupationally related inequalities in health, housing, and education. In conjunction with the symptoms of inequality such as industrial conflict, alienation, and poverty these differences show that the significance of changes in the occupational structure has to be interpreted in terms of class divisions that remain entrenched.

Commentary

The significance of changes in the occupational structure is not a subject upon which sociologists can agree. For example, A.H. Halsey distinguishes the middle from the lower-middle classes but he nonetheless follows convention in regarding all white-collar workers as in the middle of the occupational structure. On this basis Halsey is led to argue that this century has seen a shift in the occupational structure 'from the shape of a pyramid to that of an electric light bulb' (*Change in British Society*, second edition, p.25). However, John Westergaard and Henrietta Resler disagree. They argue that

it is plainly false to postulate a major shift towards 'middle' and higher-paid jobs, when the bulk of the labour force are in essentially wage-earning jobs, however those jobs are conventionally designated; and when many white-collar employees are now merely semi-skilled operatives in the world of office work.

(*Class in a Capitalist Society*, p.73)

This kind of diametrically opposed difference of opinion is not confined to the question of the contemporary significance of the division between manual and non-manual labour. It also surfaces in the debate about ownership and control. For example, Ralf Dahrendorf asserts that

> The separation of ownership and control has replaced one group by two whose positions, roles, and attitudes are far from identical.

(*Class and Class Conflict in an Industrial Society*, p.47)

Westergaard and Resler reply:

> The division is a myth. There is certainly none visible between owners and top controllers, the directors of companies. For directors in general are themselves large owners of share capital.

(*Class in a Capitalist Society*, p.161)

If this seems confusing the way to recognise how different authors line up on these issues is to see whether they refer to nations like modern Britain as 'industrial' or 'capitalist' societies.

Question 8
Technology at work: is it the main determinant of workers' attitudes and behaviour?

Technological determinists argue that a particular level of technological development imposes a corresponding work environment which governs the quality of life at work and the degree of job satisfaction. Their view can be illustrated by examining the spread of the factory system which they have explained in terms of technical innovations leading to the mechanisation of production. From this perspective social characteristics of factories like the division of labour and the bureaucratic organisation of work are regarded as necessary for industry to function effectively. However, though technically more efficient the factory system reduces opportunities for self-expression, creativity and fulfilment at work.

On the other hand, not all industries employ the same technology and those who argue that this is the crucial factor in explaining workers' attitudes and behaviour have attempted to test the hypothesis by comparing workers in different industries. For example, in his book *Alienation and Freedom* the American sociologist Richard Blauner attempted to measure the effects of four different work situations.

For Blauner the printing industry was representative of craft technology. Workers were able to control their work rate, were not closely supervised, and were required to use considerable skill in the performance of their job. In addition they worked in small groups on a variety of tasks. However, in the textile industry most workers were machine minders and the pace of their work was largely determined by the speed and number of machines they tended. Workers were expected to stay constantly by their machines performing routine operations and supervisors were employed to make sure that they did.

The third industry studied by Blauner was automobile manufacturing. This is representative of assembly line techniques of production. Here workers are almost literally 'appendages to the machine' because the speed of the line controls the rate of work and all decisions about how the job is to be done are made and enforced by management. Finally, Blauner investigated the chemical industry as an example of process technology. In this type of industry the entire production process is automatically controlled and workers are mainly employed to monitor, adjust, maintain and repair plant and machinery. Here Blauner found a more heterogeneous labour force who had jobs which gave them both autonomy and responsibility.

Blauner claimed that in each case the type of technology accounts for most of the differences in work satisfaction and industrial behaviour. For example, amongst print workers Blauner found a high degree of job satisfaction. He attributes this to the printer's freedom from external controls, ability to identify with the product, and membership of an occupational community. However, Blauner argues that the automobile worker is at the other extreme, since each worker is virtually powerless to control the work situation, is required to perform meaninglessly repetitive tasks, and is relatively isolated from other workers. Assembly line technology is thus seen by Blauner as the main source of alienation and labour unrest in the automobile industry.

However, a study of affluent workers conducted by John Goldthorpe and David Lockwood does not confirm the importance attributed to technology by Blauner. This research also studied a range of different work situations but Goldthorpe and Lockwood found that workers had very similar attitudes. On this basis the authors argue that approaches that concentrate on the implications of technology are inadequate in so far as they ignore a network of social relationships that extend beyond the factory gates.

In particular Goldthorpe and Lockwood emphasise the importance of prior orientations to work. Their research showed that most semiskilled workers did not expect their work to be intrinsically rewarding. On the contrary, most saw work as a means to an end and were prepared to accept its inherent deprivations in return for relatively high wages. They therefore had an instrumental attitude and their industrial behaviour was shaped not so much by the technology they worked with as by the value they placed upon their family life and leisure activities.

Goldthorpe and Lockwood's findings stimulated further research which also demonstrates that technology is not always the most important factor. For example, Dorothy Wedderburn and Rosemary Crompton's study showed that whilst the production technology had some effect on attitudes and behaviour it did not account for general orientations to work. As Duncan Gallie's research shows these orientations are influenced by cultural factors. He studied oil refinery workers in Britain and France but despite their use of the same technology there were important differences in attitudes and behaviour. However, one criticism of all these studies is the extent to which they rely on interviews and questionnaires. This means that when the authors claim that work often considered alienating is not necessarily experienced as such they rely on the accuracy of subjective assessments of job satisfaction made by their sample of workers. Marxists reply that what this fails to recognise is that alienation is essentially an objective condition generated by the overall position of wage labour in a capitalist society.

Marx's view was that there is nothing inherent in technology itself that causes alienation and conflict. However, under capitalism the interests of workers are subordinated to the profit motive and the character of work is shaped by a social relationship that rests on exploitation. From this perspective job fragmentation and bureaucracy appear in a new light. For example, the American Marxists Samuel Bowles and Herbert Gintis argue that the real function of these characteristics of capitalism is not to increase efficiency but to control the workforce.

The effect that managerial control can have on employees is illustrated by Huw Benyon's study *Working for Ford*. His participant observation research at Ford's Halewood plant near Liverpool discovered widespread hostility to the company amongst the labour force. However, the main complaint of workers was not the unrewarding nature of their work but the attitude of management. That attitude placed a higher value on production than on people. This is crucial because despite the relevance of factors like technology and work orientation Benyon's study shows that ultimately the attitudes and behaviour of workers are governed by the need for dignity and respect at work.

Commentary

If you have never worked in industry you may find it difficult to appreciate the stupefying monotony of the jobs performed by many shop-floor workers. This is where you will find Huw Benyon's book useful. He points out that at Halewood the men fitting gearboxes performed the same operation forty times an hour and three hundred and twenty times a shift. In a five shift week they would fit sixteen hundred gearboxes and then do the same or similar jobs in subsequent weeks, months and years. As one trim line shop steward put it:

'The point about this place is that the work destroys you. It destroys you physically and mentally. The biggest problem for people is getting to accept it, to accept being here day in and day out. So you've got low morale from every point of view. You're inflicted with a place of work and you've got to adapt because it won't adapt to you'.

(quoted in Benyon, p.188)

However, a recurring theme in Benyon's book is that the despair and resentment felt by workers was not so much caused by the assembly line itself as by the way it was run. For example, in the opinion of one worker:

'They treat their labour as machinery here. The Personnel Department just doesn't exist. In many cases they are just cruel. All they're concerned with is production problems. It's production, production all the time with them.' (p.97)

Question 9
Industrial disputes: why are they not randomly distributed between industries?

Industrial disputes take various forms but in modern western societies the most visible and dramatic symptom of labour unrest is strikes. In Britain as in other countries, strikes are commonly regarded as an index of industrial conflict and their number, size and duration are recorded in official statistics. These statistics indicate that the relative propensity to strike varies between industries. For example, statistics published by the Department of Employment show that during the period 1966–1975 the most strike-prone industries in Britain were the docks, coalmining and the automobile industry, whereas agriculture, public utilities and the service sector had generally low strike rates.

To some extent this pattern is confirmed by international comparisons. For example, in their article 'The Inter-Industry Propensity to Strike' Clark Kerr and Abraham Siegel analysed the strike records of eleven countries. They claim that the comparison shows that miners, dockers and seamen are consistently amongst the most strike-prone workers. Kerr and Siegel argue that this is because these occupational groups tend to live in communities that are fairly homogeneous and geographically set apart from the wider society. Allegedly the relative isolation of these workers increases their common awareness of grievances, enhances group solidarity and insulates strikers from the effects of social disapproval.

This explanation of the pattern of strikes seems plausible at first sight because striking is a form of collective behaviour which depends upon some degree of group cohesion. However, although solidarity amongst workers is a necessary condition of organised resistance to management this is not, by itself, a sufficient explanation of strikes. What Kerr and Siegel neglect is the fact that most strikes are calculated acts designed to enforce a demand or express a grievance. Under these circumstances the strike threat is often a tactical weapon. However, in the bargaining process on the factory floor, the opportunity to win concessions from management by taking strike action will vary because the effectiveness of strikes depends partly on the production technology.

This is illustrated by J.W. Kuhn's study *Bargaining in Grievance Settlement*. Kuhn compared the electrical and rubber industries in the US. In the rubber industry stockpiling raw materials and finished products is difficult and costly so management aims at continuity of production. However, this gives workers an advantage because unauthorised stoppages of work at strategic points in the production process can disrupt the plant's total production at a cost to workers which is small in comparison to that inflicted upon management. According to Kuhn it is this opportunity to engage in 'fractional bargaining' which largely accounts for a strike rate in the rubber industry five times as high as in the electrical industry.

Some support for Kuhn's interpretation of levels of strike activity can be found in the trend of strikes in Britain. Most strikes in Britain are not large scale, protracted disputes involving thousands of workers spread throughout an entire industry or major company. They occur at plant level when some or all the workers spontaneously down tools to express a grievance. The overwhelming majority of these strikes are unofficial, involve only a relatively small number of workers and are quickly settled. However, they are often very effective ways of winning minor concessions from management because in industries using advanced technology employers are often more vulnerable to strike activity.

One industry which seems to confirm the importance of technology in the level of industrial disputes is the automobile industry. Here a stoppage of work by only a handful of operatives can bring the entire assembly line to a halt and, as Robert Blauner has emphasised, assembly line technology also contributes to high levels of alienation which undermines the worker's moral commitment to the firm. However, the problem with this technological explanation of the level of industrial disputes is that within some industries the same technology is found in conjunction with widely varying strike rates. For example, in the automobile industry there is a much higher strike rate in Britain than in Germany or Japan and, even within Britain, there are wide variations in the industrial relations record of different firms.

Of course technology could be working in association with other variables to produce a particular level of strike activity and it has been suggested that organisational structure, the number of workers and their level of skill also affect strike rates. The problem with all these explanations is that they view the behaviour of workers as if it were mechanically determined by social forces. This ignores the fact that workers consciously interpret social situations and act in terms of the meaning they attribute to the structural characteristics of work.

The importance of the subjective dimension for the understanding of industrial conflict is illustrated by studies of particular disputes. For example, in *Wildcat Strike* Alvin Gouldner studied a strike at an American gypsum mine. Ostensibly the strike was for higher wages. However, Gouldner found that the underlying cause of the dispute was a series of changes in work practice. These had altered the traditional basis of the relationship between workers and managers and resulted in tighter control of the labour force. Informal relationships between the men and their supervisors deteriorated under the new regime and the strike was more to do with relationships which had been redefined in terms of the conflicting interests of men and management than with purely economic demands.

Gouldner's study shows that the circumstances that provoke a strike can be more complex than is commonly assumed. This point has been developed by Richard Hyman. He argues that although industrial conflict is inevitable in present-day society the level of rationality displayed by workers can vary. One consequence of this is that workers with a similar sense of grievance do not always act in the same way. However, if the same structural conditions do not always generate the same response it means that no explanation of differences in strike rates is possible without also examining forms of consciousness and orientations to work.

Commentary

Not all industrial disputes end in strikes. Sometimes it is possible to settle conflict peacefully through existing negotiating machinery. Should this not work there are various options open to employees. These can include work to rule, overtime bans, token strikes, strikes by key personnel and all out stoppages. To some extent these different forms of industrial action can be seen as alternatives and which one workers choose will depend upon local circumstances and workers' definitions of the situation.

In addition to the above types of organised conflict there are also various forms of unorganised conflict. Before collective action can take place there needs to be a shared sense of grievance, a degree of solidarity, and a belief amongst workers that by taking collective action they have the means to do something about their problem. If one or more of these conditions is not present it is likely that workers who experience deprivation at work will resort to unorganised conflict. This also comes in a variety of forms, including absenteeism, poor timekeeping, labour turnover, restrictions on output and individual acts of sabotage.

These various forms of unorganised conflict are often regarded by employers as labour indiscipline rather than industrial disputes. However, if the labour force is not sufficiently cohesive to act collectively then individual acts of defiance may be the only way of expressing a grievance. The problem, of course, is that the individual employee is then vulnerable to retaliatory action by management. This is why most unorganised forms of conflict are relatively ineffectual and Richard Hyman argues that because of this they are generally less rational responses to deprivation than organised forms of conflict. (See Richard Hyman, *Strikes*, Chapter 5.)

Question 10
The professions: consensus or conflict view?

The consensus view of the professions stems from Emile Durkheim's analysis of the implications of the division of labour in society. For Durkheim occupational differentiation was the dominant characteristic of modern society. However, although the specialisation of work roles enabled goods and services to be produced more efficiently Durkheim believed that it also weakened the normative regulation of economic activity. Whereas in pre-industrial societies the force of tradition and the power of institutions such as the family combined to foster a sense of duty towards others, this was now threatened by the individualism and self-interest which dominated the market. What was needed was a new moral framework which would reconcile the pursuit of personal gain with the needs of society as a whole. Durkheim argued that this role would be performed by professional groups.

Durkheim's ideas have been developed by functionalists such as Bernard Barber and Talcott Parsons, who both argue that the professions are a unique category of occupation with a special role to play. For example, Parsons claims that unlike the business community the primary orientation of professionals is to the welfare of others. In this way professionals ensure that the benefits of scientific and technical knowledge are shared by all. Barber, who agrees with Parsons that the professions can be objectively distinguished from other occupational groups, argues that their selflessness accounts for the prestige they enjoy. However, as well as being honoured for their devotion to the public interest, professionals are also highly rewarded materially. Barber explains this in terms of the functional importance of the work they do. Thus, because their expertise is so important to society, their earnings reflect society's recognition of the value of the contribution they make.

For consensus theorists the functions of 'true' professions are institutionalised through their structure and, in particular, through professional associations. These bodies are regarded as the guardians of the public interest with a special responsibility for ensuring that the profession renders the best possible service to its clients. One way professional associations are alleged to do this is by seeking to ensure that all practitioners are technically competent. For example, new recruits to most professions have to undergo a lengthy period of training and, before they qualify as full members, they may also have to pass professional examinations and complete a supervised apprenticeship. In addition many professional associations try to enforce a code of ethics and where the association's members have a legal monopoly on the provision of a service they can discipline members who break the code by expulsion. This effectively bars the offender from further practice.

Functionalists regard the power of the professions to insist upon standards of competence and morality as further evidence of public spiritedness. However it is equally possible to interpret these two forms of control in conflict terms. From this perspective the power of the professions to supervise entry into the occupation is seen as a way of restricting the supply of trained and qualified practitioners and manipulating the market to their own advantage. Similarly, the internal disciplinary procedures of the professions can be interpreted as a means of preventing public scrutiny of the quality of the services they provide. For these two reasons conflict theorists regard professionalism as ultimately no more than a successful occupational strategy used by professionals to ensure high income and status for themselves.

From a conflict perspective therefore the professional's alleged commitment to a higher calling is an ideology. Behind the myth lies the underlying reality of powerful vested interests out to protect themselves rather than the interests of clients. This view receives strong support from Ivan Illich. His central idea is that the professions are out of control. Teachers, doctors, lawyers and other professionals are manufacturing artificial needs which are not so much in the public's interest as in the interest of an expanding professional bureaucracy.

Illich's views can be illustrated by his critique of the medical profession. For example, in his book *Medical Nemesis* he argues that the main reason for the increase in life expectancy in industrial societies is not the skill of doctors but the improvements in sanitation, nutrition and housing that have created a healthier population. However, patients are encouraged to believe that modern medicine is the answer to all their problems and they surrender themselves into the hands of doctors because of their mistaken confidence in medical experts.

According to Illich one result of this is that many patients undergo treatment which is unnecessary, useless and even harmful to their health. This is particularly so when treatment involves drugs with dangerous side-effects. Also drugs do not always cure illnesses and sometimes seriously affect the quality of life whilst prolonging it for only a few more months. However, even more important than doubts over their effectiveness are the harmful consequences of the overuse of drugs. This has led to the 'medicalised addiction' of a growing proportion of the population and Illich claims that it is time to recognise that the medical establishment is itself now a threat to health.

Despite describing many of the potential sources of conflict between professionals and their clients Illich does not go on to analyse the position of professions in the class structure. This is an important omission because although in theory the professions provide equal services to all, in practice this is impossible in a stratified society. This is most clearly illustrated by the legal profession. It cannot dispense justice impartially, not only because of the expense of litigation but because under capitalism the law itself guarantees the rights of property owners. This means that in following their profession lawyers will cater especially for the needs of the wealthy, and, to some extent, this is true of most professions.

Commentary

You may have noticed that in this essay I do not give a general definition of the professions. This is deliberate, because sociologists cannot agree on the characteristics of the professions and, in practice, most definitions are clearly 'persuasive'. (A persuasive definition is a definition that does not just denote what something is but tries to get you, the reader, to view that something in a certain way.) For example, Talcott Parsons claims that:

> In sociological terminology a profession is a cluster of 'occupational' roles,
> that is roles in which the incumbents perform certain functions valued in the
> society in general and by these activities, typically 'earn a living' at a 'full time
> job'.
>
> (*Essays in Sociological Theory*, revised edition, p.372)

Notice that for Parsons the professions perform their functions on behalf of
'society in general', and in terms of this definition one is already committed to a
consensus point of view.

On the other hand Terence Johnson claims that professionalism is

> a peculiar type of occupational control rather than an expression of the
> inherent nature of particular occupations. A profession is not, then, an
> occupation, but a means of controlling an occupation.
>
> (*Professions and Power*, p.45)

His point is that professions are ways of managing tensions in the relationship
between practitioners and clients and in making this the most important point
his definition implies a conflict perspective.

Chapter 4

Population and the family

As you come to compare one topic with another you should notice that cutting across particular areas of specialisation are broader theoretical divisions. These divisions are commonly referred to as sociological perspectives and, if your course demands a knowledge of theory, you will need to be able to discriminate between the different perspectives. In this chapter the focus will be on one of those perspectives, namely functionalism, and how it interprets the existence and place of the family in society.

The first thing to notice about functionalism is the variety of terms that is used to describe it. It can be referred to as 'systems theory', 'a consensus point of view' or 'the holistic approach'. This can seem confusing but do not be put off. These various ways of describing functionalism highlight different aspects of the functionalist perspective.

Briefly, functionalism is referred to as 'systems theory' because functionalists describe society as a real system made up of distinct but interrelated parts. It is called a 'consensus point of view' because these various parts are seen as integrated with each other so that they function in relative harmony. It is known as a 'holistic approach' because functionalists maintain that in order to explain any one part of society one must understand its relationships with other parts.

Which of these three descriptive labels is most appropriate depends on what aspect of functionalism you are most concerned with. In particular it depends upon whether you want to emphasise the views of functionalists concerning what society is like, or their account of how it works, or their ideas about how it can be explained. Although these issues are all related they are separated in the analysis that follows in order to simplify the explanation.

The functionalist view of society as a system

To begin with the functionalist view of what society is like: why view society as a system? Three main arguments have been put forward. The first asserts that though within sociology functionalism has been regarded as a perspective it is in fact the method of science in general. This view was put forward by Kingsley Davis in his article 'The Myth of Functional Analysis as a Special Method in Sociology and Social Anthropology'. There he claimed that 'the traits most frequently cited as characterising functional analysis . . . describe what any science does'. On this basis Davis went on to argue that the only scientific way of explaining social facts was in terms of social systems and that therefore functionalism was synonymous with sociology itself.

This view is rarely heard today. Davis was writing in 1959 and then functionalism was the dominant perspective in sociology. Now that this is no longer the case the claims made by functionalists tend to be more modest. A typical example is the view of Robert K. Merton. In the introduction to *Contemporary Social Problems* (fourth edition) he argues that 'no single theory accounts for every aspect of the wide range of social problems'. Merton suggests, as many modern functionalists do, that progress in sociology will depend on combining the insights of various perspectives.

The second justification of a systems approach starts from the nature of the 'thing' to be explained rather than the method of its explanation. Usually society is compared to an organism and it is argued that you can explain both in the same way. The most extreme exponent of this point of view was the nineteenth century English sociologist Herbert Spencer. He claimed that 'So completely is society organised on the same system as an individual being that . . . the same definition of life applies to both' (quoted in N.S. Timasheff, *Sociological Theory*, revised edition, p.35). On this basis it is often argued that the science of biology acts as a model for sociology.

This argument was popularised by the English anthropologist A.R. Radcliffe-Brown and his view influenced American functionalists such as Kingsley Davis (1948) and Ely Chinoy (1954). They both describe the organic analogy as 'helpful'. However, the problem is that though in some respects society is similar to a living organism in other respects it is not. In practice this means that the argument raises more difficulties than it solves. (For an explanation see Question 39.) As a result the organic analogy has dropped out of favour and, though it still lurks in the background, most modern functionalists prefer to do without this kind of comparison.

This leaves the third argument put forward in favour of systems theory. It rests upon what has come to be known as 'the Hobbesian problem of order'. Thomas Hobbes was a seventeenth century English philosopher. He believed that people were naturally selfish. However, if everyone was allowed to pursue their own self-interest by whatever means were most effective it would lead to perpetual conflict. This was in nobody's long term interest because social life would be impossible and without society human existence would be 'solitary, poor, nasty, brutish and short'.

Hobbes said that people escape these evils by forming a social contract. He saw this as an agreement between people who formed communities by surrendering their freedom to fight one another in return for the protection of a sovereign power. However, Hobbes' claim to have discovered the basis of order is unsatisfactory. Although it may be useful to imagine a society based upon this kind of implicit agreement between its members the problem with Hobbes' theory is that it has no basis in fact. As a result it came to be realised that what was needed was a sociological solution to the problem of order.

One attempt to devise such a solution is to be found in the works of Emile Durkheim and Talcott Parsons. Both rejected Hobbes' view that social order rested upon fear and calculation and proposed instead that it depends upon a shared morality. In Durkheim this is referred to as 'the collective conscience' and in Parsons as 'a value consensus'. Both emphasise that submission to social rules does not normally depend upon self-interest but on a belief in their validity. In Durkheim the source of this belief was society itself but in the writing of Parsons society is described as a social system. This is because Parsons sees the commitment to commonly accepted values as realised in a network of roles and institutions that are constantly engaged in the normative regulation of conduct.

Parsons believed that social order was maintained by a social system adapted to produce this very result. Although his ideas have been extensively criticised this remains a popular defence of the functionalist perspective. Partly this is due to the fact that his is a more subtle justification than either of the previous two. In addition Parsons' view derives a degree of plausibility from the fact that social order is an important issue whatever perspective one takes. However, whether the problem of order is *the* fundamental issue in sociology and whether systems theory is *the* answer to that problem are matters of dispute. This has led some functionalists to favour a pragmatic point of view. Their argument is that any attempt to justify one's assumptions is ultimately fruitless. The task is to apply those assumptions in order to see if they lead to useful results. This raises issues to do with the functionalist explanation of how society works.

The functionalist view of how social systems work

There have been many attempts to explain how society functions and even more attempts to explain the contributions made by particular parts. For the time being explanations to do with the functioning of specific institutions will be left on one side. Many of these arguments are dealt with in the essays on substantive questions. Here the functionalist explanation of how society continues to operate as a 'going concern' will be examined. The most ambitious attempt to provide such an explanation is again to be found in the works of Talcott Parsons.

In his book *The Social System* (1951) Parsons stated that 'If such a system is to constitute a persistent order or to undergo an orderly process of developmental change certain functional prerequisites must be met'. Functional prerequisites can be regarded as problems that any society must solve if it is to continue to exist. Parsons believed that there were four such problems and he argued that it was in response to these problems that societies developed an institutional structure.

First, the system must be adapted to its environment. Were it not society could not provide its members with the means to survive. To ensure that they are able to live arrangements must be made to provide at least some of the population with food and shelter. For Parsons the production and distribution of these scarce resources is the primary function of the economic institutions of society.

Second, the system must make provision for goal attainment. In other words all social systems require procedures through which their members can agree on collective goals. In addition to establishing what these goals are to be there will also be a need to decide on priorities, to allocate resources, and to ensure that the resources are used for the proper purposes. For Parsons the setting of goals and the mobilisation of the resources to achieve them is the primary function of political institutions.

The third problem that must be resolved is pattern maintenance and tension management. This is to do with motivating individual actors to perform socially necessary roles. There are two aspects to this. To begin with, if a pattern of roles is to be maintained for any length of time social systems must be in a position to solve the problem of generations. This means there must be mechanisms to ensure that there is a continuous supply of competent and adequately motivated role players committed to the values of society. However, it is also necessary to maintain the motivation of existing role players. They have to cope with stresses induced by the need to live up to role expectations. This means that in addition to mechanisms that produce the kinds of personality needed to make the system work there is also a need for further mechanisms to prevent the tensions that result interfering with the continuity of effective role performance. For Parsons both these functions are mainly performed by kinship institutions.

Finally there is the problem of integration. This problem is met by institutions whose primary function is to contribute solidarity to the social system. One way in which this is achieved is by cultural and community organisations. For example, institutions like organised religion and mass education furnish members of society with collective representations. This contributes to social order because individuals who share a 'symbolic universe of meaning' find it easier to co-operate in different spheres of life. However, as well as fostering common values there is also a need to enforce common norms. This is one function of legal institutions. They are also said to contribute to social integration because the law establishes a generalised code of rights and obligations backed up by judicial sanctions.

For Parsons the four functional prerequisites described above are conditions that govern the operation of any social system. The first two, adaptation and goal attainment, are largely to do with the practical needs of individuals and society. These needs are referred to as instrumental prerequisites and the institutions which meet them are largely concerned with getting things done. However, if this is to be achieved through interaction with others there will be a need to ensure that people can and do co-operate. This depends on pattern maintenance and integration. These are expressive prerequisites and the institutions that meet them are mainly concerned with controlling emotions and injecting vitality into culture.

This leaves us with the following picture of society as a whole. It is first and foremost a system that reconciles the needs of society with those of the individual. This is achieved through an institutional structure made up of four major subsystems. The economic and political subsystems are the institutionalised means of achieving practical goals. The kinship and cultural subsystems are the institutionalised means of reducing friction. Each subsystem mobilises human resources through the performance of roles. These are the patterns of behaviour that are expected from social actors with positions in the institutional order. They are composed of more specific guidelines for action known as norms and specific norms are united in fundamental values which are the ultimate bases of the functioning of society.

In Parsons' scheme the parts of society fit together like a gigantic jigsaw puzzle. However, because societies exist over time they are dynamic systems which are not just integrated through their structure but also through social processes. The most important of these is socialisation. This is not just a matter of learning what to say and do in specific situations. To be fully effective socialisation also involves incorporating the values of society into the personalities of its members so as to bring their psyches into line with system needs. Then, when they have internalised the culture, members of society will not just conform out of expediency but will be actively motivated to uphold and defend standards that they themselves believe in.

On the other hand, not everyone can be equally committed to the values of society and some will seek to gratify their needs in socially unacceptable ways. This is called deviance. Its significance for social systems is that behaviour patterns that break the norms of society tend to disturb its equilibrium. If allowed to go unchecked this could eventually lead to social disintegration. This is why there is also a need for mechanisms of social control. These mechanisms are involved in all interactive processes and it is through them that social systems counter disruptive tendencies and seek to restore the alignment between personality and social structure.

The function of mechanisms of social control is to maintain and repair the normative fabric of society. This is only partly to do with containing deviant tendencies. Instability will also be generated by degrees of malintegration between system parts and, from outside the system, events such as natural disasters and foreign wars can also pose a threat to social order. However, once a disturbance is introduced into the system it tends to trigger the behavioural adjustments required to restore the system to relative equilibrium. In the process there will, of course, be modifications to the social structure and where this is part of an orderly sequence of changes functionalists refer to the system as in a state of 'moving equilibrium'.

The concept of 'moving equilibrium' was used by Parsons as an explanation of how structural changes occur in relatively stable societies. He was also convinced that there was a direction to these changes. This led Parsons to embrace an evolutionary theory of social change. More specifically he argued that social systems become more complex as their capacity to control their environment increases. However, in order to justify this view Parsons found it necessary to assume that social evolution was a continuation of biological evolution and that the same basic mechanisms were involved. This is significant because although he avoided direct comparisons between society and an organism, when it came to explaining social change even Parsons was forced to regard social systems as if they had a life of their own. This raises the third major issue. It is to do with the kind of explanation that functionalists offer.

The functionalist view of sociological explanation

One influential point of view is that of Robert K. Merton. In his article 'Manifest and Latent Functions' he argued that the central orientation of functionalism is 'the practice of interpreting data by establishing their consequences for larger structures'. In other words functional explanations interpret social facts by examining their effects on the system of which they are a part. Sometimes this leads to explanations that emphasise the ways in which individual members of society benefit from social institutions. However, the more common approach is to argue that it is society, rather than its members, which is both the initiator and prime beneficiary of institutionalised behaviour.

This kind of explanation is teleological. A theory is teleological if it claims to explain the existence of some phenomenon in terms of its beneficial consequences. This is what functionalists do when they interpret the characteristics of social institutions in terms of their contribution to the needs of society. Of course functionalists recognise that in addition to their useful effects institutions can have undesirable consequences too. However, there is always a tendency to assume that the very existence of an institution demonstrates that its advantageous consequences outweigh its dysfunctions. Furthermore, by weighing up the net contribution that each institution makes to the wellbeing of society functionalists believe that they are able to explain both social structure and social change.

Whether or not these assumptions are justified depends upon issues that will be dealt with later. For the time being the aim is to make the functionalist case rather than criticise it. However, part of that case rests upon the substantive contributions functionalists claim to have made to sociological theory. One substantive area where they have been particularly active is the sociology of the family and this is reflected in the subsequent essays. However, before you turn to the more specific issues dealt with in those essays it is worth getting a general view of how functionalism regards the family.

Functionalist views of the family

In an introductory text the American sociologist Alex Inkeles provides an illustration of the functionalist line of reasoning. He states that 'if a society is to continue it must periodically find new members. In all known societies this need is met by some form of family system. The family is the institution which "acts" for society to ensure fulfilment of the function of sexual reproduction, of early care of the dependent infant, and of his initial training in the ways of society in which he will live' (*What is Sociology?*, p.35). Here, in the classic functionalist manner, Inkeles is treating society as if it had a truly independent existence separate from the existence of its individual members. This is also implied in the functionalist account of how particular institutions 'act' and why they change.

The family is regarded as part of a real system. It makes a positive contribution to the survival of that system by producing the kinds of people that the system requires. This function is performed through the structure of the family. Essentially this structure consists of a framework of norms that define appropriate conduct. These norms are realised in the roles of individual family members and in their relationships with each other and with non-family members. This is institutionalised behaviour. Its observed consequences for other subsystems and society as a whole are the functions of the family. By performing its functions the family helps maintain social equilibrium. It therefore plays a fundamentally beneficial role in society.

In addition to contributing to social order the family is able to adapt to social change. In simple societies the extended family is the basic organising principle of social life and virtually all system needs are met through the kinship network.

However, evolutionary developments lead to structural differentiation. Formal organisations emerge and take over religious, political, legal and economic functions previously performed in the family. As a result the family becomes a smaller group which performs fewer functions. This makes it a more functionally efficient institution. It now concentrates on its essential functions and continues to perform a beneficial role by specialising in tasks that have become more important in a highly differentiated society.

To sum up the three aspects of functionalism as they apply to the family: the family is part of a system; it unites people through its structure; it is beneficial both to them and the system itself. This is an optimistic view, implying that it is society's self-stabilising mechanisms that ensure its members co-operate to their mutual advantage. The practical implication would seem to be that, as members of society, we should defend and even seek to strengthen social institutions, but the following essays show this is an attitude not everyone shares.

Question 11
The birth rate: what are the changes? why have they occurred?

In the last 100 years Britain has experienced a demographic transition. In the 1880s the birth rate was over thirty per 1000 population. Recent figures show that it is now about thirteen. From an average family size of about six the average number of children per family has declined to just over two. This reduction in fertility by almost two thirds is associated with an increase in the popularity of the two child family. Figures published by the Central Statistical Office show that in 1977 37 per cent of children in Great Britain lived in this type of family (*People and their Families, 1980*).

The decline in the birth rate began in the middle classes in the 1870s and it took fifty years to reach all major occupational groups. Overall the decline was fairly regular up to the mid 1950s with the exception of only temporary 'baby booms' after both world wars. Then in the late 1950s the birth rate began to increase and this trend was maintained up to 1964. Since 1964 there have been further fluctuations with a generally downward trend up to 1977 followed by a slight rise. However, although the birth rate has been more erratic since World War II, the fluctuations have been around a generally low level.

Explaining these changes in the birth rate is an enormously complex affair. Although the changes themselves are reliably documented in official statistics and government reports, an understanding of the reasons for the decline in fertility raises complex problems of human motivation. This is because most births depend upon a voluntary decision by the parents to have children. To explain the lower birth rate today one therefore needs to explain why the majority of married couples in modern Britain have decided to limit their family size.

One factor contributing to the decision to have a small family is the growth in knowledge of the means to prevent conception. Although contraception was available in the nineteenth century there was a widespread stigma associated with its use and there were difficulties over obtaining medical advice. Since then the secularisation of religious institutions and of society generally has helped make contraception more acceptable. For example, the Anglican church was converted to approval of the 'responsible' use of contraception in 1930. Although the Roman Catholic church still officially opposes artificial means of contraception, David Martin claims that one third of practising Roman Catholics approve of birth control (*A Sociology of English Religion*, p.56).

Changing attitudes to contraception have also been influenced by scientific and technical developments. These have led to an increase in the safety and reliability of contraceptives as well as to a reduction in cost. In addition the contraceptive pill is an unobtrusive method of birth control. It has been widely available since the 1960s and together with the legalisation of abortion in 1967 and the increase in voluntary sterilisation this has led to new opportunities for limiting family size.

The above are all means of preventing conception or terminating pregnancy amongst the sexually active population. In addition variations in the amount of sexual activity will have an effect on the birth rate. For example, one reason why the birth rate was so low during the interwar years was that during World War I Britain lost an estimated six hundred thousand men. This meant that after the war there was a shortage of men of marriageable age and many women who might have expected to marry and have children did not. The rise in fertility between 1955 and 1964 is partly due to similar factors. During this period marriage rates increased and the average age of marriage declined. Since about 90 per cent of births were legitimate this increased the population of women most likely to have children.

None of these factors explain why parents should want smaller families in the first place. J.A. Banks suggests that the trend in Britain began among the middle classes in the late nineteenth century because they saw family limitation as a way of preserving their economic advantages and privileged life style. At the time the incentive to have fewer children was being strengthened by the declining infant mortality rate and an economic recession. Middle class parents came to see that they were faced with a choice between limiting their family size or suffering a decline in living standards.

Economic and demographic changes also help to account for the reduction in the fertility of the working classes. For much of the nineteenth century children were an economic asset. However, the growth of restrictions on child labour and the introduction of compulsory education in 1880 meant that a large family was increasingly becoming an economic liability. This slowly led to a change of attitudes. As more parents realised that a smaller family would enable them to give more care to each child and have a higher living standard for themselves they too came to attribute greater importance to the quality of life rather than the size of their family.

This change in values has affected women most of all and their relative emancipation is both a cause and an effect of declining fertility. Although the process is far from complete, it has radically altered the position of women both in the family and the wider society. In their relationships with their husbands women now have greater equality and are less likely to have unwanted pregnancies forced upon them. In society at large there has been an expansion of opportunities for women leading to a large increase in the number of married women at work.

As a result married women today increasingly perform the dual role of mother and worker. Although, as feminists have pointed out, a woman's domestic role remains the basis of her status in society, her participation in the economy affects her role dramatically. This is because women have been able to use the available means of family limitation to plan their families in order to fit in with the demands of a career or the desire to maintain a higher living standard. This has meant that, in contrast with the nineteenth century wife who might expect to spend fifteen years in child bearing and nursing and have as many as ten pregnancies, women today concentrate child bearing and nursing into four to five years and have only two or three children.

Commentary

In *The Sociology of Fertility* Geoffrey Hawthorn invites the reader to imagine the implications of a perfect correlation between low fertility and working mothers. A positivist empiricist might argue that what this shows is that a reduction in fertility is caused by female employment. However, even if the association were perfect (which it is not) Hawthorn argues that this would still not be a satisfactory explanation. This is because

> When we say that working mothers cause low fertility we can only make the statement intelligible to ourselves by hypothesising an intervening mechanism. It is almost certain that this mechanism will refer to the mental states of the women, to their appraisal of the feelings about their roles and to the decisions that they have taken on the basis of those appraisals and feelings.
>
> (*The Sociology of Fertility*, p.54)

In other words the claim that 'working mothers cause low fertility' is really no explanation at all. This is because the statement omits to consider the motives which lead women to take up paid employment outside the home and the relationship between this and their decisions about when to have children and how many.

This is important because it also applies to other factors that are thought to have contributed to the decline in the birth rate. These factors include economic, demographic, legal and technological changes. However, in each case it is the significance of these changes that you must emphasise. If you give the impression that the decline has occurred automatically you will be deservedly penalised for not explaining the subjective importance of the various factors.

Question 12
Conjugal roles: the symmetrical family – myth or reality?

According to Michael Young and Peter Willmott a new kind of family has emerged as the dominant type in modern Britain. They consider it has three main characteristics: it is home centred, relatively isolated from wider kin, and involves a considerable desegregation of conjugal roles. Since Young and Willmott regard this third characteristic as the most important they refer to the modern family as symmetrical. This is meant to indicate that whilst some role differences remain marriage is now more equal and the relationship between husbands and wives is more of a partnership.

The concept of a symmetrical family is linked by Young and Willmott to their principle of stratified diffusion. According to this principle, industrialisation creates opportunities for a new life style and these are first taken up by the well off and then filter downwards through the stratification system. To explain their principle the authors resort to the analogy of a marching column. Just as all ranks in a column pass the same point so, they suggest, families may be at different stages in a process of evolution. This analogy is significant because in their suggestion that all groups in society are marching in the same direction and that the ranks advance in an orderly fashion they implicitly assume a consensus view of society.

The research upon which *The Symmetrical Family* is based builds on a series of family and community studies carried out by Young and Willmott in the London area. The authors argue that these studies confirm a movement from segregated to joint conjugal roles throughout the stratification system. However, they emphasise that this change has been most dramatic in the working class. Thus, they claim most working class families at the turn of the century were part of an extended kinship system whereas today the working class is increasingly adopting a nuclear family structure.

As David Lockwood has pointed out this difference between the 'traditional' and 'new' working class has been exaggerated. For example, in their study of the traditional working class area of Bethnal Green, Young and Willmott romanticise the segregated pattern of role relationships and largely ignore sources of social disorganisation and conflict. Then in the contrast they draw between this and the modern family they overemphasise the degree of symmetry in the latter. Symmetry implies that working wives receive compensation for taking a share of the role of breadwinner through greater involvement of husbands in household tasks, but this is not entirely confirmed by Young and Willmott's own data and the conclusions they draw from their evidence have been extensively criticised as biased and inconsistent.

If the degree of symmetry has been exaggerated, a point emphasised by feminists like Ann Oakley, Young and Willmott are none the less correct in pointing to genuine changes in conjugal roles. The decline in the birth rate and the mechanisation of the home have combined to release many married women onto the labour market while the reduced working week and higher wages have combined to make husbands more home centred. The fact that these changes appear to have affected the working class most of all is confirmed by John Goldthorpe and David Lockwood's study of affluent workers. Their research showed a trend towards a more home-centred existence amongst men for whom work was not a source of intrinsic satisfaction.

Other studies have also found a relationship between conjugal roles and social class. However, Elizabeth Bott's research shows that the one is not directly caused by the other. Bott's in-depth study of twenty families found too much variation and too many exceptions for this to be the case. Looking further afield for an explanation Bott focused on the characteristics of the social network through which families establish relationships beyond the nuclear boundary. A close-knit network tends to develop amongst families who have experienced little mobility. Here the marriage is superimposed upon existing relationships and this tends to lead to segregated conjugal roles and an asymmetrical husband-wife relationship.

Bott's study emphasises the way in which conjugal roles are related to patterns of normative control and social support exercised through external relationships. The husbands and wives she studied tended to regard their particular pattern of role relationships as normal, but the definition of 'normal' differed in response to patterns of social interaction. If roles are negotiated in this way it suggests that Young and Willmott's idea of a typical modern British family may well be misleading.

The significance of external relationships is confirmed by Colin Rosser and Christopher Harris's study in Swansea. They modify Bott's ideas by suggesting that rather than examine families as if they were distinct household types one should take account of the stage particular families have reached in their developmental cycle. What they argue is that segregated roles are related to the degree of domesticity imposed on the wife during the childbearing phase. This suggests that in most families the pattern of role relationships will vary throughout its life cycle.

The studies of Bott and Rosser and Harris show that the shift from segregated to joint conjugal roles is far from complete. Furthermore, to suppose that changes in the relationship between husband and wife are part of an evolutionary development towards greater equality is entirely speculative. Not only is this assumption contradicted by the institutionalisation of sex-related roles in work and education, it also fails to explain the exceptions that contradict Young and Willmott's claims. These exceptions tend to be dismissed by the authors of *The Symmetrical Family* as minority patterns. However, this is unrealistic given the instability of modern marriage and the increasing number of one parent families. These families are important because their structure is profoundly asymmetrical in that one partner performs none, or virtually none, of the social roles associated with parenthood.

Commentary

In Chapter 2 of his book *Middle Class Couples* Stephen Edgell explains some of the methodological problems raised by sociological research into conjugal roles. These problems centre on the ambiguities that surround concepts like 'joint' and 'segregated'. For example, it is not always clear whether sociologists are using these concepts to refer to attitudes or behaviour. Then there is always the possibility that roles might be organised differently in different spheres of life. If so, there are further problems which arise out of the need to make a decision about what activities to include and what importance to attach to them. This is usually solved in a very unsatisfactory manner and the use of inherently vague terms like 'often' or 'sometimes' to describe the pattern of marital relationships only increases the confusion.

Methodological criticisms like these have been frequently levelled at *The Symmetrical Family* and, summing up the views of a variety of critics, Edgell claims that Young and Willmott have used 'doubtful methods to advance highly contentious theses' (p.56). To illustrate this Edgell himself shows how Young and Willmott's data can be used to support a conclusion which is precisely the opposite of the point of view that they want to maintain. Thus,

In the 'mixed' tables, Young and Willmott show that men watch more television than women . . . men have more leisure activities than women . . . men see more friends and relatives than women . . . Young and Willmott also comment that wives mostly 'knitted or sewed more than they did anything else except watch television' . . . Thus, the leisure time and activities of husbands and wives cannot be understood in isolation from an unequal sexual division of labour that allocates the main responsibility for the home to women and the main responsibility for 'breadwinning' to men.

(*Middle Class Couples*, p.85)

Question 13
Functionalism and the family: is the family functional for its members and society?

The most important contributor to the functionalist theory of the family has been Talcott Parsons. He describes the modern family as structurally isolated from the kinship network. For Parsons the functional significance of this stems from the needs of a society in which achieved status is more important. He argues that industrial societies require considerable geographical and social mobility from a labour force which is free from binding obligations to relatives. A clear boundary between family and occupational systems means that in the latter roles are largely allocated on the basis of merit rather than family connections. As well as promoting economic efficiency this reduces the potential for conflict within the family since its isolation means that the authority of the head of the household is not threatened by other adults with a higher status.

Parsons argues that these developments mean that the modern family no longer performs its principle functions directly on behalf of society as a whole. However, far from being less important Parsons believed that the contraction of its role in the wider society made the family better able to perform its two 'basic and irreducible functions'. These functions are realised in the roles of individual family members and the most important is the primary socialisation of children. Thus Parsons emphasises that, in the first instance, families are 'factories which produce human personalities'. However, effective socialisation depends upon the emotional bond between mother and child. Only if this relationship is physically and psychologically rewarding will the child successfully internalise the values of society. Parsons therefore sees cultural reproduction as a role primarily performed by women. Their obligations are regarded as being anchored in the home where they perform an expressive role as the main providers of warmth, security and emotional support.

The second basic function of the family is the part it plays in the stabilisation of adult personalities. For Parsons the marriage relationship is the primary outlet for the affectual needs of adults and the home-centred nuclear family is seen as providing a refuge from the bureaucratic impersonality that dominates relationships in the world of work. According to Parsons this is particularly important for men because the role of breadwinner imposes upon them the obligation to provide economic support for their dependants. In an achievement orientated society this creates stress and anxiety and it is the family which compensates for these tensions. For example, in their relationships with their children parents are able to put aside their responsibilities and act in childish ways. In addition a wife's expressive role equips her psychologically to provide the emotional support that her husband needs to perform his instrumental role.

The theory as a whole seeks to demonstrate a basically harmonious relationship between individuals and society mediated by the family. The needs of children are met by their mother and father, those of parents by the complementary characteristics of conjugal roles, and those of society by the flexibility of a nuclear family structure. However, though the theory is internally logical, it achieves consistency at the expense of empirical evidence which demonstrates that the family is not always the integrative mechanism that functionalists suppose.

For example, it is by no means clear that the isolated nuclear family is well equipped for cultural reproduction. Critics of the modern family like Edmund Leach, Ronald Laing, and David Cooper have shown that the family has the potential for suppressing spontaneity, implanting guilt, and distorting personality development. This is because its structural isolation acts as a psychological barrier behind which family members grow resentful and suspicious of outsiders. Meanwhile emotional demands become focused almost entirely on other members of the nuclear family creating conflict and instability. In this atmosphere women become neurotically overprotective towards their children, men become violent, and children grow up mentally unbalanced.

Some support for this view that the modern family is more effective in creating than in dissolving tension is provided by international trends in divorce. Functionalists have tried to explain away the continuing rise in divorce rates by arguing that this is due to the increased availability of divorce and higher expectations of marriage. However, feminists have exploded this myth by demonstrating that marriage is an unequal partnership in which men gain at the expense of women. Furthermore, the complementary roles of adult men and women stressed by Parsons are questioned by research that shows that one of the effects of differences in male and female socialisation is to create incompatibility between the sexes. This makes romantic love, on which the modern family is supposedly based, increasingly difficult to attain.

For all these reasons functionalism can be criticised for idealising the modern family. It implies that the normal family is a happy, well-adjusted, two-parent family, living in their own home with the husband in employment and the wife free to provide a higher standard of comfort and care for her much smaller family. Although functionalists recognise that not all families are like this they interpret exceptions to the norm as deviant cases. This is unrealistic because, apart from anything else, the social structure denies many families the opportunity to live this way. In particular, though isolated from kin, the family is not in the least isolated from the class system.

The neglect of class differences is a fundamental weakness of the functionalist theory of the family. This is because the family reproduces two of the fundamental conditions of capitalist society. Property is transferred through inheritance, so helping to perpetuate a capitalist class, while labour power is reproduced in the family at no additional cost to employers. This helps explain some of the psychological costs of family life. For the family is at the intersection of some of the major contradictions in capitalist society. Its internal relationships are affected by divisions between the sexes and the generations while its external relationships are strongly affected by class and ethnicity. The failure of functionalism to recognise these structural bases of conflict adequately means that in practice functionalism becomes an ideological defence of the family rather than a scientific theory.

Commentary

Extracts from Talcott Parsons' writings can be found in *Sociology of the Family* edited by Michael Anderson. Alternatively, a summary, interpretation, and critique of Parsons' views are given in *Social Theory and the Family* by D.H.J. Morgan. This book also contains a description and assessment of the writings of other American functionalists such as G.P. Murdock, R.L. Coser, and W.J. Goode. However, although any or all of these writers could be used as an alternative to Parsons, Morgan points out that in the sociology of the family Parsons 'still dominates the field' (p.26).

As well as being the most important contributor to the functionalist theory of the family, Parsons has also been the most extensively criticised. These criticisms come from a wide variety of points of view. However, bear in mind that Parsons was mainly concerned with the family as a subsystem of the wider society. Following this line of thought he was led to neglect relationships between the family and the social structure. As Morgan explains, in Parsons' work

> There are no classes, no regions, ethnic or status groups, no communities. The outside world is treated as an undifferentiated environment in which the family is placed.
>
> (*Social Theory and the Family* p.42)

Question 14
The health of the family: is the family breaking up and losing its impórtance?

The family has traditionally been regarded as the most fundamental of all social institutions and its health and strength have been interpreted as crucial to social order. However, more recently its alleged role as the cornerstone of society has come under attack from critics and social reformers who see the family as an institution in a state of crisis. This view draws upon the darker side of family life and interprets evidence of marital breakdown and social problems within families as symptoms of social disorganisation. However, though modern society imposes strains upon relationships between family members, empirical evidence suggests that for most people the family is the central focus of their lives. This is significant because it implies that the family is a more resilient institution than its critics suppose and that to prophesy its impending collapse is unrealistic because of the importance of the values which the family represents.

One of the first to argue that the family is in decline was the English philosopher Bertrand Russell. He interpreted this as due to the State taking over functions previously performed in the family. This was also the view of some early American functionalists. For example, R.M. MacIver distinguished essential and nonessential functions and argued that the family's nonessential functions had been transferred to specialised institutions that performed them more efficiently. One of these institutions is the school and the rise of mass education is often put forward as evidence that the family has grown less important. However, this can easily be exaggerated because a great deal of learning still takes place in the home. Furthermore, were the educational function of the family so completely hived off one would not expect family background to have such a decisive effect on educational attainment.

There are similar doubts about the other functions that have allegedly been transferred to formal organisations. However, the most important issues arise out of the changed economic role of the family. In relation to this, those who argue that the family is in decline stress that in pre-industrial societies the family is a unit of production. This means that the roles of family members are united in shared economic activities. With the coming of industrialisation the pattern is disrupted. The home and the work-place are physically separated and families begin to buy more of what they need and make less of it themselves. However, to interpret this as a decline in the economic importance of the family is to neglect the positive implications of these changes. For example, in advanced industrial societies the family is a more important unit of consumption and roles are to some extent reunited in shared leisure activities and home entertainment.

The evolution from a subsistence to a market based economy also changes the basis of family solidarity. In pre-industrial and industrialising societies the family is typically bound together by economic necessity. In advanced industrial societies the compulsion is not so strong. Although the role of housewife is usually taken by a woman who thereby becomes economically dependent on a man, the growth of female employment and State benefits to aid in child care makes the one-parent family economically viable. This means that increasingly the main source of unity between family members is mutual affection and critics of the modern family argue that it is breaking up because its members are unable to cope with the emotional demands they make on each other.

Edmund Leach has claimed that the psychological costs of family life are too high to prevent its internal collapse. He argues that whereas in traditional societies the kinship network is able to provide continuous practical and psychological support for its members, in modern society the family cultivates an unhealthy degree of privacy. As Michèle Barrett and Mary McIntosh explain in *The Anti-Social Family*, the exclusion of outsiders can turn the family into a prison and behind its walls wives and children are especially vulnerable to physical and mental abuse. This view receives strong support from R.D. Laing who argues that schizophrenia is a reaction to living in a 'family ghetto'. With twenty per cent of patients in mental hospitals diagnosed as schizophrenic Laing claims that the family is more effective in causing madness than in educating children.

This view of the family as a source of social problems is also one interpretation of rates of abortion, illegitimacy, delinquency and domestic violence. These social problems are often seen by moral entrepreneurs as evidence of the declining standards of family life and when taken in conjunction with international trends in divorce it is often argued that statistics show that the nuclear family is disintegrating. However, although there has been a rapid increase in divorce this evidence is not conclusive. This is because at the same time that divorce has been increasing marriage has been becoming more popular and the divorced, far from giving up on marriage, remarry more often than ever before.

All of this seems to show that it is not that the values enshrined in family life are any less important but that people are finding it more difficult to realise them. This is one reason why feminism has such an appeal and it also helps to account for the increased popularity of alternatives to conventional family life. However, though there is no shortage of proposals for the reform of domestic arrangements most of these are unrealistic. This is because the family retains its importance as the basic building block of the class system.

Ultimately it is the relationship between family and class that explains the internal characteristics of the family and the problems that beset it. This is because the quality of family life is broadly governed by the characteristics of the society of which it is a part. In advanced industrial societies this means that in its internal relationships the family reproduces problems caused by class divisions in the wider society. One effect of this is to distort the most intimate of human relationships and this is why the continued importance of the family in reproducing the class system exacts such a heavy price from its individual members.

Commentary

In *Social Theory and the Family* D.H.J. Morgan argues that there are four possible positions that one can take on the alleged decline of the family. Thus,

1 It may be argued that the family is in decline and that this is to the detriment of society. Thus it will be argued that the decline of the family brings with it a whole host of other social evils such as delinquency, lack of discipline, drug abuse and so on. This is a view commonly held by certain 'moral entrepreneurs' in society.

2 It may be argued that the family is in decline and that this is either all to the good or a natural stage in the evolutionary history of mankind. Barrington Moore appears to approach this argument and it has its parallels in 'rationalistic' views of the obsolete character of religion in a scientific age.

3 It may be argued that the family is not in decline and that this is all to the

good. This is more or less the position of Fletcher, McGregor, Aron and, to a large extent, Parsons.

4 It may be argued that the family is not in decline and that this is to the detriment of the individual and society. This is the most common 'radical' perspective and is identified with the writings of Laing, Cooper and radical feminists.

(*Social Theory and the Family*, pp.88–9)

The essay above adopts position 4 and criticises 1 and 2.

Chapter 5

Social stratification

This section examines the sociologically important aspects of the work of Karl Marx (1818-83). Although Marx did not use the term social stratification, he was the first thinker to attempt to analyse systematically the inequalities in industrial society. The section should be read in conjunction with the opening section of the following chapter. That will deal with developments since Marx and with the attempts to reinterpret his ideas in order to make sense of modern societies.

Marx's thought presents several difficulties for the newcomer to sociology. To begin with, most of his books are devoted to an interpretation of the social, economic and political changes that occurred in his lifetime. His books are full of very detailed analyses of nineteenth century industries, social conditions, laws, technological innovations and ideas. Moreover, whereas most intellectuals fit into a tradition of thought Marx's contribution defies categorisation. Although its roots can be traced to German philosophy, French socialism, and British economics Marx united elements of each in an original way. His work was a synthesis on such a vast scale that it requires an effort of the imagination to comprehend it as a whole.

The synthesis embraces an interpretation of history, a critique of social institutions and predictions about the destiny of humanity. The common element is Marx's materialism. In materialism Marx believed he had discovered the key to an understanding of the processes that unite the past with the present and the future. What Marx meant by materialism is therefore the crux of the problem when it comes to interpreting his work.

Marx's materialism

The problem arises because materialism is a concept with a variety of meanings. In philosophy it is the doctrine that the only real world is the world of matter. Philosophical materialists deny the existence of divine or spiritual forces and argue that even thoughts, sensations and the like are ultimately reducible to physical processes. This view leads to the conclusion that people's ideas and beliefs are a product of the material conditions under which they exist. Or, as Marx put it, 'It is not the consciousness of men that determines their life' but 'their life that determines their consciousness' (*The German Ideology*, p.47).

Traditional materialist philosophy takes this as its point of departure and goes on to spell out the logical implications of the priority of matter over mind. However, Marx believed that in treating the material world as an abstract category previous materialists had missed the essential point. By separating their doctrine from its connection with actual experience they had dissipated its truth in sterile philosophical debate. The real task was to explain the relevance of materialism to people's lives as they actually are. For Marx this meant people 'as they operate, produce materially and hence as they work under definite material limits, presuppositions and conditions independent of their will' (*The German Ideology*, pp.46—7).

Marx's point was that in order to live people must actively reproduce the necessary means of subsistence. In other words the basis of human existence lay in the material solution to a material problem. The collective expression of this was the way production was organised in society (the mode of production). However, the organisation of production varies and Marx believed that variations in the conditions under which people labour caused variations in the culture and structure of society as a whole. Following this line of thought Marx took materialism out of the realms of philosophy and put it to work in the analysis of history.

The materialist conception of history is essentially a theory of social change. Marx believed that the form of that change was dialectical. Dialectical is another concept with a variety of meanings. It comes from a Greek word meaning to argue or to contend, and in classical Greek philosophy rational argument or dialogue had been developed into a method of philosophical enquiry. However, the important influence on Marx was not the dialectical method of the ancient Greek philosophers but the dialectical system of Hegel.

Hegel and Marx

In Germany Friedrich Hegel (1770—1831) was the most renowned philosopher of his day. He regarded history as a process that could be understood in terms of categories derived from philosophy. One of the bases of western philosophy is that the world is not as it appears to be, and this contradiction between appearance and reality is what Hegel claimed to resolve in his logic. There he had argued that absolute truth lay in human awareness of the identity of opposites. However, this 'truth' was a secret that up till then had been hidden from humanity. With Hegel's 'discovery' it was possible to reveal the meaning of history. The meaning lay in the stages through which thought had passed in its journey towards the absolute truth embodied in his own philosophy.

Hegel claimed that history (and all reality for that matter) worked in accordance with a rational plan that he had been the first to discover. His philosophy is mystical, arrogant and very obscure but in its day Hegel's thought was regarded as daring and profound. However, Marx was never overawed by another man's reputation. He believed that there was a kernel of truth in Hegel's ideas but that his philosophy as a whole was a mystification of actual experience. 'It is evident', he said, 'that the true method is turned upside down' (*Contribution to a Critique of Hegel's 'Philosophy of Right'*, p.40). Hegel was right to argue that change was a product of opposing forces but wrong to think that one could deduce those forces from the categories of philosophy. What was needed was an analysis of the contradictions people actually endured.

Marx's point was that Hegel and his followers made history with formulas and ignored the real contradictions that lay in the material and social conditions of actual existence. Hegel had fallen into the trap of believing that he could resolve contradictions at the level of thought. Marx replied that 'ideas cannot carry out anything at all' (*The Holy Family*, p.160). It is through labour that history is created and this must constitute the proper premise and object of understanding. Marx therefore rejected Hegel's idealism and turned dialectics from a philosophy of contemplation into a philosophy of action.

Marx wrote 'My dialectical method is not only different from the Hegelian but is its direct opposite' (*Capital*, Volume 1, p.19). By this he meant that his conception of history was not speculative but depended upon the empirical analysis of the processes that governed the life of humanity. To this end Marx drew a distinction between the 'forces' (or means) and the 'relations' of production. The forces of production are the raw materials, instruments and tools employed in the production process. The relations of production are the social relationships between people who work to produce goods or services. Marx believed that contradictions arose between the forces and relations of production as a result of the progressive division of labour. This was because stages in the development of the division of labour corresponded to different forms of ownership which generated conflict in society at large. Marx's materialism therefore directs attention to the economics of an epoch and regards contradictions in the mode of production as the motor of historical change.

The materialist interpretation of history

In brief, Marx's interpretation of history was as follows. In the most primitive types of society the members of society have very few tools to help them subsist and there is only a rudimentary division of labour. Every member of society has to work in order to live and the products of labour and the means of production are treated as the property of the community as a whole. However, the development of skills such as pottery making, metal working, animal husbandry and the like lead to a growth in the division of labour and to the emergence of specialist occupations. This in turn stimulates commerce, trade and the accumulation of wealth. However, with the emergence of private property ownership of the means of production becomes concentrated in the hands of the few. They no longer have to work in order to live because their control of the means of making a living means that instead of exploiting natural resources for themselves they can exploit the labour of others. Thus in moving beyond the level of primitive communism societies divide into social classes.

For Marx members of society were assigned to social classes in terms of their relation to the means of production. Those who owned or controlled the means of production, and who were prepared to back this up with force, were in a position to cream off for themselves any surplus produced by the rest. The particular form that this exploitation took would depend upon the development of the forces of production in the society concerned. Thus, reflecting on history Marx was led to emphasise how in various epochs 'Freeman and slave, patrician and plebeian, lord and serf, guildmaster and journeyman, in a word, oppressor and oppressed, stood in constant opposition to one another' (*Manifesto of the Communist Party*, p.41). In other words, the opposing forces that emerged out of contradictions in the mode of production were opposing social classes. 'History', said Marx, 'is the history of class struggles' (*Manifesto*, p.40).

Marx applied this perspective to an analysis of various economic systems including slavery, feudalism and the Asiatic mode of production. However, Marx was more interested in the present than the past and most of his life's work was devoted to an analysis of the origin and development of modern industrial capitalism.

Marx's analysis of the origins of capitalism

He interpreted the transition from the medieval to the modern social order as bound up with the development of towns. This stimulated trade and commerce and led to the growth of a class of merchant capitalists within feudal societies. When Europeans began to make voyages of discovery in the late fifteenth and sixteenth centuries they discovered gold, silver and other forms of wealth which greatly enriched the merchant class at home. This influx of precious metals provided the merchant class with the capital to move over from purely trading operations to manufacture. In the process they undermined the medieval guilds and reorganised production, initially through the domestic system and subsequently in factories. Then with the development of machinery capitalism took another leap forward. The result was the industrial revolution.

Marx saw these developments in the forces of production as the cause of changes in the class structure of society. Under the feudal regime the mode of production was based on the exploitation of serfs by the landed aristocracy. Serfs were not slaves but neither were they free. Instead of being the personal property of their masters as slaves would be, they were tied to the land by traditional and legal restrictions which meant that they were not free to move elsewhere. Exploitation generally took the form of labour dues and serfs were required to work without pay for a certain number of days each year on their lord's estate.

The growth of commerce and manufacturing within medieval societies brought the forces and relations of production into contradiction with one another. Feudal relations of production were an obstacle to capitalist development because they limited freedom of trade and placed restrictions on the right to set up factories, buy land and hire labour. This led to a struggle between the defenders of the old mode of production and the representatives of the new. The outcome was a victory for the representatives of capital – the modern bourgeoisie. However, Marx believed that 'The modern bourgeois society that has sprouted from the ruins of feudal society has not done away with class antagonism. It has but established new classes, new conditions of oppression, new forms of struggle' (*Manifesto*, p.41). This was because the growth of the factory system which created an industrial bourgeoisie also brought forth a new class of factory workers – the industrial proletariat.

Whereas under feudalism most workers were also independent producers, under capitalism workers are forced to sell their labour in order to live. However, though workers own their own labour they do not own the wealth that it produces. Their remuneration takes the form of wages and the product goes to the capitalist who produces in order to sell at a profit. Profits, Marx alleged, come from paying workers less than the value of the goods they produced. Exploitation is thus at the heart of the system and conflict the inevitable result. Those who own or control the means of production have an interest in preserving the relations of production upon which their wealth and privilege depend. In contrast productive workers who find that the fruits of their labour are being appropriated by others have an interest in overthrowing a system that oppresses and exploits them.

However, Marx's point was not just that the workers under capitalism are denied the economic rewards that are rightfully theirs. In addition labour itself is dehumanised so that work becomes a source of misery to the workers rather than a means of self-fulfillment. The fundamental reason for this is commodity production itself. In pre-capitalist societies the workers generally work either to satisfy their own needs or the needs of some other member of their community. Under capitalism they are working for wages, producing for the market and enriching only the capitalist. As a result the labourers are unable to identify with the product of their labour. It appears to them as an alien and hostile power because commodity production reproduces and expands the very conditions of the labourers' own oppression.

In his theory of alienation Marx argued that people are essentially creative beings but that under capitalism their essential nature is in contradiction with the conditions of their actual existence. This is because the organisation of productive relations in a capitalist society is not designed to cater for human needs but to maximise profitability. The inevitable result is the increased division of labour and the introduction of machinery. However, in its effort to increase productivity capitalism progressively reduces the worker to 'an appendage of the machine'. Furthermore factory labour is physically and mentally debasing so that work is experienced as 'forced labour'. Finally, the alienation of labour 'for the worker appears in the fact that it is not his own, but someone else's, that it does not belong to him, that in it he belongs, not to himself, but to another' (*Economic and Philosophical Manuscripts of 1844*, p.111).

If you now work your way back through the previous account you should notice that Marx uses the word 'contradiction' in at least three different ways. There is firstly the contradiction between human essence and human existence. That is the cause of alienation. Then there is the contradiction between the interests of the proletariat and those of the bourgeoisie. That is the cause of conflict. Finally there is the contradiction between the forces and the relations of production. That is the cause of change. However, change has so far been dealt with only in terms of the transition from feudalism to capitalism. In the three volumes of *Capital*, the culmination of his life's work, Marx set out to analyse the law of development of capitalist society itself.

Marx's analysis of the development of capitalism

Capital is a book about the economics of capitalism. In it Marx expounds his theory of economic value, of price and of the relationship between values and prices. He also explains how capitalism succeeds in extracting surplus value from the labour of the working class and how surplus value is related to profitability and capital accumulation. The social and political implications of these economic ideas are summarised in the *Manifesto of the Communist Party*.

In the *Manifesto* Marx argued that up to a point capitalism was a progressive force. This was because it organised the use of resources more efficiently than in feudal society. As a result capitalism expanded into new markets both at home and abroad until eventually it brought about the capitalist organisation of society as a whole. However, just as feudalism had nurtured the seeds of its own destruction so capitalism was doing the same. The more it expanded the more it developed its inner contradictions so that eventually the forces of capital and labour would confront each other openly.

Within the capitalist class Marx argued that competition between individual capitalists would lead to the concentration of capital in fewer and fewer hands. In their restless search for profits capitalists would be forced to look for ways of reducing the costs of production so as to capture a larger share of the market for themselves. However, unrestrained competition would lead to periodic crises of overproduction and in the ensuing slump the less efficient producers would be driven out of business. That in turn would pave the way for a further expansion of capitalism leading to an even greater economic crisis and another round of take-overs, mergers and bankruptcies.

Intermediate groups would decrease in size and importance. The peasantry had already been largely forced off the land in England and this process would continue. The petty bourgeoisie, that is the shopkeepers, small traders and family business owners, would mostly sink into the proletariat. Finally, handicraft workers (for example, handloom weavers) would find that their skills were becoming more and more obsolete. 'Thus the proletariat is recruited from all classes of the population' (*Manifesto*, p.53).

As the proletariat increased in size it would also increase in homogeneity. It would become concentrated in ever greater numbers in cities where workers and their families shared the same conditions of life. Also, in the factories machinery would obliterate distinctions between categories of labour and increase the sense of alienation felt at work. Finally, capitalism would 'nearly everywhere reduce wages to the same low level' (*Manifesto*, p.54). Although some would continue to earn more or less than the average and there might be temporary increases in living standards the rate of exploitation would continue to rise.

Overall Marx believed that as capitalism developed society as a whole was 'more and more splitting into two great hostile camps' (*Manifesto*, p.41). However, though changes in the relations of production were creating the economic conditions for a violent upheaval, the revolution still had to be fought for and won. That would depend upon the development of class consciousness amongst the proletariat leading to their realisation that the struggle was essentially a political one.

Marx argued that class consciousness develops in stages. At first conflict takes the form of clashes between individual workers and their employers. Out of these clashes workers see the need to band together to form trade unions. However, trade unions are essentially defensive organisations. What is needed is for the proletariat to go onto the attack. This will be achieved under the leadership of the Communist Party. Marx regarded this party as the only true representative of the interests of the entire proletariat. Its aim should be to convert the proletariat into a political movement and to broaden the fight against bourgeois supremacy into a national and eventually international struggle. Then, when the proletariat has been forged into a revolutionary force, the class which the capitalist mode of production brought into existence will rise up and make history for itself.

Although the bourgeoisie could delay matters by reforming capitalism from within or by exploiting weaker nations beyond their borders Marx believed that the day of reckoning would eventually come. Capitalism, like feudalism, slavery, and all other modes of production, was an historical phenomenon and, like all historical phenomena, it would pass. However, the take-over of power would be violent because the bourgeoisie would not surrender their privileges easily. On the contrary they had organised capitalist society in defence of their interests and ranged against the proletariat was not only the power of private property itself but also the social institutions and forms of consciousness associated with it.

Chief amongst these institutions was the executive arm of the State. This acted as an instrument of class domination or, in Marx's words, as 'a committee for managing the common affairs of the whole bourgeoisie' (*Manifesto*, p.44). Then there was organised religion. This was 'the opium of the people', a kind of spiritual drug in which the victims of capitalism were encouraged to find solace. Even the family was essentially a bourgeois institution and Marx described marriage as a form of private property. Through their control of the institutions of capitalist society the bourgeoisie were thus far more than mere owners of the means of production. They were a ruling class who would only be finally defeated by the total reorganisation of society as a whole.

It was to just such an objective that Marx committed his life. He was not a disinterested intellectual but an active participant in the class struggle he described. During his lifetime he worked incessantly for the proletarian revolution that he believed would lead to the liberation of mankind. This means that running throughout his work there is a commitment to revolutionary action. Marx himself was quite explicit about this and it is summed up in his phrase, 'Philosophers have only interpreted the world, in various ways; the point is to change it' ('Eleventh Thesis on Feuerbach').

Question 15
Social inequality: functionalist or conflict view?

The essential difference between functionalist and conflict views of inequality is that whereas functionalists regard inequality as beneficial to society as a whole conflict theorists see it as benefiting some groups at the expense of others. This difference leads to characteristic interpretations of the role of inequality in society. Functionalists see it as a mechanism that helps to preserve social order and promote efficiency whereas conflict theorists see it as a source of different and opposing interests which can be disruptive. Although each view claims to be a scientific explanation of inequality it is difficult to escape the conclusion that the two perspectives also perform an ideological role as a defence or critique of the status quo.

Functionalists frequently begin their analysis of stratification with the observation that all societies exhibit some form of institutionalised ranking. They suggest that the universal occurrence of socially created inequalities is evidence that stratification is inevitable in society. For Talcott Parsons this is because there is a value consensus. Stratification is then seen to follow from the fact that members of society who perform more or less well in relation to core values will be ranked accordingly. On the same basis Parsons argues that unequal rewards will normally be accepted as just and fair by members of society. However, whilst this might be plausible in simple societies where the main types of social differentiation are prestige and power, it hardly seems adequate as an explanation of the need for the massive economic inequalities which are characteristic of western industrial societies. Furthermore it is inconsistent with empirical evidence of differences in the way members of society rank occupations which indicates there is no general agreement about their value in society.

Kingsley Davis and Wilbert E. Moore's theory of stratification is subject to similar objections. However, they interpret inequality not as a direct expression of shared values but as a means to satisfy the functional prerequisite of effective role allocation and performance. Beginning from the twin assumptions that some tasks are functionally more important than others and that talent in society is scarce they go on to argue that stratification is an unconsciously evolved functional device for matching the most qualfied people with the most important positions. It achieves this, according to Davis and Moore, by offering rewards that compensate for the sacrifices made during training. These rewards act as incentives motivating members of society to compete for top positions.

This theory has been heavily criticised even from within the functionalist camp. Melvin M. Tumin, for example, points out firstly that the idea of functionally important positions is ultimately a value judgement since there is no way of measuring the relative importance of social roles. Secondly there is the question of talent. Davis and Moore's theory assumes that the function of stratification is to develop talent and put it to use for the benefit of society. However, this assumes that all members of society have the opportunity to develop and use their talents and Tumin explains that it is precisely this that a developed stratification system prevents. This is confirmed by dysfunctional aspects of stratification such as the wastage of talent in education, and barriers to upward mobility.

Fundamentally these and other objections to functionalism rest upon the argument that functionalist explanations of inequality depend upon a fictitious, idealised model of a totally integrated social system that does not and never has existed. This is Ralf Dahrendorf's view and he argues that functionalist theories are utopian because they neglect conflict, change, and coercion. This criticism clearly applies both to Parsons and to Davis and Moore since they assume that inequality in society rests upon meritocratic principles. This is to neglect the fact that in practice the rewards of major groups in society depend more on their economic power than their functional importance.

It is the crucial significance of power that is recognised by conflict theorists. David Lockwood led the way in 1956 when he criticised Parsons for concentrating only on the normative aspects of social order and the shared values transmitted through socialisation. However, an alternative perspective stems from Karl Marx. He saw that the organisation of productive activity under capitalism rested upon objective differences of interest. The interest of the bourgeoisie lay in the greatest possible exploitation of labour power so as to maximise their profits. In contrast the interest of workers lay in shorter working hours, improved working conditions and higher wages. This contradiction at the very heart of capitalism was crucial for Marx because he saw it as a source of conflict.

From this point of view it is the class struggle that governs the distribution of rewards in society. However, Marx's views, though still the basis of conflict theory, have proved to be an oversimplification. This is because economic rewards are not the only source of social differentiation and, in a development of Marx's ideas, Max Weber emphasised the importance of prestige and political power. This is a vital modification to Marx because his two class model is not equal to the complexities of modern stratification systems where criteria like race, gender, and age are the basis of further inequalities. These types of inequality rest upon status and party distinctions rather than relationship to the means of production.

Weber's theory is a more realistic account of inequality in modern society where, superimposed upon the basic distinction between capital and labour, are numerous secondary inequalities. However, despite the superiority of conflict theory over functionalism both views can be criticised. This becomes clear from their treatment of facts that do not easily fit the model. Thus functionalism, which assumes a value consensus, tends to dismiss disagreement over the relative importance of occupations as due to defective socialisation, whereas some versions of conflict theory see acceptance of inequality by the lower classes as false consciousness. Neither of these explanations is adequate and a comprehensive theory of inequality would need to go beyond functionalist and conflict views and investigate the meaning of inequality throughout the stratification system.

Commentary

During the 1950s and early 1960s functionalism was the dominant perspective in sociology and Talcott Parsons its most influential representative. However, even in their heyday the functionalists were not without their critics. For example, in his essay 'Some Remarks on the Social System' (reprinted in N.J. Demerath III and Richard A. Paterson, editors, *System, Change and Conflict*) David Lockwood argued that Parsons' excessive concern with social order had led him to neglect sources of instability within society. For Lockwood these sources of instability are seen to depend ultimately upon 'ownership patterns', that is the existence of private property. From this point of view social inequality is not an expression of unity but a source of conflict.

Summing up his idea of two alternative perspectives on inequality Lockwood stated that '

> Social stratification for Marx is the differentiation of competing economic interest groups in the society on the basis of productive relations; for Parsons it is the differentiation of individuals in terms of social superiority and inferiority on the basis of the dominant value system of the society. (p.286)

This can be roughly translated as follows. Social stratification is for conflict theorists the inequality between social classes whose rewards depend upon their relation to the mode of production; for functionalists it is the inequality between individual role players who are rewarded in terms of the value society places upon their skills and achievements.

Although there can be little doubt that Lockwood's sympathies lie with the conflict approach, in his 1956 article he was prepared to concede some of Parsons' basic arguments. However, it was not long before sociologists like Ralf Dahrendorf (*Out of Utopia*, 1958) and John Rex (*Key Problems of Sociological Theory*, 1961) were claiming that conflict theory was not merely an alternative to functionalism but a superior form of analysis.

Certainly the criticisms levelled against functionalist theories of inequality have been fairly devastating. However, do not feel you have to accept the conflict view uncritically. The essay indicates that it is possible to go beyond both consensus and conflict models and you will find a brief critique of both in Percy Cohen's book *Modern Social Theory* (pp.166–72).

Question 16
Social inequality: could it be abolished?

A commitment to equality has been the inspiration of revolutionaries and reformers in various societies at different historical periods. It is present in Karl Marx's principle that under communism the distribution of material goods would be 'to each according to his needs'. Equality was also one of the goals of the French revolution of 1789 and the Russian revolution of 1917. The construction of an equal society is enshrined in clause four of the constitution of the British Labour Party and was part of the philosophy upon which many of the Israeli kibbutzim were founded.

Despite this there is not a single known society which is egalitarian in all respects. Functionalists see this as empirical support for their view that inequality is necessary for social equilibrium and they dismiss the views of those radicals who have worked for the creation of an equal society as utopian ideology. However, as Alvin Gouldner has pointed out, the theory of the functional necessity of stratification is itself little more than an article of faith and can be interpreted ideologically as a justification of privilege.

In view of the scale of its reforms and its international importance the Soviet experiment is of crucial significance. With the coming to power of the Bolsheviks the socialist reconstruction of Russian society was begun. Ownership of the means of production was transferred from private hands to the State, eliminating inequalities of wealth stemming from production for profit. Lenin was also able to reduce inequalities of income drastically and additional measures were taken to ensure equal rights for women. Early Soviet intellectuals, such as Nikolai Bukharin (in *The ABC of Communism*, 1919), proclaimed the equality of all workers under Communism.

However, particularly under Stalin, the earlier egalitarian tendencies were halted and partially reversed. Although in the USSR today the extremes of wealth and poverty common to western societies do not exist there are substantial income inequalities. David Lane points out that an industrial director can earn up to thirteen times the wages of the lowest grade of manual worker. To this has to be added a variety of fringe benefits, such as official cars and holidays, that further increase the privileges enjoyed by the elite. In addition to economic inequalities surveys show differences in occupational prestige which are broadly similar to those in western societies. Although there is some evidence of greater social mobility in the Eastern bloc inequalities of educational opportunity remain and differences in power are even more marked than in the west.

Whether the Soviet Union is a crucial test of Communism is open to dispute. Many Marxists in the west follow Leon Trotsky's interpretation and argue that the revolution was betrayed. This idea of betrayal by the leadership is a constant theme in Marxist thought and is frequently put forward as an explanation of why successive Labour governments in Britain have failed to eliminate economic inequalities. However, whilst neither Communist nor Labour governments have fully realised their ideals each has brought about radical transformations of society. It may well be that it is partly the size and complexity of advanced industrial societies that make greater equality difficult to achieve.

If this is the case small scale societies may provide a clearer answer to the question of whether an egalitarian society is practical. Marx himself claimed that in societies living at subsistence level a form of primitive communism did prevail, but in recent years attention has focused on the social structure of the kibbutz. This is typically a settlement of several hundred members and some have abolished a money economy in the internal relationships between kibbutz members. Property is held in trust for the community as a whole so private wealth is eliminated. Commodities and services are distributed on the basis of need so no one earns, or needs to earn, an income. Full political participation is ensured by a system of direct democracy and each member of the kibbutz is entitled to a vote on all major decisions.

Despite the surface image of an egalitarian society Eva Rosenfeld claims to identify a stratification system. She points to the existence of social differentiation between leader-managers and the rank and file. Despite the virtual elimination of economic inequalities differences in status, power and job satisfaction remain. If even here one still finds inequality it might seem to confirm the functionalist case that inequality is inevitable. However, this is not necessarily so, for the idea that inequality is necessary implies not merely that it is found in all known societies, but that it will be equally necessary in all future possible societies as well.

It is here that the functionalist case is on its weakest ground. Parsons, for example, argues that stratification is inevitable because it derives from the common values in terms of which members of society rank each other. He conveniently forgets that equality itself is a value and that a commitment to this is incompatible with ranking. Davis and Moore present a somewhat different argument. They claim that inequality plays a crucial part in role allocation by ensuring that the most able are motivated to strive for the most important positions. However, experience shows that stratification systems actually inhibit the development of the abilities of some members of society.

These criticisms have never been fully answered from a functionalist point of view and although the elimination of inequality would clearly involve many problems, the case that it is impossible to do this has never been adequately made. At the back of the functionalist case lies a view that it is human nature that would make an equal society unworkable. However, comparative studies suggest that human nature is infinitely variable and it is likely that the potential for reorganising society in order to bring about equality and social justice has not been exhausted.

Commentary

In the Programme of the Communist Party of Russia, adopted at its eighth party congress (1919), it is stated that

While striving to secure equal remuneration for all labour, and while aiming at the establishment of complete communism, the Soviet Power cannot endeavour to effect the full realisation of this equality at the present moment . . . . Hence it will be necessary to maintain for a certain time the system of specially high remuneration for experts.

In the Constitution of the Labour Party (adopted 1918) it is stated that one of the objectives of the Party will be

To secure for the workers by hand or by brain the full fruits of their industry and the most equitable distribution thereof that may be possible upon the basis of the common ownership of the means of production, distribution and exchange, and the best obtainable system of popular administration and control of each industry or service.

Both these statements are ambiguous. Notice how they each begin by endorsing the principle of equality and then go on to qualify this by claiming either that it cannot be achieved now or that it might only be achieved to a degree. This means that supporters of the policies of such parties can always argue that it is practical difficulties that have prevented their party from achieving equality when in office. However, radical critics of allegedly left-wing governments are rarely convinced by arguments such as these. They have tended to argue that it is a lack of commitment to socialist principles by the party leadership that is responsible for the persistence of social inequality in societies that are or have been governed by parties that in theory are committed to equality.

Question 17
Embourgeoisement and proletarianisation: social processes or sociological myths?

To Karl Marx, writing in the nineteenth century, it was clear that there were two main classes in capitalist society: a propertied bourgeoisie and an impoverished proletariat. However, since Marx was writing, there has been a rapid increase in the number of workers who occupy intermediate positions in the class structure. Two groups that have attracted particular attention are affluent manual and routine non-manual employees. Their ambiguous position is illustrated by the fact that though the Registrar General's scale places white collar workers higher up the occupational hierarchy, official statistics show that the average pay of clerical and sales staff is well below that of many manual workers.

Supporters of the embourgeoisement thesis have interpreted this as evidence that the leading edge of the working class is becoming middle class. In contrast the proletarianisation thesis alleges that the class position of lower middle class employees is merging with that of manual workers. However, the problem with both these theories is that although today class boundaries are blurred most empirical evidence shows that between manual and non-manual workers there remains both a material and an ideological divide.

Embourgeoisement was the conventional wisdom of the early 1960s, when many people believed that class distinctions were withering away. The Labour Party had lost a third successive general election in 1959 and some political commentators suggested that social and economic changes were eroding the traditional basis of its support. For example, during the 1950s there had been a general rise in living standards and many manual workers were earning what had previously been regarded as a middle class income. In *The Worker in an Affluent Society* (1961) Ferdinand Zweig claimed that these affluent workers were abandoning traditional working class values and becoming almost socially indistinguishable from the lower middle class.

The affluent worker studies carried out by John Goldthorpe and David Lockwood tested this theory in a setting favourable to its confirmation. Their research was carried out in the prosperous new town of Luton amongst relatively highly paid employees working in industries using advanced technology. However, the results of the study showed that these affluent workers were not middle class in a number of crucial respects.

The material basis of this difference lay in the way these workers earned their living. Although they received more for their labour the work itself brought little intrinsic satisfaction. Furthermore, in return for a 'middle class' income they typically worked longer hours in unpleasant conditions at monotonous jobs, which gave them little sense of achievement. Finally, they had less job security, fewer fringe benefits, and little prospect of advancement.

The industrial and political attitudes of Luton workers reflected the fact that they were still essentially wage earners. They mainly saw themselves as working class, joined trade unions, supported the Labour Party, and subscribed to a collectivist philosophy. Although their solidarity with the labour movement had been weakened by their instrumental attitude to work and privatised family life, in their leisure activities and friendship patterns they showed little desire to mix with middle class neighbours.

Goldthorpe and Lockwood's study suggested that a new working class was emerging. Not all subsequent research bears this out. However, what the evidence does show is that changes in the working class are not leading to widespread embourgeoisement. For example, in *The Fragmentary Class Structure* Kenneth Roberts reports that most of their sample of workers still held traditional working class beliefs about the class structure.

Roberts also found little support for the view that a substantial part of the lower middle class is now working class in all but name. This claim is often made by Marxists. For example, in *Class in a Capitalist Society* John Westergaard and Henrietta Resler stress the erosion of the economic advantages of many white-collar workers and argue that their working conditions are becoming more like those on the factory floor. In addition it is sometimes argued that the increasing size and militancy of white-collar unions is evidence that a proletarian consciousness is spreading amongst non-manual workers.

The Blackcoated Worker by David Lockwood casts doubt on this interpretation. Certainly there has been some decline in the market position of clerical workers. However, Lockwood argues that when the full range of economic benefits are taken into account the relative decline in the rewards of white-collar work is not so great as income statistics suggest.

There are also important differences in the work situations of factory and office workers and the office environment normally allows greater freedom for expressing individuality at work. One example of this is that whereas most manual workers are supplied with protective clothing, non-manual workers are allowed to wear their own clothes. This tends to create social distance between the two groups and this is reinforced by management when it provides separate canteen and washroom facilities.

The differences in work situation act as disidentifers and this is reflected in the status aspirations of clerks. They frequently work in close contact with management and it is from this genuinely middle class group that they tend to draw their values. Studies of clerical workers show that though their income may be low the majority describe themselves as middle class, vote Conservative, and, if they join a trade union, tend to do so for different reasons from manual workers.

The problem with both the embourgeoisement and proletarianisation theses is that they operate with too narrow a definition of class. However, when class is seen to involve market situation, work situation, and status aspirations, it is clear that there remain real differences between manual and non-manual workers. The significance of these differences is illustrated by Peter Willmott and Michael Young's study in the London suburb of Woodford. This was a middle class area into which affluent manual workers were moving. However, this did not lead to a merging of classes. On the contrary it created tensions between middle class residents who believed that the newcomers 'lowered the tone' of the neighbourhood and working class families who resented what they saw as the 'snobbish' attitudes of their neighbours.

Commentary

A particularly useful study for both sides of this question is *The Fragmentary Class Structure* by Roberts, Cook, Clark and Semeonoff. In this book the authors write up the results of a survey carried out in 1972. The survey consisted of interviews with a random sample of 474 working males living in a mixed housing area on Liverpool's suburban fringe. They found that in response to a direct question nearly every subject acknowledged the existence of social classes, that in over four out of five cases respondents used the term 'middle' or 'working' to describe their class position, and that there was a strong (but by no means perfect) association between self-assigned class and occupation.

Roberts et al. argue that their survey shows that the dichotomy between the middle and working classes is a real division within modern Britain which involves both a difference in rewards and opportunities and a difference in values. Attributing particular importance to the latter they claim that

Self-assigned class, party political loyalties and trade union membership, therefore, are not only all similarly associated with occupational status but are also related to each other, thus producing syndromes characteristic of the working and middle class respectively. (p.24)

Later, they show how this can be reconciled with economic changes. Thus,

Just as blue-collar affluence produces an affluent working class rather than bourgeois manual workers, therefore, so it is arguable that denying white-collar workers former privileges leads not to proletarianisation but simply to a more militant middle class. (p.128)

Question 18
Social mobility: is Britain becoming a more open society?

Social mobility refers to the movement of individuals and groups between social strata. A society which allows or encourages such movements is referred to as an open society whereas a society which prevents them is said to be closed. There is a widespread belief that industrialisation creates a more open society and that in modern Britain there has been an increase in mobility rates. Functionalists see a link between this and the rise of mass education. They argue that we now live in a more meritocratic society in which achievement has replaced ascription as the institutionalised basis of role allocation.

One of the problems involved in testing this theory is that it is very difficult to get accurate quantitative information on the extent of mobility and even more difficult to make comparisons over time. There are no reliable statistics on the amount of mobility in pre-industrial Britain or in Britain in the nineteenth century. However, what information there is shows Britain was never a completely closed society. For example, there is evidence that even in feudal England there was considerable mobility through marriage into the nobility. Furthermore, the decline of feudalism and the rise of a commercial and later industrial bourgeoisie implies considerable mobility in the transition to an industrial society.

The first national survey to measure the extent of mobility in Britain was carried out by D.V. Glass in 1949. The study provides a retrospective view of mobility in the first half of the twentieth century. Glass found a fairly high rate of intergenerational mobility and nearly two thirds of the men interviewed were in a different occupational category from that of their fathers. Most mobility was shown to be short range with the highest rates occurring in the middle of the stratification system. This pattern was partly confirmed by the Oxford mobility enquiry carried out in 1972. However, in comparison to Glass's study this showed an overall increase in social circulation and more long-range mobility. In addition the research showed that a lot more people had been upwardly than downwardly mobile.

Two factors work in combination to explain why the balance of movement has been upward. Changes in the occupational structure since the nineteenth century have increased the demand for higher grades of worker and reduced the demand for unskilled and semiskilled labour. Over the same period reductions in fertility have restricted the number of children born to non-manual workers. Since the increased demand for middle class workers could not be met from within the middle class itself there has been a net influx of men and women from working class backgrounds into middle class occupations.

Despite relatively high mobility rates in the middle of the stratification system sons continue to follow fathers into occupations at the top of the hierarchy. For example, Glass's study showed that on his occupational scale the son of a father in category one had thirteen times the average chance of following his parent into this privileged group. Evidence derived from the Oxford mobility enquiry seems to show that the relative advantage of sons of parents in top positions has since declined to less than four times the average. However, one reason why the self-recruitment ratio appears to have fallen is differences in the size and composition of the occupational categories used in the two surveys. More precise studies of particular elite groups show that amongst the top decision makers and the very wealthy the inheritance of cultural capital and material advantages can still be decisive.

Although the evidence on elite mobility shows that the route to the top is not entirely closed it is probable that inequalities of opportunity increase the further up the ladder one goes. Frequently the crucial mediating agency is a private education and the evidence of the Public School Commission shows that elite positions in the judiciary, armed forces, civil service, economy and church continue to be dominated by ex-public school boys. However, only about six per cent of children receive a private education. The rest are educated at State schools. These schools are regarded by functionalists as 'the proving ground for ability'. They argue that increasingly roles are allocated on the basis of merit and that therefore education is breaking down the barriers to mobility.

Certainly research does show that the link between educational achievement and occupational status is growing stronger. This is because entry into higher status occupations and promotion at work has become more dependent upon examination passes. However, the tightening bond between schooling and work is likely to restrict opportunities for upward mobility by other routes. For example, as more firms recruit managers with professional or scientific qualifications promotion from the factory floor is likely to become rarer. This is not a change from ascription to achievement but the substitution of one form of achievement for another.

In addition educational attainment is strongly associated with social class. This is illustrated by the results of the Oxford mobility enquiry. Comparing those educated before the 1944 Education Act with those educated after it was found that an extra one and a half per cent of children of semi-skilled and unskilled workers achieved a university degree. However, over the same period the increase amongst children of parents in category one was a massive thirteen per cent. As A.H. Halsey has argued the expansion of educational opportunity has not led to any reduction in inequality of educational attainment.

In combination with the effects of credentialism this means that the expansion of education has benefited the privileged more than the deprived. The impression that Britain has become a more open society is largely an illusion caused by differential fertility and changes in the occupational structure. If one leaves these out of account then the relative chances of children from different social classes shows no trend towards equality of opportunity. On this basis A.H. Halsey argues that the British data supports 'a model of constant social fluidity'. However, even this might be over-optimistic. If mobility rates during the depression of the 1930s are a guide to the present, it is likely that in recent years economic recession has reduced the opportunity for moving up and increased the amount of downward mobility.

Commentary

Before one can measure how much mobility there is in a particular society at a particular time it is necessary to devise a scale against which movement can be measured. This is where the problems begin. For example D.V. Glass looked at movement between seven 'status categories' distinguished in terms of their social prestige. This led him to place routine non-manual workers in the same status category as skilled manual workers and to rank both below shopkeepers and foremen. However, in his work for the Oxford mobility enquiry John Goldthorpe looked at movement between seven social classes distinguished in terms of economic rewards and work situation. This led Goldthorpe to place clerical workers, foremen, shopkeepers and skilled manual workers in four distinct classes at the same level.

In his book *Social Mobility* Anthony Heath comments on the problem of classifying occupations into categories. He explains that

Exactly how much mobility and stability we find will depend on the number, size and character of the categories we distinguish. (p.55)

As a result

We cannot possibly take a single figure as 'the' rate of social mobility in a specific country. It would not be too far-fetched to suggest that we can get almost any answer we want simply by fiddling with the categories. (p.56)

Chapter 6

Education and the mass media

Marx, the nineteenth century intellectual, inspired what has since become the most powerful political ideology of the twentieth century. Today Marxism as a doctrine seeks to cover the entire life of humanity. This section provides a general exposition of some of the major developments in Marxist thinking, focusing in the essays that follow on Marxist contributions to the understanding of cultural phenomena, especially education and the mass media, in a capitalist society.

One popular prejudice to dispel straight away is that Marxism is synonymous with Communism and that Marxists are necessarily supporters of the Soviet system. Certainly it is true that in the USSR a version of Marxism, mainly derived via Lenin, is the official ideology of the State. Furthermore, Soviet power has ensured that the Moscow line is followed in other Eastern bloc countries. However, elsewhere more recent social movements like the Chinese revolution, African socialism, and Eurocommunism have prompted very different interpretations of Marx. International developments like these are one reason for the continuing relevance of Marx's thought. You will find it useful to know something about the way neo-Marxists in the west have explained developments in countries such as Britain and the US.

These developments are important to academic Marxists because the revolution that Marx predicted has not come about in the countries that he regarded as the most likely candidates. This fact alone has led some non-Marxists to argue that the materialist conception of history has been refuted in the twentieth century. However, Marxists argue in reply that Marx's analysis was basically correct and the fact that revolution has not occurred in societies like our own can be accounted for in line with Marx's ideas by bringing them up to date.

They say that we still live in an essentially capitalist society and that what is needed is to extend Marx's work to embrace current realities. In practice this has led neo-Marxists to concentrate their attention on three areas. These are: developments in the economic organisation of capitalism, the growth in the power of the State and the crucial role of ideology in modern capitalist societies.

Developments in the capitalist economy

From a Marxist point of view the capitalist economy evolves through different stages. Although this does not eliminate the contradictions that the system generates, as part of this process new institutions are developed. These help to stave off the collapse of a mode of production still based on private ownership of property and geared to the pursuit of profit. The most important of these institutions in the economic sphere are the giant corporations with the power to control entire sections of the economy.

When Marx was writing capitalism was still in an early stage of its development and at the time it was characteristic for unrestrained competition to hold sway between individual capitalists. However, competition leads to the concentration of capital in fewer and fewer organisations and concentration in turn produces the opposite of free competition, namely, monopoly. Where there are just a small number of very large producers they can make agreements amongst themselves to keep up prices and guarantee profits. In this way capitalism has largely superseded the market and in doing so it has strengthened its hold over society.

It is often argued that the process has gone furthest in the US, now the leading capitalist power in the world. Two influential American Marxists to put forward this point of view are P.A. Baran and P.M. Sweezy. In their book *Monopoly Capital* they argue that the capitalist tycoons and family businessmen who used to own and control industry in the US have been increasingly overtaken by public, and often multinational, corporations. These corporations operate rather differently from the old-style capitalist entrepreneur.

For a start they are generally run by organisation men who typically do not own the businesses they work for. Non-Marxists sometimes interpret this separation of ownership from control as signifying the supersedence of capitalism. However, Baran and Sweezy interpret it as a development within capitalism. Whereas in the past the expansion of capital was subject to the whims of individual entrepreneurs it is now institutionalised through the bureaucratic organisation of production. This means that business activity has been professionalised and whilst pursuing the same goal of profit maximisation the large corporation takes a long term view.

Partly it is able to do this because where there are a small number of producers they are able to form a cartel that effectively outlaws price cutting as a legitimate means of economic competition. One cartel that you may have heard of is OPEC, the Organisation of Petroleum Exporting Countries. It has been very successful at raising the price of oil, which is no longer related to the costs of extraction, refining, and distribution but is instead fixed in terms of the price that the market will bear. Baran and Sweezy argue that the same principle is increasingly the norm under monopoly capitalism. The result is that where new technology lowers the costs of production, price-fixing by producers leads to wider profit margins. However, the profitability of monopoly capital increases only in so far as large corporations are able to maintain demand for the products they sell at inflated prices.

This is achieved in a variety of ways. To begin with the corporations constantly bombard domestic consumers with advertisements designed to encourage them to believe that they need the products and services that only monopoly capital is equipped to provide. However, the largest single consumer is the government and Baran and Sweezy interpret increased government expenditure as a mechanism for bringing idle capital and labour into production so as to maintain profitability. Of course some of the government's income is derived from taxation on industry and some is spent on benefits which go to the disadvantaged. However, the effects of government intervention do little to reduce inequality. Rather than threatening the interests of capital, social and economic policies generally help to preserve capitalism by defusing the opposition and stimulating a demand for products at the cheaper end of the range.

In addition much of the expansion in government expenditure is due to increased spending on defence. This has various consequences. First, it directly benefits those corporations engaged in research, development and manufacture of armaments. Second, it provides the most powerful nations with the military strength to bring weaker nations into their sphere of influence. Third, it creates a permanent arms race. This in turn stimulates further increases in the military budgets of nations throughout the world, fuels a series of wars in South East Asia, the Middle East, Central America and elsewhere, and leads to the mass deployment of nuclear weapons. These consequences are interpreted by Marxists like Baran and Sweezy as the inevitable outcome of capital expansion. From this point of view international conflict is not the exception in an otherwise peacefully determined course of development. On the contrary, it is argued that the efforts of monopoly capital to stave off economic collapse play an essential role in creating political instability and enhancing the risk of global destruction.

Growth in the power of the State

All this is bound up with the Marxist theory of the role of the State. This has had to be considerably modified since Marx was writing because Marx's analysis of nineteenth century capitalism was conducted at a time when the prevailing political ideology was laissez faire. In terms of that doctrine the major functions of government were seen as foreign policy, external defence, and law and order and it was widely believed that the most prudent social and economic policy was nonintervention. This was justified by arguments that claimed that individuals were the best judges of their own interests and that government meddling would disrupt the market, undermine initiative, and threaten individual freedom.

Marx interpreted this policy as implicitly representing the interests of the bourgeoisie. This was because government nonintervention meant that capital expansion could proceed relatively unhindered by restrictions on the exploitation of labour. The individual freedom championed by the apologists of capitalism was thus a very one-sided affair. Whilst the bourgeoisie were free to use their economic power to increase their wealth most of the rest of the population were condemned to a life of squalor and poverty. However, even in Marx's lifetime laissez faire was opposed by the beliefs that produced a succession of Factory and Public Health Acts, and it was subsequently abandoned altogether. The result has been that in advanced capitalist societies like modern Britain the State now plays a more important role in social and economic affairs.

This development has received a great deal of attention from left-wing scholars in recent years. One influential figure is the English socialist Ralf Miliband. In his book *The State in Capitalist Society* he tends to agree with Baran and Sweezy's analysis of the economics of monopoly capital. However, in Miliband's work the emphasis is shifted onto the ways in which political power is exercised in advanced capitalist societies.

Miliband argues that capitalism is able to accommodate itself to a variety of political regimes including the parliamentary democracies of western industrial nations. In these societies political power is vested in the State elite. This is made up of people who occupy the top positions in central and local government, the civil and armed service, the judiciary, and the police. Most are not themselves members of the capitalist class. However, Miliband argues that in societies like modern Britain the State elite is permanently allied to the interests of private property.

For a start politicians, on both the left and the right, are mainly recruited from the upper and middle classes. This means that they tend to share a similar cultural horizon and educational background with other members of the elite and sometimes they have family and financial connections too. Despite this voters are given the impression that politicians are deeply divided on matters of policy and political ideology. However, Miliband argues that the disagreements between political leaders bearing different labels are seldom as fundamental as they seem. For the most part their differences of opinion can be reduced to arguments about how best to run the capitalist system rather than how to bring about radical change.

This is partly because governments themselves depend on the private sector for most of their revenue. This means that their autonomy of action is limited by their dependence on the health of the capitalist enterprise and when they intervene to manage the economy it is largely with the purpose of helping business to prosper. Despite this political leaders usually see themselves as serving the national interest rather than the interests of a particular class. However, Miliband points out that whenever there is an industrial dispute the national interest is identified with the interest of employers and workers are interpreted as behaving unreasonably. In practice government intervention is therefore mainly partisan and this is reinforced by the fact that the State is itself now the largest single employer.

When the democratic process leads to a left-wing government being voted into office there is often some attempt at reducing inequality. However, though Labour and socialist politicians may in theory be committed to the transcendence of capitalism Miliband argues that they rarely pose a threat to the dominant classes. One reason is that the leadership of allegedly left-wing parties is generally to the right of the rank and file and though leaders often indulge in radical rhetoric when in opposition they tend to follow moderate policies when in office. As a result the aspirations of the supporters of socialism are so scaled down by their political leaders that the party ends up preserving the very social and economic conditions it was pledged to oppose.

Another way in which the dominant classes are able to preserve their privileges is through control of the means of public administration. Although popular mythology has it that civil servants are politically neutral Miliband argues that in practice they generally play a conservative role. Partly this is because most top civil servants come from upper and middle class backgrounds.

In addition candidates for the civil service and members of it are subject to screening and those whose attitudes and behaviour depart from the prevailing conservative consensus tend to be weeded out as security risks. However, even more important is State intervention in the economy. This has led to an increasing collaboration between businessmen and civil servants and to a constant interchange of personnel between the private and the public sector. This, more than anything else, helps to ensure that the national interest is defined in terms favourable to the capitalist enterprise.

In a similar vein Miliband goes on to develop his analysis by extending the Marxist concept of the State to embrace the military and judicial elites, legislative assemblies, and local and regional government. The general drift of his argument is against what is commonly known as a pluralist concept of power. According to pluralism power in advanced western industrial nations is dispersed between a variety of interest groups and governments arbitrate in the competition between them. However, Miliband replies that though there is competition between organised interest groups in these societies they do not compete on equal terms. This is because the strategic position which the capitalist enterprise enjoys in its dealings with the government ensures that this interest group has a decisive and permanent advantage.

This also fits in with the views of Baran and Sweezy, who stress how monopoly capitalism evolves ways of superseding the market. One of these ways is through agreements between major producers. Economic planning by governments can now be interpreted as the extension of this on a national scale. From this point of view giant corporations and governments are in collusion with one another; the capitalist enterprise as the producer of wealth, the State as the guarantor of its profitability.

However, there is still something missing from this analysis. This is because capitalism must not only reproduce the forces of production, it must reproduce the existing relations as well. A Marxist might put this as follows.

Role of ideology

Capitalism is a dynamic system which not only sells goods to produce profits but in the process reproduces itself. This is because part of the income from an enterprise is reinvested in the continuation of the business. For example, it is used to buy raw materials, meet tax obligations, service debts, and pay wages. In these and other ways capitalism reproduces itself economically. As raw materials are used up more are bought. As labour power is consumed it is bought again the following week with wages.

So far this only describes part of what capitalism does. Factors of production like raw materials, labour etc. have only entered the equation as commodities; that is things with a price that the capitalist has to buy in. However, one of these factors of production is different from all the rest. This is labour power and although it is a commodity under capitalism the crucial point is that it is not just a commodity. It resides concretely in the person of the labourer who exists historically as a member of a class – the proletariat in Marx's formulation, the working class as we know it today. The last chapter described how Marx believed that this class, realising its exploitation under capitalism, would rise up and seize power in a violent revolution. According to the French Communist Party member Louis Althusser it is precisely this that the capitalist class seeks to prevent.

In the 1970s Louis Althusser was one of the most influential exponents of a rather theoretical brand of continental Marxism. His article 'Ideology and Ideological State Apparatuses' (reproduced in his book *Lenin and Philosophy*) is a useful introduction to Marxist views on the cultural characteristics of capitalism. Althusser's main point is that the reproduction of labour power under capitalism not only requires the reproduction of the workers and their skills but also the reproduction of their submission to the rules of the established order. To explain how this is accomplished and revolution thereby avoided Althusser argues that it is necessary to add something to Marx's definition of the State. What is missing in Marx, according to Althusser, is a theory of how the State uses its power. With the aim of contributing to such a theory Althusser introduced a distinction between the repressive and the ideological State apparatuses.

The repressive State apparatus consists of those institutions controlled by the State that embody the means of coercion. They include the army, the police, the courts and the prison service. Through these institutions the State seeks to establish a legal monopoly on the use and threat of violence. However, the ideological State apparatus functions quite differently. Its principal role is not to repress dissent but to manufacture consent and it does this by disseminating ruling class ideology.

In precapitalist societies the dominant ideological State apparatus was the Church. This encouraged men and women to think about the real (i.e. material) conditions of their existence in an imaginary way. For example, by means of religious ideology we may be taught that suffering is just retribution for sin rather than due to material causes. This encourages an attitude to life that is materially embodied in practices such as prayer, penance, confession and charity. Althusser's point is that these practices serve to channel social energy into activities that do not constitute a threat to the established order, and that it can adapt and even use for its own ends.

However, the technical and scientific revolution brought about by the development of capitalism makes religion less effective as an ideological force. As a result the legitimation of the established order is brought from heaven down to earth and the Church is replaced by education as the dominant ideological State apparatus. Education takes children from all classes of society and then for the years in which they are most vulnerable it drums into them the attitudes and values that make the relations of exploited to exploiters seem natural and inevitable to the next generation of workers. Through education, backed up by the mass media and the other cultural institutions in a modern capitalist society, Althusser argues that the State fosters false consciousness in society at large and succeeds in ensnaring us all in ruling class ideology.

Question 19
Education and occupation: functionalist or Marxist view?

As industrial societies advance education assumes a more important role and eligibility for entry to particular occupational specialisms comes to depend to a greater extent on paper qualifications. This process, whereby examination passes become a more important determinant of occupational status, is known as credentialism. It means that for more and more members of society there is a tightening bond between attainment in school and subsequent work roles.

According to Emile Durkheim the relationship between industrialisation and mass education can be explained in functional terms. His view can be illustrated by the way developments in technology and the division of labour are related to the growth of the educational system. The relative decline of the traditional nineteenth century industries and the rise of the tertiary sector led to demands for new and higher levels of skill. The response was a rapid expansion of higher education, innovations in the curriculum, and the raising of the school leaving age.

In addition functionalists have argued that education and occupation are linked through the connection they both have with the central value system. This point was stressed by Talcott Parsons. He saw the school as a bridge between the family and the wider society. Within the family a child is largely judged in terms of particularistic values. These are values that apply only to specific individuals, in this case individuals who have the ascribed status of son or daughter. However, although the bond between parents and their children is important in the process of primary socialisation, Parsons argued that it does not adequately equip the child to perform work roles in modern industrial society.

According to Parsons one reason is that in the wider society individuals tend to be judged in terms of universalistic values. These are values that are applied to everyone irrespective of kin. Parsons argued that the standards that these values imply are fostered in schools. In particular the examination system helps young people internalise the values of individual achievement and equality of opportunity. For Parsons this prepares them psychologically for the competitive environment that they will face at work.

The idea that the educational system is increasingly linked to the occupational structure by means of meritocratic standards that apply to both is also associated with the work of Kingsley Davis and Wilbert E. Moore. They assumed that certain roles are more functionally important than others and that therefore it is vital that they be performed by able and highly motivated individuals. By selecting and grading young people the educational system identifies talented individuals and develops the skills that they will need if they are to occupy elite positions. In this way Davis and Moore saw education as the means by which modern societies allocate their most talented members to the most important occupations.

Running through the functionalist accounts is the view that in advanced industrial societies education performs a beneficial role both for society and its members. However, although conflict theorists would agree that education contributes to the relative stability of western industrial societies, they argue that this is not because it meets the functional prerequisites of this type of society but because it plays a role in reproducing the class system. For example, the French Marxist Louis Althusser emphasises that education reproduces labour power. This is only partly to do with reproducing the skills necessary to the current development of the forces of production. It also, and more importantly, involves the reproduction of ruling class ideology and false consciousness in capitalist society.

One way that the school does this is through the hidden curriculum. This refers to all that is learned informally rather than what is officially timetabled and taught as part of a formal syllabus. In practice this informal learning is structured through the peer group, teacher-pupil relationships, and the organisation of the school. For example, in the peer group students develop strategies to cope with boredom. Meanwhile staff-student relationships stress submission to authority through the respect pupils are expected to show for teachers. Finally, the school as a whole emphasises conformity by enforcing seemingly pointless rules, particularly those relating to appearance and the wearing of uniforms.

The relationship between these characteristics of education and the occupational structure is stressed by the American Marxists Samuel Bowles and Herbert Gintis. In *Schooling in Capitalist America* they point out that social relationships at work and in schools tend to replicate each other. Just as the principle of hierarchy is embedded in the organisation of the factory and the office so too is it embedded in schools and colleges. In this way submission to authority at work is maintained by anticipatory socialisation at school. The result is to encourage the development of personality traits in young people which are favourable to the persistence of inequality. The most important of these personality traits is the acceptance by pupils of alienation as a normal, necessary, and inevitable aspect of life.

Alienation involves the inability to identify with, or find self-fulfilment in, work roles. However, powerlessness, meaninglessness, isolation, and self-estrangement are not only characteristic of many occupational roles but also of the process of schooling. For both the student and the employee of the large bureaucratic organisations that dominate the world of work extrinsic satisfactions, like the hope of examination success or higher wages, become a substitute for self-fulfilment. At the same time the myth of the meritocracy is perpetuated by a system that provides equality of opportunity in theory but not in practice.

This is demonstrated by the continuing importance of ascribed statuses such as race, gender and social class background. These statuses still exert a decisive influence on both educational attainment and occupational status. For the most part therefore education serves to confirm members of society in their existing status and thus legitimates the unequal distribution of rewards in capitalist society. From this point of view the meritocratic explanation of the link between schooling and work assumes the role of an ideology. Thus Marxists reject functionalist accounts and argue that instead of promoting efficiency the increasingly close connection between education and occupation is a symptom of the extension of class control.

Commentary

Functionalists tend to argue that the educational system does in reality do what it is officially supposed to do. For example, Kingsley Davis talks of education as 'the proving ground for ability and hence the selective agency for placing people in different statuses according to their capacities' (*Human Society*, p.219). Of course functionalists recognise that education does not always do this as efficiently as it might. However, they interpret this as due to dysfunctional consequences of education or malintegration between system parts.

In contrast Marxists tend to argue that there is a difference between how education is officially supposed to work and how it actually works. For example, they regard the meritocratic principles that education is supposed to foster as a facade, which disguises the 'real' role of education in a capitalist society. This point of view is strongly associated with the ideas of Samuel Bowles and Herbert Gintis. They claim that

> The educational system serves – through the correspondence of its social relations with those of economic life – to reproduce economic inequality and to distort personal development ... It is precisely because of its role as producer of an alienated and stratified labour force that the educational system has developed its repressive and unequal structure.

(Schooling in Capitalist America, p.48)

Question 20
Social class and differences in educational attainment: what explanations have sociologists offered?

Twenty five years ago research into the reasons for social class inequalities in educational achievement was largely positivist in general orientation. Working class underachievement was interpreted as a wastage of talent, an effect that was seen as caused by the material circumstances of children brought up in relative poverty. In particular, factors like low income, large families, poor housing and urban decay were supposed to be affecting the performance of many working class children. Then research carried out by J.W.B. Douglas added a new dimension. His studies appeared to indicate that the most important factor was the degree of interest that parents take in their children's education. This led some sociologists to adopt a subcultural approach to differences in educational attainment. They moved the emphasis from the economic constraints faced by the underprivileged to values which allegedly act as a self-imposed barrier to educational success. Through their 'present orientation', 'fatalistic attitudes' and patterns of 'immediate gratification' lower working class children were thought to possess personality attributes which made them less educable than middle class children.

Although studies by John and Elizabeth Newson confirm that there are social class differences in child rearing practices much of the early research was inadequate because it tended to ignore how the process of schooling affects achievement. In the attempt to get round the limitations of the subcultural perspective sociologists began to focus on the way language and communication can influence educational attainment. Research was begun in this area by the English sociologist Basil Bernstein. He developed the concepts of a restricted and an elaborated code. Bernstein sees the restricted code as a kind of shorthand speech in which meanings are not explained and communication depends upon the shared experiences of those involved in interaction. In contrast, the elaborated code is a universalistic order of discourse in which meanings are spelled out and the sense can therefore be conveyed in principle to anyone who shares the vocabulary and grammar.

Bernstein associated the restricted code with the speech patterns of working class children and the elaborated code with the middle classes and with teachers and schools. At first sight this only appears to add another deficit, linguistic deprivation, to the list of material and cultural factors mentioned previously. However, in his later work

Bernstein emphasised that it is not that working class speech is intrinsically inferior but that it is interpreted as being so by teachers. This is confirmed by William Labov's research into the speech patterns of Harlem ghetto children. In *The Logic of Non-standard English* he demonstrates that the ghetto child is able to comprehend and reason about abstract ideas. However, such children often appear to be linguistically deprived in the classroom because they define the situation as hostile and potentially threatening.

Labov's work highlighted the importance of studying interaction in schools. This is because it is in schools that children are processed into achievement rates, and pupil-teacher relationships can have a crucial effect on their attitudes to education and subsequent level of attainment. During the late 1960s this led to another change of emphasis and sociologists increasingly switched their attention to the ways in which relationships in classrooms were structured. For example, in America Howard Becker showed that teachers work with a notion of the ideal pupil and that they tend to perceive lower working class children as furthest from it. The effect that this can have is demonstrated by studies of schools in England carried out by Julienne Ford and Stephen Ball. Both showed that working class children whose measured ability is equal to that of middle class children tend to be perceived as less able and are more likely to be placed in a lower stream.

Furthermore the evidence on streaming suggests that the organisation of the school can itself act as a barrier to progress amongst children allocated to the lower ability bands. Partly this is due to the fact that it is lower streams that tend to be taught by the least experienced and most poorly qualified teachers. However, David Hargreaves' study, *Social Relations in a Secondary School*, showed that there were other social processes at work too. For example, Hargreaves' research indicated that children segregated into ability bands tend to form stream bound friendship groups. Lower stream pupils, who were effectively denied an institutional source of self-respect, responded by developing anti-school attitudes. This led to the development of a delinquent subculture in which status was awarded to those who broke school rules and disrupted lessons.

In the early 1970s research into the social processes involved in schooling was a much needed corrective to the one-sidedness of previous work which had emphasised the background of the child and neglected the way education was experienced. However, it soon became evident that studies which focused on classroom interaction and the organisation of the school were inadequate in so far as they ignored the relationship between schooling and society. This led to a renewed interest in Marxist interpretations of educational inequality. For example, the French sociologist Pierre Bourdieu has argued that the main role of the educational system is cultural reproduction. However, in practice decisions about what is taught in schools and how it is taught are imposed by the dominant classes in society. One result is that their children have a built-in advantage. They possess the cultural capital necessary for educational success whereas working class children, whose style departs from the dominant culture, are mainly eliminated from the higher levels of education.

By stressing the ways in which education reproduces culture in a stratified society sociologists such as Bourdieu have emphasised how patterns of inequality in educational attainment depend upon factors that go far beyond either the home or the school. This has led to an increased awareness of the relationship between differences in the provision of educational opportunity and the distribution of power in society. In Britain today this relationship is still directly observable in the social background of entrants to fee-paying schools. However, it is indirectly responsible for inequalities throughout an educational system geared to the class structure of capitalist society.

Commentary

In *The Sociology of Educational Inequality* William Tyler lists five different explanations of how social class background influences scholastic achievement. They are

(a) The 'culture of poverty' thesis which states that the poor are kept in their position because their children learn a culture of failure ...

(b) The 'material disadvantage' thesis which puts forward the view that the cultural disadvantage of the poor is only a mask for their structural and material handicaps ...

(c) The 'good home' thesis: this states that ... the processes of socialisation, the value orientations of the family, and the level of parental involvement tend to be the most important predictors of success....

(d) The 'self-fulfilling prophecy' thesis: teachers hold to certain stereotypes of what is valuable knowledge and what constitutes an 'ideal' pupil. They apply these stereotypes, often unconsciously, to discriminate against pupils who do not fit their models....

(e) The 'cultural capital' thesis: ... it proposes a radical, class conflict explanation of 'social reproduction'. . . . Culturally privileged children internalise this code and consequently do well in school and in later life.

However, whilst the differences between these types of explanation seem clear enough in principle, in practice the debate over educational inequality is full of ambiguities. A case in point is the work of Basil Bernstein. Thus Tyler points out

In the first place one could claim that Bernstein's 'restricted code' was a part of the 'culture of poverty' ... One could also claim that such a mechanism could help to explain what constituted a 'good home'. .... Finally one could claim that Bernstein had hit upon a very important aspect of 'cultural capital' ...

(*The Sociology of Educational Inequality*, pp.101–3)

Question 21
The mass media: why have sociological approaches changed since the war?

Most of the early postwar research into the mass media was carried out in America. It was strongly influenced by positivist assumptions and sociologists at the time were obsessed with the problem of quantifying the effects of exposure to the media. This led many researchers to adopt a model of explanation in which audiences were treated as if they were made up of isolated and passive individuals 'injected' with media messages. Then the researchers attempted to judge the consequences of media exposure by measuring attitude changes over a period of time. Much of this research was carried out under artificial laboratory conditions or through the use of questionnaires and market research techniques. The approach was social-psychological, the focus was on the short term effects of the media, and the research was mainly concerned with estimating the effectiveness of direct attempts to influence people's spending patterns and voting habits.

Since much of this research was unrelated to the social context in which members of society experience the media it yielded results which were often contradictory and largely inconclusive. However, one finding which did emerge from the early studies was that direct attempts to persuade people through the media are less effective than had previously been supposed. One influential study to show this was *The People's Choice* (1944) by Paul Lazarsfield and his colleagues. They used a panel sample to assess the impact of the 1940 presidential election campaign on political opinion. However, the research appeared to show that the campaign had had a negligible effect on voting behaviour. For the most part it had merely reinforced the political opinions people already held.

In the course of this research Lazarsfield introduced the 'two step flow hypothesis'. Up till then sociologists had tended to conceptualise the power of the media in terms of a simplistic stimulus response model borrowed from behaviourist psychology. However, Lazarsfield proposed a model of the effects of the media in which the main influence was seen as diffused through 'opinion leaders'. This hypothesis was later tested by Elihu Katz and Paul Lazarsfield in their book *Personal Influence*. This confirmed that face-to-face communication was the most effective means of persuasion and that the influence of the mass media was channeled via interpersonal relations.

Another finding to emerge during the 1950s was the importance of audience selectivity. Communication research consistently showed that, in the main, people tend to read, watch, and listen to messages that present points of view with which they agree. Also people do not just select which material they are exposed to; they remember it better if it coincides with their own views. Finally, even when people are exposed to communications with which they disagree they tend to reinterpret the content and often end up perceiving the message as supporting their beliefs. All this makes it very difficult to measure the effects of the media. For example, there is some evidence to show an association between exposure to violence on television and violent behaviour. However, no one has yet conclusively demonstrated that violence on television causes violence in society and what correlations there are could be due to people of a violent disposition seeking out violent images.

It was partly the difficulty of resolving problems like this that led to a growing disenchantment with efforts to measure the effects of media exposure. Furthermore, research that had shown that the audience were not isolated individuals had revealed a need to examine how use of the media was related to membership of social groups. This contributed to a change of approach during the 1960s. No longer was the most important question interpreted as being, 'What do the media do to people?' It was seen as more relevant to ask, 'What do people do with the media?'

Early research along these lines tended to operate with a 'uses and gratifications' model of explanation. Members of society were interpreted as using the media to gratify a variety of needs and this was seen to account for different reactions to media messages. However, this approach was of limited usefulness. Although there is evidence to show that people generally take what they want from the media their needs are themselves conditioned by membership of society. This is illustrated by research into the broader implications of media dependency. This shows that members of society are relying on the media for information more and more. As a result the ideas they have about society are increasingly derived from images manufactured by media organisations.

Much of the recent research has interpreted this in phenomenological terms. From this perspective the social world is seen as a creative accomplishment constructed out of the beliefs and values of its members. However, today the social world is largely experienced indirectly and is brought to members of society second-hand through the intervention of television, radio, and the press. As providers of knowledge and experience the media are thus in a position to shape the very beliefs and values upon which social reality depends. The main way they do this is not through direct attempts at persuasion. It is rather that the media provide a framework for making sense of experience and in indirect yet pervasive ways they organise the public's understanding of events.

One consequence of studying the media from this perspective has been that sociologists have switched their attention from media consumption by the public to media production by organisations. The most heavily researched area has been news, and research shows that news bulletins reproduce a variety of social myths. Perhaps the most powerful of these is a consensual model of society. This is the implicit guideline that journalists use when choosing and interpreting newsworthy material, and though they may not intend to manipulate public opinion the result is that the media tend to present a selective image of reality structured in terms of dominant values. This is crucial to many contemporary researchers who in seeking to probe the underlying meanings in the output of the media are increasingly being led to ask, 'Whose interests do the media serve?'

Commentary

Even media sociologists admit that much of the research into the mass media has been of poor quality. This is particularly so with much of the early quantitative research. Commenting on this, in a cynical vein, Brian Winston writes

> It might well be true, as somebody once suggested, that if you asked a communications researcher to define measles, he would find a sample of subjects with measles and count the spots on their faces.

(*Dangling Conversations*, Book 1, p.24)

However, in recent years there has been a major shift in emphasis in the sociology of the media. The attempt to measure attitude changes has largely been abandoned and sociologists have turned their attention to the content of media messages and the models of society which the media present. This approach is strongly represented in *The Manufacture of News* edited by Stanley Cohen and Jock Young. They argue that the media are in the business of reproducing an image of society and that this image rests upon the assumption of an underlying consensus. Thus, for example, Young writes

> the mass media offer an amazingly systematic frame of reference. It is not random bias but a consistent world view which is purveyed. The model of society held by the mass media, and implicit in their reporting of both deviant and normal, I will term consensualist. Its constitution is simplicity itself: namely, that the vast majority of people in society share a common definition of reality.

(*The Manufacture of News*, second edition pp.326−7)

Question 22
The manufacture of news: is the reporting of news inevitably biased?

The main sources of news in advanced industrial societies like Britain are the press, radio and television. Of these the most important is television. For example, each night the two main news bulletins put out by BBC 1 and ITN attract an estimated sixteen million viewers. This popularity is partly due to a widespread belief that television news is more objective and neutral than the news output of other media. This was confirmed by a BBC survey carried out in 1972. It found that few people were concerned about bias in television news or even believed that it existed. Television news is thus regarded as an authoritative source of information and precisely because television broadcasters have been so successful in putting over an image of trustworthiness their output is largely accepted uncritically. However, recent research has begun to show that confidence in the impartiality of the news is seriously misplaced.

To begin with the popular conception that news is discovered by intrepid journalists who diligently search out 'facts' which they then faithfully report to the public is a myth. As Stanley Cohen and Jock Young point out there is a sense in which news is manufactured rather than discovered. That is not to say it is invented by journalists and presenters themselves. However, what they call news is inevitably partial, selective and packaged for public consumption. Partly this is because there is just too much material and there have to be filters to select what is to be shown, in what order, at what length and with what stress. This filtering is the job of the editorial staff. They are the gatekeepers of the news, and in his article 'Decision Making in Network Television News' Malcolm Warner estimates that a group of less than fifty people has the power to shape the form and decide on the content of the news output of American network television.

Two further factors that influence the way news is structured and presented are periodicity and television values. Periodicity refers to the frequency of news communications, and television news, which is gathered and reported on a daily basis, stresses immediate events and neglects the long term processes that led up to them. Television values are bound up with the fact that television is a visual medium of communication which derives much of its impact from filming individuals who allegedly make the news. The effect of periodicity and television values is that the public is presented with an unhistorical view in which events occur suddenly and unexpectedly through the dramatic intervention of important people. In the process the underlying causes of economic and political changes and their impact on the social structure disappear beneath a welter of incidents and personalities.

However, technological, organisational and financial factors are only part of the reason for selective reporting. A more important barrier to impartiality is the values of professional journalists and the interests of the organisations they serve. These values and interests are built into the norms of journalistic practice and realised in the framework of interpretation that the media place round events. With the output of television news as their starting point the Glasgow Media Group set out to decode the news and thus to reveal the underlying norms governing its manufacture.

The group videotaped all television news broadcasts between January and June 1975. They were particularly interested in the way the media reported industrial news. Their study demonstrated that anyone relying on television for information about the British economy would get a very distorted picture. For example, industrial accidents are consistently under-reported. On the other hand, industrial disputes, which are heavily reported in general, were not covered systematically during the period studied. Comparing the Department of Employment's record of strikes with media coverage it was found that there was no consistent relationship between the two. However, that did not mean that the reporting was purely random. On the contrary, what was regarded as newsworthy were the strikes which caused most public inconvenience or which could be most effectively used to epitomise 'the British economic crisis'.

These examples illustrate that it is the media themselves and not the outside world that set the agenda for news. However, even more important than the amount of coverage given to particular aspects of the news is the manner in which events are reported. For example, industrial conflict and civil unrest are almost always defined as bad news; that is, of course, unless they occur in Eastern bloc countries. Then in terms of the anti-Communist stance of the western media these phenomena are translated into good news.

However, the process of imparting values through the news is best illustrated by the way the media report trade union activities at home. In the media trade unions are almost exclusively seen as dispute organisations and their wider economic and social role is consistently disregarded. When disputes do occur media coverage tends to focus on the effects of strikes and the causes are largely ignored. Deprived of essential background information the audience is invited to regard striking as senseless and irrational behaviour rather than as a response to a genuine grievance.

Of course ritual attention is given to the point of view of trade unionists. However, the hierarchy of access to the media ensures that their views receive less exposure. Furthermore, even when trade unionists are interviewed, media interviewers set the agenda. One effect is that though trade unionists' attitudes are frequently reported the reasons they have for holding them tend to be suppressed. This means that the blame for industrial conflict and economic problems tends to be imputed to the workforce, their elected representatives, or militant agitators. Meanwhile critiques of the economic system that produces conflict are conspicuous by their absence. In other words the media perform an ideological role by disseminating a one-dimensional view of reality. They organise news coverage so as to portray the establishment as rational, reasonable and fair whereas dissenters are interpreted as ignorant, unbalanced, or just plain evil.

Commentary

In *Bad News* the Glasgow Media Group describes two case studies that illustrate the way the media handle industrial disputes.

The first was a strike by heavy goods vehicle drivers working for Glasgow City Corporation. It lasted for three months and was caused by a belief amongst the workers that their employers had reneged on a promise of negotiations towards parity with drivers in the private sector. However, the media never reported the point of view of the strikers (none were interviewed), interpreted the strike as a wages claim and from the very start organised their coverage in terms of the 'health hazard' caused by rubbish piling up in the streets.

The second was a strike by engine tuners at British Leyland's Cowley plant. This received extensive coverage over a five week period and time and again the media took the line that a strike-prone work force was the root cause of British Leyland's problems. This was despite the fact that in the period leading up to the strike half of all lost production had been due to factors like component shortages and machinery breakdown. However, the possibility that the company's problems could be due to a lack of investment and bad management was an explanation that the media ignored.

Commenting on these two cases, the Glasgow Media Group states

> Our analysis goes beyond saying merely that the television news 'favour' certain individuals and institutions by giving them more time and status. Such criticisms are crude. The nature of our analysis is deeper than this: in the end it relates to the picture of society in general and industrial society in particular, that television news constructs. This at its most damaging includes, as in these case studies, the laying of blame for society's industrial and economic problems at the door of the workforce. This is done in the face of contradictory evidence which, when it appears, is either ignored, smothered, or at worst, is treated as if it supports the inferential frameworks utilised by the producers of news.
>
> (*Bad News*, pp.267–8)

A critique of the media along similar lines can be mounted in respect of the reporting of international relations, social problems, crime, deviance, race and women.

Chapter 7

Gender divisions in society

Class is not the only form of social inequality. There are also inequalities between the sexes, generations and races in Britain and elsewhere. Some sociologists argue that it is difficult to account for these divisions from a Marxist point of view and a number have turned to a perspective commonly known as 'conflict theory' or 'conflict structuralism'. Typically, Marx is interpreted as the founder of conflict theory and it is often said that his ideas were developed by Max Weber and turned into a sociological perspective by Ralf Dahrendorf. Sometimes a number of contemporary British sociologists are also associated with this point of view and names that you are likely to come across include David Lockwood, John Goldthorpe and John Rex. The ideas of these sociologists will be dealt with here.

What is distinctive about these sociologists is that though they all stress the importance of Marx's contribution to sociology they also believe that Marx's system of thought contains serious flaws and inadequacies. The task, as they see it, is to separate Marx's sociological insights from his philosophy and economics. In the process two of the principle elements in Marx's thought are dropped. These are his commitment to revolutionary action and his materialist perspective. For Marxists this involves dropping precisely what is practically and theoretically most important in Marx's work. However, conflict theorists maintain that it is necessary to recast Marx's ideas in order to make sense of the changes that have occurred since his death.

As well as being revisionists conflict theorists tend towards reformism rather than revolution. Their political commitment is to social democracy rather than the class struggle and their academic interest is in inequality rather than exploitation. Whilst they are often critical of the existing social order, and even more so of functionalist explanations of it, they tend to regard Marxism as a political ideology rather than as a sociological perspective. To provide intellectual support for this attitude conflict theorists frequently make use of the ideas of the German sociologist Max Weber (1864–1920).

Max Weber is sometimes said to have engaged in a lifelong dialogue with the ghost of Marx. The most famous aspect of that dialogue is Weber's research into the relationship between religion and modern capitalism. This research is often held to refute the materialist conception of history. It will be dealt with in Chapter 10. However, Weber is almost as renowned for his conceptual analysis of the principles of stratification. This analysis is sometimes alleged to undermine the grounds of Marx's belief in the inevitability of revolution. It will be dealt with here. Although it occupies but a small part of Weber's overall output his ideas on stratification are important to the development of conflict theory because of the distinction he made between class, status and party. (For the following quotations, see 'Class, Status and Party', reproduced in H.H. Gerth and C. Wright Mills, *From Max Weber: Essays in Sociology*, pp.180–95.)

Weber's view of class

Up to a point Weber agrees with Marx's analysis of class. For example, he accepts that 'the factor that creates class is unambiguously economic interest'. He also agrees with Marx that 'Property and lack of property are, therefore, the basic categories of all class structures'. However, whereas in Marx class is defined in terms of one's relationship to the means of production, for Weber class is governed by one's relationship to the market. By 'the market' he means the market both for goods and for labour. This leads Weber to view 'class position' as a function of the economic power of social actors who compete to buy or sell goods or services for the sake of an income or a profit.

On the basis of this Weber argues that in addition to the division between the propertied and the propertyless there are significant class divisions within each group as well. Amongst the propertied Weber attributes considerable importance to capital liquidity. This refers to the degree to which assets can be transformed into cash. At one extreme there will be those whose assets are tied up in fixed term investments, trust funds and the like. Their economic power is often limited to the power to dispose of only the income on their capital. At the other extreme there will be those who can transfer their assets into cash easily and at any time. Their economic power is limited only by the size of their fortune.

Amongst the propertyless Weber emphasises the importance of differences in skill. This is because in market economies skill is a commodity and those who possess skills that are in demand also have a source of economic power. This is one of the causes of differences in the price at which labour power is sold. However, it also means that there are corresponding differences in the class position of various categories of worker. For example, members of powerful professions such as doctors and lawyers are able to secure for themselves a relatively privileged position by virtue of their specialised skills and monopolistic control over the provision of medical and legal services. Their class position will therefore be very different from that of unskilled workers who, except in times of a general labour shortage, do not possess the economic leverage that comes from control of a scarce resource.

For Weber, then, factors other than ownership or non-ownership of the means of production influence class formation. This leads him to very different conclusions from those drawn by Marx. In particular whereas Marx predicted that there would be a polarisation of social classes Weber maintains quite the opposite. This is because as capitalism develops the scope and scale of bureaucratic organisation increases and there is an expansion in the size and significance of intermediate groups. Thus instead of society more and more dividing into 'two great hostile camps', as Marx held, Weber sees a developing plurality of economically determined aggregates of individuals differentiated from each other in terms of market advantages and disadvantages that flow from different types of capital and levels of skill.

In addition Weber does not accept that a shared class situation always leads to a sense of common identity, a recognition of mutual interest, and a realisation of the advantages of acting collectively. Although communal action stemming from a shared economic position is a possibility, countervailing forces often prevent this from happening. One such force can be the presence of status distinctions in society.

Weber's view of status

Whereas class divisions are to do with the unequal distribution of economic rewards and opportunities for gain, status distinctions are bound up with the unequal distribution of social honour. Those who are honoured have prestige in the eyes of other members of society and are generally treated with respect. Those who are dishonoured are stigmatised by others and are thought worthy of contempt. In principle any characteristic which sets one group apart from others can act as a focus for status distinctions and frequently sexual, racial, religious, cultural and educational differences do so. However, when a status group is formed it is normally expressed 'by the fact that above all else a specific style of life can be expected from all those who wish to belong to the circle'. Status groups are therefore normally communities and to a greater or lesser extent they seek to preserve their exclusiveness by placing restrictions on social contact with outsiders.

In extreme cases status groups evolve into castes. The classic example is in India. Here members of castes are typically united by endogamous marriage (i.e. marriage is permitted only between members of the same caste), a traditional occupation, separate religious rituals and a variety of restrictions on touching, associating with, dining with, or even eating food prepared by, outsiders. Should these rules be broken and prohibited contact between a high and low caste member occur the high caste member is considered to be polluted and must undergo a purification ritual before being fully readmitted to the life of the community. Although this is an extreme example of status segregation restrictions on, or at least disapproval of, certain kinds of contact between members of different status groups are found in all societies.

For Weber these divisions are not reducible to class. This is because members of society are looked up to or looked down on for a variety of reasons, of which economic standing is only one. It thus follows that whilst there is likely to be some association between wealth and honour there will also be individuals who share the same class position but not the same status group. For example, amongst the wealthy there is normally a degree of status distinction between established wealth holders and the *nouveaux riches*, with the latter often being excluded from high society because they are judged to lack the taste, etiquette, or refinement necessary for social acceptance as equals. Studies also show the presence of status distinctions within the working class in Britain. For example, in her study of Banbury Margaret Stacey reports that it was common to find manual workers making a distinction between 'rough' and 'respectable' families.

Weber's view of party

Whereas classes are determined by the economic organisation of society, and status groups by the distribution of positive and negative evaluations, parties are orientated toward the acquisition of legal and political power. According to Weber this third dimension to stratification arises in communities that 'have some rational order and a staff of persons who are ready to enforce it'. In other words parties are only possible in societies and organisations in which decisions affecting the members as a whole are made and enforced by an administrative body. This is because the aim of a party is to influence the staff of that administrative body and, if possible, get their own members recruited to it.

Parties are therefore 'always structures struggling for domination'. In the case of a pluralistic democracy like modern Britain this means that politics becomes a matter of the play of interest. In the foreground are the major political parties which compete with each other for office. However, in Weber's terms pressure groups are also parties. These enter directly into competition for power by seeking to get their own members elected or appointed to positions in the governing elite. Indirectly they seek to exert an influence over policy and its implementation either by legitimate means (such as force of argument or political lobbying) or illegitimate means (such as political terrorism or bribery and corruption).

For Weber parties 'are always directed towards a goal which is striven for in a planned manner'. In any particular case they 'may represent interests determined through class situation or status situation'. However, in practice parties usually recruit their members from and represent the interests of a mixture of class and status groups. This means that just as status distinctions can cut across class divisions so party allegiance can cut across both class and status.

The picture of the stratification system that we are left with is more complex than Marx's two class model of society. Basically this is because, whilst accepting that money is a source of power, Weber believed there were other sources as well. Status and party therefore assume the form of distinct dimensions to stratification. However, although he defined these conceptually distinct types of power, Weber recognised the presence of empirical links between them. Where he disagreed with Marx was in the way he interpreted these links.

Interpretations of class conflict

Marx interpreted the relationship between economic, social, and political power in terms of his materialist conception of history. This led him to reduce questions raised by the struggle for power to class conflict. On this basis he predicted that revolution was inevitable. However, Weber argued that the relationship between different types of power was empirically variable. This led him to argue that social classes were not the only significant groups in society. From this point of view the nature and direction of class conflict cannot be deduced from philosophical premises. It has to be discovered empirically by examining the relationship between classes and other forms of inequality in particular societies at particular times.

This is also a theme taken up by modern conflict theorists. For example, in *Class and Class Conflict in an Industrial Society* (1959), Ralf Dahrendorf set out to separate the sociological and philosophical elements in Marx's theory of class. This, in effect, was what Weber was doing in his analysis of class, status, and party. However, Dahrendorf felt that it is necessary to go further.

Dahrendorf also believed that Marx was wrong to tie economic, social and political power to ownership of the means of production. However, whereas Weber follows Marx in seeing class in economic terms Dahrendorf argued that 'Classes are neither primarily nor at all economic groupings' (p.139). He also stated that, 'By social class shall be understood such organised or unorganised collectivities of individuals as share manifest or latent interests arising from and related to the authority structure of imperatively co-ordinated associations' (p.238). In other words, for Dahrendorf classes are any groups in any organisations that have different interests due to their occupancy of positions of domination or subordination.

Like Dahrendorf, Lockwood is also interested in the ideas of Marx and Weber. However, whereas Dahrendorf's main work has been in the area of conceptual and theoretical issues, Lockwood is best known for his empirical research. This research has been mainly concerned with the analysis of the class position of particular occupational groups in the stratification system of modern Britain.

For example, in *The Blackcoated Worker* (1958) Lockwood set out to explore the class position of clerks. Following Weber he distinguished between the market situation, work situation, and status aspirations of clerks and then went on to examine their position in terms of these three dimensions. A similar approach was used in *The Affluent Worker* (1968, 1969). This research was carried out by Lockwood in collaboration with John Goldthorpe and others. It also involved a multidimensional approach to stratification organised in terms of a distinction between the economic, normative, and relational aspects of class. (For further treatment of these issues, see Question 17.)

The significance of these studies has to be seen against the background of the debate over changes in the stratification systems of advanced industrial societies. This was one of the main issues in British sociology during the 1950s and the 1960s. Some Marxists were claiming that routine non-manual workers were undergoing a process of proletarianisation. Others argued that these workers had a 'false consciousness' of their 'true' class position. Amongst non-Marxists embourgeoisement was fashionable, and to some it even seemed that class divisions were disappearing. However, none of these ideas is supported by the empirical studies of Lockwood and his co-researchers. They therefore made a contribution to sociology by laying to rest some of the widely accepted myths about the class structure of an advanced industrial society.

Another interesting development is represented by John Rex and Robert Moore's book *Race, Community and Conflict*. This is an empirical study of race relations in Birmingham in the 1960s, and Rex and Moore also claim to be following Weber in their use of the concept of class. However, whereas Lockwood's interest is in stratification by occupation, Rex and Moore focus on the stratification system of the city. In relation to this they argue that 'there is a class struggle over the use of houses and that this class struggle is the central process of the city as a social unit' (p.273). On this basis they distinguish different types of access to domestic property and show how the bargaining position of various individuals and groups in relation to the housing market affects the formation of different types of neighbourhood. However, Rex and Moore are not just making a sociological statement. Like some other conflict theorists they also advocate reforms for dealing with the social problems that class produces.

At the heart of the debate with Marx is the meaning attached to 'class'. For Marx class was a question of relationship to the means of production. The important point is that conflict theorists regard this as unsatisfactory. So, in one way or another and with varying degrees of success they have set out to reformulate the idea of class. In attempting to do this they are in effect following the same path as Weber. He is therefore the crucial figure when it comes to understanding conflict theory. However, Weber's ideas on stratification are also very useful in the analysis and interpretation of substantive inequalities in any society.

Nowhere is this better illustrated than in relation to gender divisions. The key point here is that these divisions must be seen as part of stratification theory. In the following essays this is emphasised. However, from Weber's point of view, gender is a status distinction. This means that in order to account for the social inequalities between men and women one has to examine the way members of each sex are regarded in society. On the other hand, Weber also argues that 'the social order is of course conditioned by the economic order'. In other words status has to be seen in relation to class. This is why the role of housewife is so important to an understanding of women's position in society. Third, there are parties. These are groups 'oriented towards the acquisition of social power'. This is the point of view from which the Women's Movement is treated.

Question 23
Sex role differentiation: biologically or culturally determined?

The genetically determined differences between men and women are the basis on which humans are classified as male or female. However, in every known society the biological division between the sexes is also embodied in social structure and culture. Materially this is realised in the different roles of men and women, ideologically in the myths about their different qualities, and psychologically in the beliefs and attitudes of individuals themselves. Sex is not therefore just a matter of physiological differences; it is also the basis of an organising principle of social life. This has led some scientists to argue that biological differences ultimately govern social roles. They claim that masculine and feminine traits are founded upon natural differences, the most important of which is that only women can bear children.

In recent years this view has been popularised by naturalists such as Konrad Lorenz. He argues that the principles that have been applied by natural scientists in the study of animal behaviour can also be applied to humans. For example, in *On Aggression* Lorenz argues that natural selection governs the evolution of cultures in the same way as it does that of species. From this point of view patriarchy is often interpreted as due to innate differences between the sexes carried over from the primeval past. Whilst it is usually acknowledged that culture may shape specific behavioural characteristics the implication of this view is that it goes against nature to suppose that there could ever be an end to gender divisions.

The anthropologists Lionel Tiger and Robin Fox have a similar theory. They argue that much human behaviour is governed by a 'human biogrammar'. This is a genetically based predisposition to behave in certain ways and Tiger and Fox believe that the biogrammars of men and women are different. They allege that this is part of the legacy of humanity's primate ancestors and that it developed during the evolution of primitive societies. According to Tiger and Fox this explains man's dominance over woman in all known societies. Both sexes are programmed by prehistoric conditions when men were the protectors and leaders of the band and women cared for the children. Applying this to industrial societies it is sometimes argued that gender divisions today are still rooted in this difference between man the hunter and woman the home-maker.

However, explanations of sex role differences in terms of humanity's evolutionary past are always speculative because of the lack of evidence about social life in prehistoric times. This has led some anthropologists to turn to the comparative method for evidence of the influence of biology on culture. One classic example of this type of research is George Peter Murdock's cross-cultural survey of 224 societies. Murdock claimed that the comparative evidence shows a universal differentiation of sex roles. He attributed this to men's superior physical strength and to women's biological role in child-bearing and nursing. According to Murdock women are more dependent on a home base and because of this different social roles are the most practical way of performing socially necessary tasks.

The idea that female domesticity is beneficial to society is also inherent in the work of Talcott Parsons. He argued that because women bear and nurse children they have a stronger bond with them. This is the natural basis of their expressive personality. This assumption led Parsons to claim that the main role of women is to provide the warmth, security, and emotional support necessary for the effective socialisation of children. This argument is sometimes used to justify the assertion that a woman's place is in the home. For example, the psychologist John Bowlby has argued that children separated from their mothers in infancy grow up psychologically disturbed. However, the research into children of working mothers has not revealed any detrimental effects. This has led feminists to question whether a woman's biological role in reproduction need determine her social role in the way that Parsons and Bowlby imply.

The evidence that natural differences do not impose a cultural pattern has been growing since the pioneering work of Margaret Mead in the 1930s. Mead studied a variety of Pacific island cultures and found a complex and variable relationship between biological constants and forms of social organisation. Furthermore, if the tribes studied by Mead are any guide to humanity's prehistory, there are no genetically determined masculine and feminine behaviour patterns. For example, amongst the Arapash women do most of the heavy work and members of the tribe believe that they are naturally equipped for this. In addition research by Colin Turnball into the Mbuti pygmies of the Congo basin shows that sex-differentiated roles are neither natural nor inevitable. In this tribe both sexes hunt and infants are mainly cared for by older relatives who are often male.

Fieldwork studies also raise doubts about the significance that Murdock attributed to practicality. For example, the kinship system of the Mundugamor of New Guinea thoroughly divides man from man and turns every son into the enemy of his father. This poses a constant threat to social order, but Mead's research demonstrated that this kinship pattern was institutionalised in Mundugamor society. This shows how considerations of pure practicality do not always govern human relationships and Mead proposes that it is cultural evaluation of human biology rather than biological differences themselves which are the cause of sex role differentiation.

This point has been developed by Sherry Ortner. She argues that in all human societies culture is evaluated as superior to nature. Women are also generally regarded as closer to nature than men and are therefore evaluated as inferior. This implies that gender divisions are not biologically determined. They only appear so because the ideology of female domesticity rationalises sex role differentiation by explaining it as natural. However, experiments in communal living such as the Israeli kibbutzim show that progress can be made in reducing sexual divisions. This system was a product of human inventiveness and though only partially successful it demonstrates that biology is always subordinate to the specifically human capacity to create new forms of social organisation.

Commentary

Functionalists tend to explain the existence of institutionalised behaviour in terms of its beneficial consequences for individuals and society. Margaret Mead's research shows that this explanation will not always work. For example, amongst the Mundugamor

> The boys' whole concept of their identity is that of fighting males tied precariously through women to other fighting males. Women are masculin-ised to a point where every feminine feature is a drawback except their highly specific genital sexuality, men to a point where any aspect of their personalities that might hold an echo of the feminine or the maternal is a vulnerability and a liability. The division of society into two groups, grown men on the one hand, women and children on the other, has been practically shattered but at a price which . . . threatens the very survival of the group. For the Mundugamor's habits of hostility were such that they had begun to eat people of their own language group. There was virtually no tribal solidarity, and it was probably a mere accident of history that they capitulated to the mission before they were destroyed by marauding neighbours.

(*Male and Female*, pp.108–9)

In the above case the culturally determined roles of men and women actively threatened the survival of society. Many modern feminists believe that in a society that possesses the means of mass destruction the institutionalised dominance of male aggression and the corresponding devaluation of 'feminine' qualities threatens the survival of us all.

Question 24
Education and gender: how does sexism influence the schooling of girls?

Sexism involves taking the attitude that certain behaviour patterns are natural to one sex or the other. In our culture sexist attitudes are embedded in sex stereotypes. These are representations of what is considered ideal or typical in males and females. They underlie the norms that enforce a gender division in society that is internalised by adults and communicated to children. This is particularly important in families and schools where adults are able to use their power to shape the identity of young people. The effect on girls is that they are channelled into a narrow range of school subjects, their aspirations are limited, and they are encouraged to view education as a preparation for a domestic role.

The different attitudes that parents have towards their sons and daughters are evident from studies of parents' sex preferences (see Ann Oakley, 'What makes girls differ from boys?', *New Society*, 21 December 1978). These show that parents want boys more frequently than girls and that they are more likely to try for a third child if they already have two girls. The importance of the sex of a child to its parents is further emphasised by the 'colour coding' of babies (pink for girls and blue for boys), and the toys given to children of each sex. Toys are important because play influences the imaginative development and children's games often anticipate the stereotyped adult roles of men as breadwinners and women as housewives.

Throughout childhood, the importance of parents as role models is particularly great and a mother's domestic responsibilities continually influence her daughter's interests and activities. This is confirmed by John and Elizabeth Newson's research. They showed that sex-related variations in behaviour increase between the ages of four and seven. One tendency was for girls to stay indoors more. As Rosemary Deem points out, parental expectations are already pushing girls into a home based subculture.

Formal education reinforces this and encourages girls in the belief that their goal in life is to love others, marry, and have children. Eileen Byrne attaches particular importance to the way teachers tend to think of boys and girls as separate species. This contributes to the division between 'boys'' and 'girls'' subjects. This goes back to the nineteenth century when a separate curriculum was established for girls, who had less instruction in science and mathematics. The justification for this was that science was more important for boys because they would be entering paid employment whereas girls would need domestic skills.

Despite the move towards joint conjugal roles and the expansion of female employment the same attitudes persist today. Partly this is due to the hidden curriculum. This ensures that boys and girls are treated differently in schools. For example, the organisation of most schools emphasises sex divisions through different treatment for boys and girls. Many of these differences carry the implicit message that girls are of less importance. An instance of this is the common practice of dividing registers by sex; almost invariably boys' names are put first.

Sexist assumptions also structure classroom interaction. Studies of teachers show they typically praise girls for being helpful, polite, clean and lady-like, whereas boys are praised for toughness and initiative. One result is that children themselves divide into male and female peer groups. Amongst boys this leads to a need to demonstrate masculinity. This is one explanation of their higher accident and delinquency rate. However, in girls' peer groups it is often appearance rather than prowess that is a source of status. This helps explain why girls are gradually overtaken by boys in secondary education. Although more girls leave school with at least one O level, a higher proportion of boys leave with two or more A levels.

Even more marked than sex-related differences in achievement are the differences in the subjects young people choose to take. For example, boys outnumber girls three to one in O level physics examinations. This is part of an overall pattern in which girls are concentrated in arts subjects while boys are over-represented in sciences. The major exception is biology. This is often regarded as a girls' science, and at most schools and colleges biology has a lower status than other sciences.

One effect of this division is to reinforce popular stereotypes of women as intuitive and men as rational. However, even more important is the way sexism in education is connected with role allocation. This is illustrated by Sue Sharpe's study of working class girls at secondary school in Ealing. Most of these girls had little interest in school and frequently left early with few qualifications for a narrow range of jobs. For them marriage was usually the over-ridingly important goal and they tended to take jobs with few career prospects because they saw work as a temporary expedient before starting on their main career as wives and mothers.

Amongst middle class girls the pattern seems different at first sight because more girls than boys enter further and higher education. Despite this the sex-related differences in courses and subjects in higher education are even more marked than at school. Partly this is because options are limited by previous subject choices. However, there is also a strong tendency for middle class girls to aim for careers that are extensions of a woman's domestic role. Many of these adolescent girls are in vocational training for traditional female professions like nursing, catering, and teaching.

Far from bringing about equality between the sexes the universities are the final link in the chain connecting women's education with gender divisions in society. As late as 1981 women made up only 37 per cent of undergraduates and R.K. Kelsall's research shows that married women graduates are less likely than women as a whole to be in employment. In line with this some feminists interpret universities as institutions where women are encouraged to compete to be the partners of a predominantly male elite.

Commentary

Despite some progress since the nineteenth century sexism remains institutionalised in British education, as it does in society at large, and Rosemary Deem quotes several interesting examples. The 1943 Norwood Report (on the curriculum in secondary schools) stated that

> The grounds for including Domestic subjects in the curriculum are variously stated in the evidence submitted to us; briefly, they are, first that knowledge of such subjects is a necessary equipment for all girls as potential makers of homes.

The Crowther Report published in 1959 (on the education of fifteen to eighteen year olds) argued that

> all schools can and should make adjustments ... to the fact that marriage now looms much larger and nearer in the pupils' eyes than it ever has before ... there is a clear case for a curriculum which respects the different roles they (i.e. boys and girls) play.

The Newsom Report of 1963 (on the education of children of average and below average ability) even claimed that

> A boy is usually excited by the prospect of a science course ... He experiences a sense of wonder and a sense of power. The growth of wheat, the birth of a

lamb, the movement of clouds put him in awe of nature; the locomotive he sees as man's response; the switch and the throttle are his magic wands ... The girl may come to the science lesson with a less eager curiosity than the boy but she too will need to feel at home with machinery.

(quoted in Rosemary Deem, *Women and Schooling*, pp.17, 59, 60–1)

Notice in the last quotation how the stereotype of excited and eager boys is contrasted to that of the lack of interest shown by girls. If educationalists and administrators themselves uncritically accept traditional sex stereotypes and persist in regarding boys and girls as if they were separate species, they are likely to add another factor to those influencing the subject choices and educational attainment of pupils.

Question 25
Women and work: why has government legislation not brought about equality between the sexes?

The 1970 Equal Pay Act covers contractual aspects of employment such as rates of pay, and terms and conditions of work. Officially it came into full operation in 1975. Since then employers have been legally obliged to pay women equal rates to men if they do jobs which are 'the same or broadly similar'. Also in 1975 the Sex Discrimination Act was passed. This deals with non-contractual aspects of employment such as job advertisements, and hiring and promoting workers. It makes it illegal to discriminate against women or men on the grounds of sex. Under the Act the Equal Opportunities Commission was established. This is a statutory body with responsibility for monitoring the law, combating discrimination and promoting sexual equality. However, these measures have been relatively ineffective in reducing the male earnings advantage and overcoming gender divisions in the labour market.

One reason is that employers have been very successful in finding loopholes in the law. For example, during the five years during which equal pay was to be phased in some employers regraded workers and segregated male and female jobs. This prevented many women from benefiting under the Equal Pay Act because by the time it was implemented there were no equivalent men's jobs with which to make a comparison. Although some women did gain, the legislation did little to change the economic position of women as a whole. Their average hourly rate of pay remains less than three quarters of the rate for men and the Act itself seems to be a spent force since the gap between male and female earnings has recently been widening.

The Sex Discrimination Act has also done little to reduce inequalities. This is partly because unlawful discrimination is difficult to prove. However, many feminists have also criticised the Equal Opportunities Commission for being half-hearted in its attempts to combat discrimination. Whilst a lot of effort has been put into research and some progress has been made in reducing sex discrimination in advertisements the Commission has been unwilling to confront the vested interests served by the current sexual division of labour. This has meant that, although there have been cases of women entering traditionally male occupations, the overall position of women in the occupational structure has not altered. They are still concentrated in a narrow range of mainly low-paid occupations and it has been left to individual women and voluntary groups to take the lead in campaigning for equal rights.

However, it is not just the difficulty of enforcing existing legislation that is responsible for continued inequality. The law itself only deals with part of the problem. This is because it does virtually nothing to counter the effects of past discrimination or change sexist attitudes. It is these two factors that are mainly responsible for the persistence of sexual divisions in income and employment and they are both related to the role of women as housewives. Ann Oakley refers to this as 'the dominant mature feminine role'. She claims that this is confirmed by surveys that show that 85 per cent of adult women are housewives and that on average they spend over seventy hours a week on housework.

Housework differs from most other types of work because it is performed on the basis of personal rather than contractual relationships. It is also mainly performed in the home and on behalf of the family. This means that housewives are relatively isolated from other workers and the boundaries of their work are blurred by its integration with family roles. Both factors contribute to a tendency for the time and effort spent on housework to go unrecognised. However, the more important fact is that housework is unpaid labour. This is the main reason for the economic subordination of women and the cultural devaluation of their role in society.

Women who combine paid employment with the role of housewife are particularly vulnerable to exploitation. For example, approximately 40 per cent of women workers combine their two roles by working part-time. Typically part-time employees are paid less and have little job security and few chances of promotion. However, they are better off than homeworkers. There are at least 150 000 of these and they are mainly women with children for whom homeworking is the only means of supplementing their income. In 1979 the Low Pay Unit reported that almost half of these earned less than forty pence an hour. In addition they are rarely entitled to basic employment rights such as holidays or pensions and have to pay overheads like heating and lighting themselves.

A woman's domestic role also affects her earnings if she is in full-time employment and statistics show that women do less overtime and have more time off than men. This partly explains why only six per cent of wives earn more than their husbands. However, the main cause of inequality is the dual labour market. This channels most women into unskilled or semiskilled manual jobs or routine non-manual occupations. In these areas many do jobs which involve clearing up, waiting on, and looking after others. These tasks are extensions of a woman's domestic role and this devalues the status of predominantly female occupations. Furthermore the same pattern is found in the professions. Here women are concentrated in lower-paid professions such as primary school teaching and social work and even the small minority who enter the high status medical and legal professions tend to be concentrated in 'female specialisms' such as gynaecology and family law.

To add to all the other disadvantages women's careers are typically discontinuous, because of periods away from paid work to bear and rear children. This makes them ideal candidates for the industrial reserve army. This is a reserve pool of cheap labour used by employers to keep down wage rates. It is also labour that can be drawn upon during times of expanding production and is easily made redundant during recession. To some extent this sums up the experience of women this century. They were drafted into industry during two world wars and into the expanding service sector during the postwar economic boom. However, in recent years economic recession has led to women losing their jobs at a faster rate than men.

Commentary

Women are themselves divided over what should be done to reduce inequality between the sexes. Some favour extending existing legislation and increasing the power of the Equal Opportunities Commission. Others favour a programme of positive discrimination designed to increase the representation of women in top jobs. A third proposal is wages for housework. However, none of these remedies is likely to be effective so long as women continue to bear the main burden of housework and the rearing of children. This has led some feminists to argue the case for a more radical approach. For example, after quoting Lenin's view that 'No nation can be free when half the population is enslaved in the kitchen', Ann Oakley goes on to claim that

> Three political statements point the way to the liberation of housewives:
>
> > The housewife role must be abolished.
> > The family must be abolished.
> > Gender roles must be abolished.
>
> (*Housewife*, p.222)

Question 26
The emancipation of women: what are the myths? what is the reality?

The subjugation of women in Victorian England extended to every aspect of their lives. Legally and politically women had virtually no rights. In the family they were subject to the authority of male relatives. Upon marriage that authority was transferred to their husbands. Although many women worked as wage earners this was often forced upon them out of economic necessity and was widely regarded as a misfortune. Ideally, a woman's place was thought to be in the home, her main role to bear and look after children. This left many women with little freedom to do anything else. Domestic drudgery, paid or unpaid, was their main work role and when a woman married she could expect to combine this with a life of constant childbearing which often led to an early grave.

Since then legal and political reforms have brought about an improvement in the status of women. For example, a series of property acts between 1870 and 1893 gave married women the right to their own earnings and the right to retain whatever property they possessed at marriage or acquired thereafter. Women have also benefited from legislation which has extended the franchise and in 1928 they gained equal voting rights to men. In addition women now have the legal right to an abortion, increased rights in the area of divorce, and the right to equal opportunities in education and employment.

There have been changes in marriage and the family too. For example, Ronald Fletcher argues that there has been a qualitative improvement in family life in Britain since the nineteenth century and that women have benefited most of all. According to Fletcher the modern family is managed democratically and wives have equal status to their husbands', an equal share in taking decisions, and more opportunity for self-fulfilment. Michael Young and Peter Willmott are broadly in agreement with this and in their community studies they contrast the segregated conjugal roles of traditional working class families with the egalitarian conjugal relationship that they see as typical of the modern symmetrical family.

Even more important is the decline in the birth rate. According to Richard Titmuss this is the main cause of 'a revolutionary enlargement of freedom for women'. This view receives support from A.H. Halsey who claims that the control of fertility is as important a social change as any this century. Whereas in the past it was common for women to have unwanted pregnancies forced upon them this is now less likely because of the increased reliability and acceptance of contraception. In addition the contraceptive pill, now the most widely used means of preventing conception in Britain, places power over reproduction in the hands of women.

All these changes have contributed to a radical alteration in the pattern of women's lives. However, both the social reformers who passed legislation to give equal rights to women and the sociologists who have interpreted this as part of a march of progress towards equality are mainly men. They have tended to define what women can hope for or have a right to expect from the point of view of their own sex. This has helped foster the myths that emancipation is a natural and inevitable process, that it is now virtually complete, and that it is men who have emancipated women.

Typically these myths are justified by comparisons between the position of women today and in the nineteenth century. However, if one compares the contemporary position of women with the ideal implications of complete emancipation a different picture emerges. Thus, full emancipation would imply that the ascribed status of sex was no disability whatsoever. This has not yet been achieved even in relation to the law. For example, women are still legally barred from entering some occupations and in the fields of taxation, national insurance and social security there are different and unequal regulations. Furthermore, some of the gains, particularly in the areas of divorce and abortion reform, remain precarious.

Even more significant are the substantive social and economic inequalities that remain untouched by legislative changes. Chief amongst these is the systematic exclusion of women from positions of power. For example, less than 4 per cent of the Members of Parliament elected in the 1983 general election were women and in 1980 women made up under 3 per cent of the membership of the Institute of Directors. Even in traditionally female occupations there is a tendency for men to occupy positions of responsibility. For example, although most office workers and primary school teachers are women the majority of office managers and primary school head teachers are men.

This exclusion of women from positions of authority both reflects and contributes to their continued subordination in society. In modern Britain this is institutionalised throughout the social structure and is particularly evident in the way images of women are socially manufactured. For example, in the mass media women tend to be ignored, stereotyped, or trivialised. However, their cultural devaluation is at its most obvious in pornography. This helps to create and sustain attitudes amongst men that lead to the sexual harassment of women at work, on the streets, and in other public places.

In addition, changes in the family have not all been to the advantage of women. The conventional view espoused by march of progress theorists is that smaller families, the mechanisation of the home, and the sharing of household duties, have all benefited women. However, women still shoulder the main burden of household tasks, are expected to provide higher standards of child care, and spend as much, if not more, time on housework.

Finally, there is no evidence of a qualitative improvement in relationships between husbands and wives. The number of divorces continues to rise and official statistics for

1978 showed that 71 per cent of divorce petitions were filed by women. This is in line with studies of attitudes to marriage. For example, in *The Future of Marriage* Jessie Bernard argues that surveys show that wives are more likely than husbands to be dissatisfied. One reason is likely to be that in addition to doing most of the housework married women are also more likely than in the past to be breadwinners as well. Rather than bringing about emancipation this has tended to 'free' women for a double exploitation in the home and at work.

Commentary

Most members of society internalise their sexual identity to such an extent that they tend to take sexual divisions in society for granted. Professional sociologists are no exception and it is possible to trace the influence of sexism in sociology by looking for what sociologists have neglected to study. For example, in the sociology of work most of the research has been into work performed by men. In the sociology of deviance it is the male crime and suicide rate that has been the focus of attention. In social mobility studies movement between social strata has conventionally been measured by comparing the positions of fathers and sons.

Sometimes even female sociologists fall into this same trap. For example, Olive Banks' book *The Sociology of Education* is often regarded as a standard text. However, if you turn to this for an account of the issues raised by the education of women then you will be disappointed. In a nearly three hundred page book this is dealt with in a subsection of one chapter where in less than three pages the author deals with women's education as 'a special case'.

However, in recent years this has been changing and feminism is now a perspective within sociology. For Sarah Delamont this means

that more women should engage in research and teaching, that research should be conducted into all aspects of women's lives, and that all social science theory and research should be rigorously scrutinised for explicit or implicit assumptions about women. This last point is in effect a call for a more scientific attitude amongst social scientists: a call for them to ask searching questions about sex differences and similarities rather than taking them for granted as natural. Thus a sociology without sexism would be a better sociology.

(*The Sociology of Women*, p.4)

Chapter 8

Social problems and deviance

Which types of behaviour are regarded as social problems or as deviant by members of a society depends upon the values and norms that they accept as valid, and the standards that people apply to evaluate their own behaviour and that of others vary. This means that it is impossible for a purely empirical subject to define once and for all what types of behaviour are social problems and what are deviant acts. However, what one can do is to seek to understand how these or any other evaluations come to be applied to social phenomena and what the effects of the application of positive or negative evaluations are. This is at the heart of a perspective in sociology known as symbolic interactionism.

A symbol is a sign, a token, something that represents or stands for something else. Language is one such sign system. Interaction is the mutual or reciprocal influence of two or more forces on each other, and social relationships are a case in point. Put the two words together and you get symbolic interaction; that is social relationships between social actors who act in terms of the meaning they attach to their behaviour and that of others. According to symbolic interactionists this is the stuff of which social reality is made.

This is very different from the perspectives we have looked at so far. To begin with, functionalism, Marxism and conflict theory are all macroperspectives; that is to say they focus on the nature and characteristics of society as a whole. They are also sometimes referred to as 'systems' or 'structural' perspectives, 'systems' because they emphasise the relationships between different parts of society, and 'structural' because they aim to explain how social structure shapes human attitudes and behaviour. Of course when it comes to describing what the system is like or explaining what its effects are these perspectives disagree strongly. However, for all their disagreements they are at least united in seeing social forces ('society', 'the social system', 'social class') as the cause of individual action.

Symbolic interactionists approach the study of social action the other way round. In place of structure they emphasise consciousness. If they refer to systems at all 'the system' is seen as the outcome and not the cause of action. Furthermore, they do not focus on society as a whole but on face-to-face relationships between individual actors. This perspective is often regarded as a branch of interpretive or phenomenological sociology. It is also sometimes described as an individualistic, a humanist, or a social psychological approach. Its central theme is that ultimately the 'solid facts' of society are mental and not material. In other words symbolic interactionists see the social world as constructed by individuals whose actions are orientated to the behaviour of others.

The origins of this perspective go back to developments in American philosophy at the turn of the century. Its founders are often said to include Charles H. Cooley, George Herbert Mead and William I. Thomas. They attempted to explore the way in which personal identity is shaped by social interaction.

Origins of symbolic interactionism: Cooley

Charles H. Cooley (1864–1929) is best known for his concept of the primary group. Primary groups are small groups characterised by face-to-face association and a high degree of involvement. They are intimate collectivities made up of social actors who express themselves as individuals. Typically members of a primary group achieve a personal rapport with each other, and theirs is an informal relationship. It does not depend upon a body of explicitly formulated rules but is rather kept alive by the spontaneous give and take generated through the free play of personality. Examples of primary groups include play groups, teenage gangs, families, and friendship groups.

Cooley emphasised that primary groups are ubiquitous. Every human being tends to be drawn into some primary group attachments and these tend to be the most significant relationships in their lives. Furthermore it is in such groups that individuals learn basic social values like loyalty, kindness, justice and freedom. By providing individuals with their earliest and most complete experience of social unity the primary group acts as a building block for more complex forms of social organisation.

Primary groups are also the main source of an awareness of personal and social identity. For example, through the medium of language we become acquainted with ideas which we then adopt as our own. Our attitude towards ourselves and others, our actions and our appearance are similarly affected. In all these cases we are responding to what Cooley called the 'imaginations' we have of one another. He believed that this was the way in which both society and the individual were sustained and to convey their ultimate unity he coined the term a 'looking glass self'. By this he meant that social interaction is like a mirror. By entering into social relationships we are able to see ourselves as others see us, and that shapes the ideas we have about the kind of person we are. In other words we are what we think we are and what we think we are depends to a large extent on what others think of us.

Origins of symbolic interactionism: Mead

George Herbert Mead (1863–1931) was a philosopher rather than a sociologist. However, his ideas have had a greater impact on the development of symbolic interactionism than Cooley's and he is often regarded as its real founder. Like Cooley, Mead also argued that our self image is derived from our relationship with others. However, he explored the implications of this in greater depth.

Mead emphasised that no hard and fast line can be drawn between our own self and the selves of others. Although we conventionally think of a person as someone who exists as a separate, autonomous and unitary being Mead invites us to question all these assumptions. His argument was that self exists only in and through interaction. It is the social process itself which is responsible for the self's emergence and Mead set out to comprehend how this could come about.

Now the self has a unique quality which sets it apart from all other phenomena; it is an object to itself. For example, we are able to remember what we did in the past, imagine what we will do in the future, reason with ourselves, criticise our actions, scrutinise our motives and hold an imaginary conversation with ourselves. In other words we are not just conscious of objects and events, we are also self-conscious beings. Through our eyes and other senses we gather the material with which to comprehend the external world. In our mind's eye we can comprehend our own inner subjectivity.

This capacity to reflect upon ourselves implies that individuals are able to take the same attitude toward themselves as others take toward them. However, Mead claimed that individuals are never able to experience themselves in this way directly. Individuals become objects to themselves only by adopting the standpoint of other individuals. That implies that members of society can communicate with one another and communication is achieved by means of common symbols. Following this line of reasoning Mead was led to attribute particular significance to language. For him this was the only medium in which the self appears as an object to itself. A simple example illustrates the point: 'I scored a goal' (self as subject); 'They applauded me' (self as object).

The above example illustrates that human beings can both undergo an experience and simultaneously be aware of it. The reason why human beings are able to do this is because they are the only life forms to have developed language. Although animals can and do communicate with each other, what they communicate to each other is, as far as we know, purely instinctive or imitative behaviour. This is why in the explanation of animal behaviour many scientists assume a stimulus-response model. However, human conduct is different. Here there is no fixed relationship between genetic or environmental stimuli and the way human beings respond. Individuals may thus behave in very different ways under what seem essentially the same circumstances. The reason is that interposed between the circumstances that prompt action and the action is the self. This is the organising principle of experience.

Thinking, said Mead, is preparatory to social action. That is to say, in human beings reactive behaviour has to a large extent been replaced by meaningful action. In this way human beings construct their own world. By selecting goals, choosing appropriate means to achieve them, and sometimes weighing up possible alternative courses of action and their consequences, action is organised through the self. However, the newborn baby cannot do this, because it has no self. Its first actions are instinctive. A self is something that is acquired.

Mead was particularly interested in the way self-consciousness develops through socialisation. In general terms the process is bound up with the imagination and involves learning to take the role of the other. This occurs in two stages. The first of these is the 'play stage'. This is when a child learns to adopt the roles of 'significant others'. For example, children play at being a parent, a teacher, a postman, a nurse. However, their make-believe world is not just a childhood fantasy. It is part of the process of learning how others feel, of anticipating their actions, of responding to them meaningfully. In other words the play stage establishes the basic co-ordinates of social experience.

In the 'game stage' the process is taken one stage further. This involves adopting the attitude of all the others participating in a social situation. For example, in a game of football it is not sufficient for individual children to be aware of their relationship to just one other player. If a child is to play the game well each act will need to take into account the actions of all the other players and the rules of the game as well. Young children find this difficult, but as they develop they become more adept at participating in groups. Their reference points are freed from dependence upon any particular significant other and come to be located in the collective point of view of the group, community or society as a whole.

In Mead's terms the individual is now acting in response to the expectations of 'the generalised other'. An example will illustrate the change. A child's morality is initially fixed through its relationship to significant others; for example, it might tell itself or others that 'Mummy wouldn't want me to do this'. However, adults faced with moral decisions generally act without reference to the attitudes of any particular other. Instead we simply say 'This is wrong', and in doing so we respond to the attitude of the collectivity of which we are a part.

Origins of symbolic interactionism: Thomas

William I. Thomas (1863–1947) agreed with Mead that thinking is preparatory to social action, that people's memories carry the records of past experiences, and that their actions are in part determined by a process located in the mind. Thomas referred to this process as 'the definition of the situation'. This led him to argue that in order to explain action one has to understand how the individual makes sense of 'reality'. However, for Thomas it was not only individual acts that are dependent upon the definition of the situation; a series of such definitions condition our whole attitude to life and our personality. Furthermore, individuals have always lived together in groups. They therefore tend to construct a normative order based on shared definitions of the situation. This is the source of a moral code in society, a code which is informally realised in folkways and mores and formally embodied in law and religion.

The definition of the situation, be it a personal or a shared view, is thus the proximate cause of any self-determined action. It does not matter whether that definition is true from a scientific point of view. The only important question is whether or not it is believed to be true by individual social actors. This becomes clear from a saying of Thomas which has since become one of the most famous axioms in sociology. He said, 'If men define situations as real, they are real in their consequences'. In other words belief is the impetus for action and action has real consequences, though not necessarily ones that are anticipated or desired.

If you now cast your mind back you will see that, despite differences in phraseology, Cooley, Mead and Thomas all had a common interest in understanding the interface between individual and society. However, even this is, strictly speaking, a false way of stating their case. This is because the distinction between individual and society really belongs to the structural perspectives. For symbolic interactionists society is symbolic interaction; nothing more and nothing less.

Implications: Blumer

The implications of this have been developed by Herbert Blumer. He was a pupil of Mead and in his book *Symbolic Interaction: Perspective and Method* (1969) he outlines what symbolic interactionism means for sociology. First, human society is seen as consisting of acting people and the life of society as consisting of their actions. In other words sociology has to be about individuals rather than social classes, social systems, or society as a whole.

Second, social action is formed by interpreting the situation. In other words individuals acting alone or in concert act in terms of the significance they attribute to the situation in which they are placed. Furthermore, if sociologists are to explain the action of individuals they must 'catch the process of interpretation through which they [i.e. the individuals] construct their actions' (ibid. p.86). That is, it is not sufficient to know merely the social conditions associated with certain types of social action. One also needs to know the attitude that social actors take towards those conditions; action must be interpreted from the subjective point of view.

Third, social organisation is the framework of action and not the determinant of it. In other words structural features of society are only general conditions of action. They are, so to speak, the contours of interaction shaping the situations in which people act and supplying them with the common symbols to do so meaningfully. However, within those contours action and meaning vary considerably. There is also always a possibility that social action may go beyond or depart from existing organisation and induce changes in the configuration of social relationships.

All of this leaves us with a very different picture of social reality from that espoused by structural sociologists. Social order is no longer seen to depend upon a value consensus or upon coercion by the powerful. It depends upon individuals who take the role of the other. Similarly socialisation is not down to society stamping passive individuals with its norms and values. It is a process in which individuals actively learn to take the role of the other. Roles thus appear, from the interactionist point of view, in an entirely new light. They are not 'given' once and for all but are 'negotiated' in everyday interaction.

Social change is another key sociological concept that changes its meaning. It is no longer seen to stem from structural differentiation or contradictions between social classes. Social change is now seen as an indigenous property of all social relationships. This is because no social situation is ever so structured that individuals act as if they were reading their parts from a prepared script. Individuals are always improvising, imbuing their world with new meaning and devising novel forms of action. It is the same with social disorganisation. No longer is it interpreted as due to a breakdown in the social structure. It occurs when individuals are unable to devise an interpretation leading to effective action.

Finally, there is the individual. From the point of view of the other perspectives individuals are relegated to the sidelines while attention is focused on the impersonal forces that constrain them to act in certain ways. For interactionists individuals construct their own social world which only has the appearance of a given natural order. However, this reality is not as solid as it looks. It is ultimately no more than a collection of arbitrary conventions precariously sustained by the meaningful interaction of self and other.

Implications: Goffman

Researchers in this tradition include Erving Goffman, who has been one of the most influential interactionists in recent years. As we have seen individuals do not just 'have' an identity; the self is constructed out of relationships with others. However, in practice social actors seek to manage those relationships in order to project a favourable self image. Goffman's book *The Presentation of Self in Everyday Life* is 'concerned with some of the common techniques that persons employ to sustain such impressions' (p.26).

Sometimes maintaining a favourable self-image is difficult or impossible because of some physical or moral blemish which is regarded as discrediting. In *Stigma* Goffman describes the typical problems and solutions of those who have to cope with a spoiled identity. What does it mean to be blind, disfigured, an ex-mental patient, a homosexual, or have any other characteristic that makes you seem abnormal to most other members of society? Goffman describes what it is like to be regarded as 'not quite human'.

Sometimes changed circumstances can threaten one's former social identity. Unemployment, bankruptcy, divorce and the death of a loved one are all situations that often involve making painful adjustments in both one's life style and social relationships with others. In *Asylums* Goffman describes a particularly extreme case of learning to live with a new social identity, that of a patient in a mental hospital. On entering the institution the inmate may be subjected to a process of disculturation. The patient's self-image, previously sustained through interaction with others on the outside, is now under attack. What social processes are involved, what typical strategies patients adopt and with what results are portrayed by Goffman in an artistic reconstruction of the life of an asylum as seen from the patient's point of view.

However, Goffman's work is not necessarily typical of all interactionist research. This is an ill-defined area of sociology and there is no single set of common assumptions and concepts shared by all those who adopt the general approach. Partly this is due to the intangibility of the mental realities that interactionists seek to comprehend and partly to their use of metaphors to explain their point of view. An example of different metaphors used to describe the same phenomenon is Cooley's 'looking glass self' and Mead's concept of the self 'as an eddy in the social current'. However, although differences of literary style contribute to the ambiguities that bedevil this area of sociology, there are substantive differences of emphasis as well. For example, whereas Mead stressed the importance of language Goffman's main interest has been in developing a framework for understanding nonverbal means of communication.

To what extent differences like these are matters of style or substance is something you will have to decide for yourself. Textbooks will not be much help because although their descriptions of this perspective overlap there is no general agreement about what the most important ideas are. However, one way of gaining insight into symbolic interactionism is to study a particular area in depth, and nowhere have the interactionists been more active than in the sociology of deviance. This is reflected in the essays which follow. These place the emphasis on the contrast between symbolic interactionism and other perspectives.

Question 27
The nature of social problems: why do sociologists disagree?

According to Robert Merton a social problem 'exists' whenever there is a sizeable discrepancy between what 'is' and what 'people' think ought to be. This definition implies that there is both a factual and an evaluative aspect to social problems and it is how these two aspects are combined that is the source of disagreement among sociologists. One reason for this is that the designation of an issue as a social problem has further implications. It suggests a need for change, it implies a judgement concerning social priorities, and it prompts calls for the allocation of resources. These three implications mean that social problems are inherently political phenomena.

This was never fully appreciated by Emile Durkheim. He believed that it was possible to identify social problems objectively. In *The Rules of Sociological Method* this led him to define pathological social phenomena as social facts that disturb the normal functioning of society. Since, for Durkheim, this normal functioning depended on the power of the collective conscience he saw social problems in modern societies as stemming mainly from the decline in the moral force that society exerts over the individual. Thus, in his theory of anomie Durkheim argued that social stability was threatened because in complex societies the integration of the individual with the demands of collective life was weakened.

Durkheim's ideas were developed by Merton who argues that where societies and institutions work inefficiently one can describe them as dysfunctioning. Merton applied this to the study of deviance which he saw as a response to a breakdown in the relationship between culturally valid goals and institutionally approved means. Similarly in organisations the position of officials within a bureaucracy may encourage behaviour patterns that actively prevent that organisation from achieving its goals. In both cases Merton argues that a major function of the sociologist is to make these latent social problems manifest.

The ideas of both Durkheim and Merton rest upon a consensus view of society. In Durkheim the overriding need for social order is assumed and in Merton the goals of American society and its bureaucratic apparatuses are never questioned. This leads both theorists to identify the needs of society with the interests of its ruling groups. However, although it may well be true that a concern for social order and efficiency is a fundamental social problem to those who stand to gain from existing arrangements, to disadvantaged groups it often seems that it is radical social change that is needed.

It is the 'pseudo-objectivity' of those who claim to take the point of view of society that is stressed by interactionists such as Howard Becker. Unlike the functionalists, who focus on the objective consequences of institutionalised behaviour, interactionists emphasise its subjective meaning. From this perspective a social problem is anything that is so labelled. On this basis interactionists recommend that sociologists should concentrate on researching how social problems come to be defined as such.

In practice this has led them to identify with the underdog and to examine ways in which social institutions create problems for their clients. The difference between this and functionalism is well illustrated by the study of poverty. For functionalists the problem of poverty is the problem of the poor themselves and of the dysfunctional aspects of their culture. However, when viewed from the standpoint of the poor it is often the inadequacies of welfare provision and their stigmatisation by social workers that are seen as the problem. It is the same with crime and mental illness. Although it is commonly the people to whom these labels are applied who are regarded as the social problem, interactionists emphasise that the 'problems' are identified, explained and sometimes even created by the experts themselves.

One of the most extreme exponents of this view is Edwin Lemert. He claims that social control leads to deviance. However, if one were to take the point of view of the underdog to its logical conclusion it would imply, for example, that the courts create crime, welfare services create poverty, and the psychiatric profession creates mental illness. There is certainly evidence that these institutions can be counterproductive. For example, police action can lead to deviancy amplification, the welfare services do undermine the self respect of claimants, and the psychiatric profession does sometimes diagnose as ill people who merely act unconventionally. However, it is a mistake to consider that there is nothing more to social problems than mere labelling. Apart from any other consideration, this is to overlook the material basis of suffering and its relationship to the distribution of power in society.

It is the wider implications of power that are neglected by both functionalism and interactionism. For functionalists power is the generalised capacity of society to bring about beneficial social change and the application of this perspective to poverty in the US led to efforts to change the values of the poor. The futility of this approach stems from the fact that it is very often situational constraints that prevent the poor from realising the values of the wider society and interactionists have pointed out how the authors of many of these constraints are the welfare services themselves. However, what is needed in addition is an explanation of the relationship between the institutionalised means for dealing with social problems and the interests of particular social classes.

From this point of view Marxists recognise that the idea of specific social problems is itself ideological. This is because in practice which types of social behaviour are defined as problems depends upon the unequal distribution of power. For example, those in positions of authority have the power to define riots, terrorism and illegal drug use as social problems. This then provides the ruling class with the excuse to extend their control whilst simultaneously diverting attention from the class system as a whole and focusing it on the casualties that are produced. Thus, the underlying objective element in the nature of social problems is the interests of groups in society affected by the selective use of this evaluation. These interests depend mainly upon the class structure and just as class is a focus for disagreement in sociology, so also are its side effects and especially social problems.

Commentary

There is a similar debate over the concept of deviance. Thus, Howard Becker argues that functionalists

> use a model of deviance based essentially on the medical notions of health and disease. They look at a society, or some part of a society, and ask whether there are any processes going on in it that tend to reduce its stability, thus lessening its chance of survival. They label such processes deviant ...
>
> (*Outsiders*, p.7)

Becker rejects this and proposes instead that

> social groups create deviance by making the rules whose infraction constitutes deviance, and by applying those rules to particular people and labelling them as outsiders. From this point of view, deviance is not a quality of the act the person commits but rather a consequence of the application by others of rules and sanctions to an 'offender'.
>
> (*Outsiders*, p.9)

However, this relativistic notion of deviance has in turn been criticised by radical criminologists. For example

> It is only by crudely opposing physical to social action that the social reaction approach can claim that an action is only deviant when so defined by others ... But most deviant, and especially criminal, acts are physical acts which have quite clear social meanings. Where is the criminal who engages in the robbing of banks and who is unaware that he is engaged in the social act of stealing? Taking an object (a physical act) without the owner's permission will always be described as stealing in those societies where the institution of private property exists.
>
> (Ian Taylor, Paul Walton and Jock Young, *The New Criminology*, p.146)

Question 28
The functionalist theory of deviance: what are its strengths and weaknesses?

Functionalists regard crime, suicide and other forms of deviance as social facts. This leads them to reject explanations that appeal to the psychological or biological characteristics of individuals and propose instead that 'society' is the cause of deviance. For example, Emile Durkheim saw the key factor as the degree of social integration. He also argued that the emergence of complex societies based on organic solidarity led to societies becoming less effective at regulating human desires. This led Durkheim to suggest in his theory of anomie that the personality of the individual was in danger of becoming disassociated from the needs of society. In other words social order in modern society was threatened by the decline in the power of society to regulate the aspirations of its members.

The ideas of Durkheim were developed by Robert Merton, who laid the foundations of the modern functionalist theory of deviance in his article 'Social Structure and

Anomie'. Merton refined Durkheim's theory of anomie by describing the malintegration of individual and society as a means-end relationship. In a perfectly integrated society common ends or goals of social action are accepted by all members of society and the means to achieve these goals are available to the entire population. However, in the modern US Merton argued that there is undue emphasis on the ends of action at the expense of making the means of success universally available.

For Merton, success in life in the US is overwhelmingly defined in monetary terms. The result is that the desire to make money, and to impress others with a life style built around conspicuous consumption, becomes the overriding goal of most Americans. The institutionalised means for achieving this success are educational qualifications and career mobility. However, in a highly unequal society where life chances are not distributed evenly certain groups find that legitimate opportunities for advancement are denied them. This creates psychological strain amongst the members of these groups and this is accentuated by the fact that US society fosters the myths that the country is a land of opportunity and that relative poverty is caused by individual moral failings.

Deviance, according to Merton, can be explained as a response to the pressures generated by this discrepancy between culturally approved goals and institutionally available means. This interpretation has been a focus for debate in US sociology since Merton's ideas were first published in 1938. Although functionalist these ideas cannot be lightly dismissed as a conservative justification of US institutions nor as a simplistic consensus theory. This is because Merton recognises the importance of inequality, conflict, and ideology to the sociology of deviance. He also adopts a critical perspective on US society and recognises its dysfunctional aspects. Furthermore, although Merton ignores the cultural transmission of deviant adaptations his theory can be linked with the concept of subculture. This would help to explain how social groups that share a similar position in the social structure collectively evolve solutions to common problems.

The most influential development of Merton's ideas along these lines is Richard Cloward and Lloyd Ohlin's book *Delinquency and Opportunity*. Their point is that individuals are not merely socialised into the norms and values of the wider society. They also learn deviant behaviour in broadly the same way. Cloward and Ohlin were thus led to extend Merton's theory and relate deviance not just to the legitimate opportunity structure but to the illegitimate opportunity structure as well. Thus they accept that there is greater pressure on ethnic minorities and the disadvantaged classes to deviate from the norms of society because they have less opportunity to succeed by other routes. However, they go on to emphasise that the availability of illegitimate means depends upon a learning environment in which young people can acquire criminal skills. Where this occurs subcultures evolve based on professional crime. However, in other areas where both legitimate and illegitimate opportunities are unavailable delinquent gangs turn to violence or evolve into retreatist subcultures.

Although the subcultural approach seems to dispose of one problem raised by Merton's anomie theory it does so at the expense of creating another. Even more than in Merton's theory, in Cloward and Ohlin's deviants are seen as produced and directed by forces beyond their control. This determinist view over-predicts deviance since whilst some individuals do move from strain to deviance the majority do not. Were society in Merton's theory or subculture in Cloward and Ohlin's to exert such a powerful force as is implied one would expect even more deviance than there is. In addition both theories fail to take account of the fact that deviance is not a way of life for most rule breakers but rather a sporadic and infrequent activity which most find easy to give up as they grow older.

If, as David Matza has suggested, most young people simply drift into deviance and have no real commitment to deviant values or solutions then the deviant may not be as different from the non-deviant as functionalists imply. This point of view can be supported by considering how evidence on deviance is collected. Both functionalists and subcultural theorists are implicitly taking for granted the official statistics that show higher crime rates amongst the disadvantaged. However, it may well be that this is an illusion created by systematic bias in law enforcement rather than greater criminality amongst these groups.

This point of view is one which is often taken by Marxists and symbolic interactionists. They have pointed out that, though not obviously defending US justice, Merton's criticism is only that the system is not working as efficiently as it might. As Ian Taylor, Paul Walton and Jock Young put it, Merton is 'the cautious rebel' (*The New Criminology*, p.101). Whilst recognising that US society is not meeting the social needs of all its members he fails to extend criticism into the politically sensitive areas of law enforcement, the labelling of individuals as offenders by the courts, and the role of these instruments of oppression in the protection of privilege.

Commentary

Merton sees deviance as a response to strains that are experienced by individuals as a result of their position in the social structure. However, a variety of responses are possible and Merton distinguishes four deviant adaptations to the imperfections of US society.

The most important of these is 'innovation'. This is the adaptation of those who accept the goals laid down by society but not the institutionalised means for their achievement. Most crimes against property fall into this category, and so does cheating in examinations. In both cases individuals adopt illegitimate means to achieve success. 'Ritualism' is the second adaptation. This involves abandoning the goals of society whilst compulsively and often over-zealously conforming to the means. The bureaucrat's strict adherence to rules without taking into account what the rules are for is regarded as an example of this form of deviance by Merton. This is because although conforming outwardly, such an official has abandoned the fundamental values of US society which involve being achievement orientated. Third there is 'retreatism'. This involves a rejection of both the cultural goals and the institutionalised means. Vagrants, alcoholics and drug addicts fall into this category. Finally there is 'rebellion'. This involves confronting society, for example through acts of terrorism pursued in an effort to undermine existing values.

Commenting on this typology Laurie Taylor writes

It is as though individuals in society are playing a gigantic fruit machine, but the machine is rigged and only some players are consistently rewarded. The deprived ones then either resort to using foreign coins or magnets to increase their chances of winning (innovation) or play on mindlessly (ritualism), give up the game (retreatism) or propose a new game altogether (rebellion). But in the analysis nobody appeared to ask who put the machine there in the first place and who takes the profits.

(*Deviance and Society*, p.148)

Question 29
Symbolic interactionism: what has it contributed to the sociological interpretation of deviance?

Symbolic interactionists see the social world as actively constructed out of the shared definitions of social actors. Thus, they focus attention on how social actors come to be defined as deviant and what the consequences of this are for their self-image and social relationships with others. This is why interactionism is sometimes referred to as labelling theory or as a social reaction perspective. It makes a contribution to our understanding of deviance by investigating the relationship between rule breaking and agencies of social control. This has enabled interactionists to reveal, first, how social control works selectively and, second, how labelling can reinforce deviant behaviour.

Interactionists emphasise that in modern societies formal mechanisms of control become more important and the power to label individuals as deviant is concentrated in the hands of professionals. They have considerable discretion about when and how to enforce rules. Furthermore US research into teachers, probation workers, psychiatrists and the police all confirms that the experts work within a taken-for-granted conceptual framework about what constitutes deviance and what deviants are like. This means, for example, that law enforcement is inevitably biased because individuals who conform more closely to criminal stereotypes are more frequently labelled as offenders than those whose social characteristics do not fit officials' preconceptions.

What the US research shows is that rates of deviance are socially constructed out of interaction between officials and potential deviants. This perspective has influenced British sociologists such as John Lambert. In his article 'The Police can Choose' ('Society Today' No. 5, 3 December 1976) he explains that if, for example, the police have stereotyped views of the young or of immigrant communities they may choose to enforce laws against these groups more vigorously. Examples of how this can lead to the amplification of deviance are provided by Jock Young's study of drug control in Notting Hill and Stan Cohen's study of Mods and Rockers.

Young explains that the police are particularly susceptible to stereotypes because their job isolates them from the community. In responding to these stereotypes by more positive policing to combat what they saw as the 'drugs problem' in the Notting Hill area of London, they unearthed more examples of drug abuse which gave the impression that crime was increasing. This led to even more resources being diverted to drug control and to the setting up of specialist drug squads. This further contributed to the apparent upward spiral in crime and shows how a 'crime wave' can be artificially, though not necessarily intentionally, created by the police themselves.

However, it is not just the role of the police that can lead to the amplification of deviance; the mass media also play a role. This is stressed by Cohen in his study of societal reaction to the riots that occurred in British holiday towns in 1964. An initial disturbance was so exaggerated by the media and played upon by moral entrepreneurs that it led to a change in attitudes. Cohen describes this as a 'moral panic'. It resulted in increased policing of the young and in deterrent sentences for those convicted of offences.

Studies by Young and Cohen show how societal reaction to deviance, manifested in new laws and regulations, more intolerant public attitudes, intensification of stereotypes, and additional powers and resources for the police, can lead to an apparent increase in deviance. However, societal reaction can also lead to a real increase in deviance either through publicity-seeking behaviour or through the stigmatising of deviants through the labelling process.

In the US this is a theme that has been taken up by Howard Becker and Edwin Lemert. They point out that being caught and publicly labelled as deviant means that others tend to relate to the labelled individual differently. Furthermore, since our personal identity is shaped by our interaction with others those who are labelled as deviant may come to identify with the label. In other words one effect of labelling is to create a self-fulfilling prophecy in which a deviant identity is built out of the reaction of others, so confirming labelled individuals in deviant roles, closing down legitimate opportunities and projecting them into a deviant career.

British research confirms that societal reaction can create more deviance and that the process often begins in schools. For example, David Hargreaves shows that when negative evaluations are applied to children by teachers the children often respond by committing more acts of deviance. This is made even more likely by streaming, which concentrates those whom teachers regard as troublemakers in the lower forms where they form a delinquent subculture in which status is awarded to those who break school rules.

Out of school behaviour often follows a similar pattern. Thus Cohen's study showed that the effects of arbitrary arrests, heavy sentences, and the lumping together of young people who shared a certain life style as 'deviants', were to strengthen feelings of solidarity and provoke a defiant attitude to authority. Similarly in the Notting Hill area of London the effects of a more active police presence were to raise drug prices, put trafficking on a more professional basis, and facilitate the entry of organised crime into the drug market.

These examples confirm Lemert's point that social control leads to deviance. However, although this is certainly a contributory factor the interactionist perspective is at best a partial explanation. This is illustrated by two points that interactionists neglect. First, they concentrate on marginal or exotic crimes, whereas almost 95 per cent of indictable crimes known to the police in Britain are crimes against property. Second, they ignore the initial motivation to commit acts of deviance and give no convincing explanation of why people choose to break norms.

These omissions point to a more fundamental failing of this perspective. This is because it is precisely the two problems above that raise questions about the wider social structure, which acts as a framework within which interaction between potential deviants and representatives of agencies of social control takes place. By ignoring the relationship between deviance and structural inequalities of power they romanticise deviance by failing to relate it to the fact that social control is an integral part of the role of the state in capitalist society.

Commentary

A useful introduction to the interactionist approach to deviance is *Images of Deviance*, edited by Stanley Cohen. In the editor's introduction Cohen writes

> The same act — shall we say a homosexual encounter — is not defined in the same way by all societies, nor are all persons breaking the rules (in this case, the rules governing sexual encounters) officially defined and classified as deviants. One must understand deviance as the product of some sort of transaction that takes place between the rule breaker and the rest of society. (p.14)

However, once that 'transaction' has taken place

> We must also be alerted to the effects of the reaction of others on the individual's concept of himself. Indignation, punishment and segregation from the community might mark the person out in a special way, and, together with others in a similar position, he might eventually act in ways which resemble society's stereotype of him. (p.17)

In other words, one of the effects of labelling is that individuals who are labelled sometimes come to be more like the kind of person they were originally thought to be. Jock Young refers to this process as 'the translation of fantasy into reality' (ibid. p.44).

Question 30
Suicide: how successful is Durkheim's explanation?

In *Suicide* Emile Durkheim sought to demonstrate the validity of an argument he first put forward in *The Rules of Sociological Method*. There he had claimed that sociology could be just as 'scientific' as the natural sciences and that it had its own separate subject matter consisting of social facts. For Durkheim these were objective properties of collective life which could be studied independently of individual cases. One such social fact was the suicide rate and Durkheim attempted to show that this could be explained in terms of underlying causal laws which originated in the force that society exerted over the individual.

Durkheim begins by defining suicide as an intentional act of self-destruction. The problem with this is that court procedures aimed at ascertaining the cause of death vary between and within societies. This means that the official quota of voluntary deaths will be influenced by the way the information was processed. In practice Durkheim ignored this problem and took official statistics on suicide for granted. However, in *The Social Meanings of Suicide* Jack Douglas argues that this means Durkheim does not really study suicide as such but rather a socially constructed abstraction with an unknown relationship to the underlying realities it is supposed to reflect.

On the basis of the assumption that the rate of frequency of death by suicide can be measured Durkheim goes on to draw three conclusions from the statistics. First, that suicide rates are remarkably constant within a particular society, second, that there are wide variations between societies and, third, that there are marked differences in the suicide rates of various groups within a society. However, as Maxwell Atkinson has emphasised, the characteristics of suicide rates will be influenced by the fact that categorisation of death by suicide will partly depend upon the state of medical knowledge at the time and the thoroughness of medical examination.

In addition to court procedures and the state of medical knowledge there is also the question of 'the meaning we give to suicide'. In an article under this title ('Society Today' No. 4, 19 November 1976) Douglas argues that Durkheim's basic error is to assume implicitly that suicide means the same thing to everyone. However, if moral attitudes to suicide vary then the incentive to disguise a suicide as death by natural causes or as due to accident will also vary. This is significant because Durkheim attaches importance to the fact that Protestants have a higher suicide rate than

Catholics. However, this may be partly due to the fact that there is also evidence that the stigma of suicide is greater amongst Catholics.

Although interactionists and ethnomethodologists are correct in pointing out the inadequacy of Durkheim's evidence, this does not mean that there are not genuine differences in the propensity to take one's life. Furthermore, many of the differences Durkheim claims to identify have been confirmed by more recent research in a variety of countries. Probably the debate over the reliability of this evidence will never be finally resolved. However, a separate question is the use Durkheim makes of these statistics to construct a general theory of suicide. Thus, in classic positivist fashion he proceeds to eliminate climate, heredity, alcoholism, and insanity as possible causes of variations in suicide rates by showing how in each case any correlation they may have with suicide is casual rather than causal. Having in this way disposed of non-sociological explanations Durkheim then introduces the crucial concepts of social integration and social regulation.

By social integration Durkheim means the degree to which individual members of society are enveloped by the collective conscience. Where social integration is weak individuals feel they have the right to take their lives and suicide becomes an expression of personality. Durkheim calls this egoistic suicide. The opposite occurs where social integration is too strong. Here individuals feel they have a duty to take their lives. This is altruistic suicide, so named because it involves the sacrifice of life out of a sense of duty to others.

Social regulation refers to the degree to which society is effective in controlling the desires of individuals. Durkheim believed that our tastes and appetites are largely formed by society and should society be unable to regulate them effectively our aspirations would become unlimited and life would be a perpetual struggle to achieve the unobtainable. Anomic suicide occurs when this happens. Individuals no longer restrained by an effective normative order take their lives out of a sense of anger, bitterness and frustration.

In this explanation Durkheim related the incidence of suicide to the nature and degree of social solidarity which he saw as generating suicidogenic currents in society. In modern societies characterised by organic solidarity and a declining collective conscience Durkheim believed there were relatively high suicide rates because of currents of egoism and anomie. In simple societies with a strong collective conscience and mechanical solidarity it was altruism that accounted for the incidence of suicide.

The adequacy of this theory depends ultimately upon the assumptions embodied in Durkheim's social realism. Durkheim adopted a holistic approach and this led him to argue that the causes of suicide are external to the individual. Thus, in his theory it is society that is responsible for voluntary deaths and not individuals. This involves reification because, whilst general social variables may be precipitating factors, the decision to end one's life depends upon the significance of social facts for the individual.

It is this systematic neglect of the empirical meaning of suicide that is the fundamental weakness in Durkheim's study. His belief that society was more real than the individual led him to reject any role for the analysis of motives. In place of this Durkheim substitutes his psychology of collective life in which power is attributed to the collective conscience. However, he makes no attempt to explain how this can contribute to the analysis of individual cases. This means that Durkheim never relates the structural features of society to the determinants of individual action. The voluntary aspect to suicide thus disappears from Durkheim's work to be replaced by the coercive power of social facts.

Commentary

According to Durkheim

> At any given moment the moral constitution of society establishes the contingent of voluntary deaths. There is therefore, for each people a collective force of a definite amount of energy impelling men to self destruction.
>
> (*Suicide*, p.239)

For Durkheim the suicide rate was the quantified expression of that collective force. This led him to adopt a positivist position and to argue that a nation's rate of suicide is determined by its social characteristics.

However, in *Discovering Suicide* Maxwell Atkinson proposes to study how some deaths get categorised as suicide. His research indicates that factors such as the existence of a suicide note, evidence of previous suicide attempts, the mode of dying, location and circumstances of death, and biographical details of the deceased, all influence the decisions arrived at in coroners' courts. Furthermore the evidence is sometimes ambiguous. For example, Atkinson quotes one coroner who in deciding between accident or suicide said

> 'My real problem is when someone has taken less than ten barbiturates. That's when I have to be on the lookout for special evidence. If he takes more than ten, I can be almost sure that it was a suicide.' (p.123)

Evidence like this leads Atkinson to the conclusion that coroners and their officers categorise deaths in terms of taken-for-granted assumptions about what constitutes a 'typical suicide'. This raises the possibility that

> By showing relationships between variables like marital status, mental illness, alcoholism, economic disaster and so on with suicide, it is arguable that all the researchers [in the Durkheimian tradition] are doing is to make explicit the explanations used implicitly by coroners in their everyday work. (pp.143−4)

This leads Atkinson to propose an ethnomethodological approach. From this point of view a nation's suicide rate is governed by its procedures of categorisation. The focus of attention is then switched to the way members of society make sense of death.

Chapter 9
Social policy

Auguste Comte (1798 – 1857) 'invented' sociology as an instrument of social reform. He believed that once theoretical sociology had discovered the laws governing social phenomena it would be possible to apply the findings to the solution of social problems and to the creation of a more free and rational society. The improvement of society by providing a scientific basis to social policy was thus, from the very beginning, the inspiration of sociology.

Comte's faith in social progress through the application of sociology is still shared by many sociologists today. However, during the 1960s there was a growing feeling that some sociologists had been naive about the moral and political implications of their work. The American sociologist C. Wright Mills was one of the first to voice disquiet when, in 1959, he wrote, 'Just now, among social scientists, there is a widespread uneasiness, both intellectual and moral, about the direction their chosen studies seem to be taking' (*The Sociological Imagination*, p.26).

The unease felt by Mills in 1959 stemmed from what he interpreted as distortions of the sociological imagination. He described the most important of these distortions as 'grand theory' and 'abstracted empiricism'. By 'grand theory' Mills meant systems theory and, in particular, the ideas of Talcott Parsons. By 'abstracted empiricism' he meant the collection of information for its own sake rather than for the purpose of contributing to our understanding of substantive problems. According to Mills these tendencies were 'parasites living off the classical social science tradition' (p.139). However, it was not primarily for intellectual reasons that Mills launched his assault on establishment sociology. More importantly, he believed that there was a danger of sociology being used to manipulate people. Summing up his views on this Mills wrote, 'Theory serves, in a variety of ways, as ideological justification of authority. Research for bureaucratic ends serves to make authority more effective' (p.131).

The theme of Mills' critique was that the heirs of the sociological tradition had neglected their social responsibility. This theme was also taken up by other sociologists. For example, in *Out of Utopia* Ralf Dahrendorf accused functional-ists of inventing an entirely fictitious and idealised model of how social systems worked. According to Dahrendorf this was responsible for a sense of complacency within sociology and a 'loss of problem consciousness'. Alvin Gouldner has since extended this critique into the realms of methodology. In *Anti-Minotaur: the Myth of a Value Free Sociology*, he argued that value freedom had become a mere 'token of professional respectability'. Whilst initially a commitment to this principle had helped sociology establish itself Gouldner argued that value freedom has since become the altar on which many American social scientists sacrifice their critical integrity.

The initial effect of these and other critiques of sociology was to damage the image of scientific and political respectability cultivated by the post-war generation of sociologists. However, it was not sufficient for critics merely to find fault with the establishment. They also had to show that they had an alternative strategy. The result was a surge of publications by authors who claimed to have a 'new', 'radical' or 'critical' approach to pure and applied sociology.

Origins of ethnomethodology

In the midst of this upheaval in attitudes and ideas ethnomethodology was born. The term itself was coined by the American sociologist Harold Garfinkel and it appears in the title of his influential book *Studies in Ethnomethodology*. Sometimes this perspective is regarded as an offshoot of symbolic interactionism. However, whilst both share an interest in understanding interaction they have independent roots. Symbolic interactionism, which grew out of the contribution of Cooley, Mead and Thomas, traces its ancestry back to the American pragmatists William James (1842–1910) and John Dewey (1859–1952). In contrast ethnomethodology developed out of European phenomenology. Its growth has been influenced by the ideas of Edmund Husserl (1859–1938), Max Weber and Alfred Schutz (1899–1959). Its ancestors are eighteenth century German philosophers such as Immanuel Kant and Friedrich Hegel.

Phenomenologists regard reality as an appearance. Their point is that we conventionally regard the natural world as made up of objects and events that exist or occur independently of our will. However, when we inspect this common-sense view more closely it becomes apparent that our very apprehension of objects and events depends upon our ability to organise the sum total of sensory data available to us into a conscious experience. There is thus a sense in which the ordered characteristics of reality are put there by us. It is only because we become so used to taking the familiar world for granted that it appears to us as reality itself rather than as a reality shaped by our act of understanding. Husserl referred to the former attitude as 'the natural standpoint'. The first premise of his philosophy was that one has to disconnect oneself from the natural standpoint in order to grasp the essence of experience.

Husserl's aim was to construct a transcendental phenomenology. To this end he asks us to suspend belief in all the everyday assumptions that we make about the natural world, other people and ourselves. For Husserl this was just so much bric-a-brac, which had to be removed in order to reveal subjectivity in its pure form. When the bedrock of experience had been reached it would be possible to reconstitute the world on the basis of a 'science' free from all presuppositions.

Alfred Schutz was strongly influenced by Husserl's philosophy. However, he developed phenomenology in an entirely different direction, being primarily concerned with the natural attitude itself. The important point for Schutz was not that we are able to suspend belief in the 'real world' but that as a matter of ordinary practice we invariably suspend doubt that the 'real world' is anything other than it appears to be. What was needed, thought Schutz, was a way of systematically describing what the natural attitude assumed. He believed that this would yield a phenomenology of social life and that that would act as the basis of a reconstituted sociology.

Weber, as we have already seen, emphasised that the social world was a world of meaning. On this basis he was led to define action as 'all human behaviour when and in so far as the acting individual attaches a subjective meaning to it' and social action as action which 'takes account of the behaviour of others and is thereby oriented in its course' (*The Theory of Social and Economic Organisation*, p.88). Schutz claimed that these definitions were inadequate because they did not see action in the context of the natural attitude. One result was that Weber was led to picture social actors as if they were isolated individuals who each devised their own subjective interpretation of events. However, experience is intersubjective. That is to say, experience is shared and, through communication with others, we come to possess the same stock of common-sense knowledge as other members of our society or group.

What Schutz was in effect trying to do was to synthesise elements of Husserl and Weber in a new approach to studying social reality. To summarise Schutz's views: first we are told that reality is an appearance. It seems other than it is because of the strength of the natural attitude, which is the constitutive principle of everyday experience. Furthermore it is an attitude we share with others, and people therefore make sense of the world in basically the same way. These shared procedures are what Schutz called 'typifications' of experience. Upon them depends the semblance of order that members of society construct for themselves, and in terms of them we act either alone or in concert with others. What these typifications are is as yet undetermined. However, Schutz thought that if we can uncover them we can uncover the phenomenological basis of experience and reveal what makes people act and think the way they do.

Ethnomethodological interpretations and methods

Ethnomethodology seeks to do precisely this. The prefix 'ethno' means pertaining to or characteristic of races or people. Methodology is the study of rules. The two together mean the study of the rules used by people to make sense of experience. For Garfinkel these rules are embedded in the organisation of everyday affairs. Thus he recommends that we give 'the most common-place activities of daily life the attention usually accorded to extraordinary events' and 'seek to learn about them as phenomena in their own right' (*Studies in Ethnomethodology*, p.1). In other words sociologists should treat as problematic what ordinary members of society treat as obvious.

For Garfinkel the first step in doing this lay in recognising that 'the activities whereby members produce and manage settings of organised everyday affairs are identical with members' procedures for making those settings "account-able"' (ibid. p.1). To explain his ideas Garfinkel introduces the concepts of reflexivity and indexicality.

Reflexivity refers to the fact that the accounts by which members make sense of the social world are at the same time actual constituents of that world. To take suicide as an example: the accounts in this case are provided by coroners, and their task is to make sense of death. The result is that suicide is situated in the social world as a 'fact'. Mainstream sociology then goes on to look for explanations of this 'fact'. However, ethnomethodology proceeds differently. It regards the categorisation of deaths as suicides as a practical accomplishment. The result is that suicide is treated as an inference. The task is to reveal how that inference is made; that is to say, to reveal the procedures through which members produce accounts of their social world.

Indexicality refers to the fact that the meaning of an account is not independent of the circumstances of its use. This time take accounts of suicide as the example. The key point is that what these accounts refer to varies according to the occasion. For example, one coroner may decide to categorise as suicides only those deaths in which the victim left a suicide note. Other coroners may to varying degrees accept different types of evidence. Thus 'indexical particulars' like whether or not a suicide note was found and which coroner takes the case will affect how deaths are categorised in individual cases. Suicide is not therefore something that 'exists' independently of our ways of discovering it. It is rather a product of the methods used by members to decide what particulars are relevant, how to recognise those particulars in specific instances and when to subsume them under general categories.

These sense-making activities are sometimes referred to as procedures for repairing indexicality. They are operations that we are all constantly and routinely performing, so much so that we do not even notice that we are doing them. It is the same with any seemingly simple everyday activity. In one of his empirical demonstrations of how such practical activities are accomplished Garfinkel studied jurors at work.

According to Garfinkel 'the jury has the task of deciding the legally enforceable situation that exists between contenders' (ibid. p.104). In short it has the task of reaching a verdict. In order to do this jurors see themselves as having to solve the problem of deciding between 'what is fact and what is fancy'. However, that in turn involves being able to identify what is at issue, what is and is not relevant to the case, what are facts and what are opinions, whose evidence is credible and who is lying or mistaken and, having sorted out the rival claims, being able to come to a collective decision concerning guilt or innocence, extent of harm, appropriate damages, etc. Garfinkel argues that his research shows that jurors 'do this by consulting the consistency of alternative claims with common-sense models' (p.106). In other words jurors tend to assume that the interpretation that makes good sense must have been what actually happened and on the basis of this they go on to infer what they see as the correct verdict.

However, in the course of becoming a juror, jurors also become acquainted with 'the official juror line'. This is a body of rules that governs how a juror is supposed to behave. For example, Garfinkel's jurors recognised that a 'good' juror does what is legal rather than what is fair, and that a juror should decide on the basis of the law and the evidence rather than in terms of personal sympathies. Now, these and other rules were those which the jurors generally believed that they had actually been following. However, Garfinkel claims that though jurors identified with the official line in theory there were discrepancies between their ideal accounts and their actual practices. In other words jurors who mainly relied on common sense felt obliged to justify their decisions in terms of the official line so as to give their verdict the appearance of rationality.

This is a case of repairing indexicality. The jurors were concerned that they should arrive at the 'correct' decision. What they were not clear about was how this was to be achieved. Only after the event were they able to decide what it was that made their decision 'the right one'. Thus in this case the rules of decision making employed by the jurors were largely to do with 'assigning outcomes their legitimate histories' (ibid. p.114). Furthermore the same principle underlies the everyday decision making of lay and professional members generally.

On the other hand a jury is something of a special case. It is always faced with an ambiguous situation since if matters were regarded otherwise it would not be required to sit in the first place. However, in most everyday situations matters are clear-cut, or at least they are conventionally so regarded by the people involved. How in these circumstances can we identify what the participants take for granted? One way might be to disrupt their common-sense world and see how they react.

Garfinkel attempted to do this in a number of famous (some would say infamous) 'experiments'. In one of these a number of students 'were asked to spend from fifteen minutes to an hour in their homes imagining that they were boarders and acting out this assumption' (ibid. p.47). The results were dramatic in every 'experiment' that was 'successfully' completed. Family members responded with 'astonishment, bewilderment, shock, anxiety, embarrassment and anger'. However, in addition to generating these emotions family members felt an overwhelming need for explanations. They asked, ' "Did you get fired? Are you sick? What are you being so superior about? Why are you mad? Are you out of your mind or are you just stupid?" ' They offered their own explanations, 'the student was "working too hard" in school; the student was "ill"; there had been "another fight" with a fiancée'. Finally, when all else failed they 'attempted isolation of the culprit, retaliation and denunciation' (ibid. pp.47, 48).

What Garfinkel's experiment showed is how deeply we are attached to our common-sense view of the world, so much so that the behaviour of these students in their own homes created a virtual panic amongst other members of their families within a matter of minutes. Furthermore the students were not behaving in what we might conventionally regard as a threatening manner. On the contrary they tried at all times to be polite and avoided retaliation. However, in another sense their behaviour was threatening. What it threatened was the shared trust we have in the familiarity of the everyday social world and the routine practices through which it is accomplished. Threaten that and you threaten members' methods of accounting for anything. Normally, of course, that possibility is shut out by the strength of our common-sense beliefs. However, if one introduces even the slightest doubt in the reality of these appearances it creates a ripple of anxiety and Garfinkel argues that the ensuing disorganisation 'should tell us something about how the structure of everyday activities are ordinarily and routinely produced and maintained' (ibid. p.38).

However, although Garfinkel claims that ethnomethodology should be able to reveal these seen but unnoticed practices, the question still remains as to whether it does. Some critics have argued that there is a basic flaw in the whole enterprise. Their argument goes something like this. The ethnomethodologist claims that the 'real' task of sociology is to reveal the background expectancies through which members create an appearance of order. However, the sociologist is also a member, whose account of action has to be understood in terms of background expectancies. For Anthony Giddens, 'the result is an infinite regress. The background expectancies of the observer, analysing the background expectancies of the actors, would have to be analysed by a second observer, who of course necessarily draws upon his own background expectancies in doing this, and so on without end' (*New Rules of Sociological Method*, pp.41 – 2). In other words the attempt to pursue ethnomethodology to its logical conclusion leads to a 'hopeless relativism' and ultimately undermines the rationality of all knowledge, and thus of any attempt to formulate policy at all. As Giddens puts it, 'Yonder lies the abyss!'

Question 31
Social policy: what is its relationship to sociology?

One of the differences between pure and applied science is that whereas the former seeks answers to theoretical questions the latter seeks solutions to practical problems. For example, pure sciences such as organic chemistry and theoretical physics aim at discovering explanatory laws. In contrast, applied sciences such as medicine and engineering consist of techniques for imposing human control over natural processes. However, if technology is to be the means for bringing about change this raises the question of the purpose to which theoretical knowledge is to be put. This question has recently come to the fore in the natural sciences because of developments such as genetic engineering and nuclear technology. However, in sociology a concern about developments in society has always been present, not as a result of sociological discoveries but as their source and inspiration.

In the nineteenth century this concern was focused upon the social and economic consequences of industrialisation and the political instability of modern societies. This prompted social thinkers to put forward grand designs for the total reconstruction of society on 'scientific' principles. One example is Auguste Comte. He proposed a religion of humanity which would harness the spiritual power of ideas to create a new society. Karl Marx, who was sceptical of the power of ideas to change society, attached greater importance to the development of the forces of production. For him capitalism rested upon an inner contradiction that made its collapse inevitable. However, out of this would come the opportunity for the socialist reconstruction of society.

Both Comte and Marx had every confidence in the power of science to transform society because they believed that social change was governed by invariable laws which they had been the first to discover. For Comte this was his law of the three stages, for Marx the materialist conception of history. Both principles are the basis of a theory of social change and a policy for action. Having 'discovered' the fundamental law of social evolution they believed this made possible scientific predictions about the future course of history and gave people the opportunity to shape human destiny consciously.

The belief in the perfectibility of humanity through the scientific reorganisation of society still remains the goal of some sociologists today. However, Comte's and Marx's beliefs about how this was to be achieved rest upon a nineteenth century view of science which Karl Popper calls historicism. This is an approach that assumes there is a predetermined pattern to historical change and that sees the social sciences as engaged in prophesying the course that events will take. Popper rejects this because it is logically impossible to predict a future which will be shaped partly by scientific discoveries which have not yet been made. However, his real objection to historicism is that it is used to justify the need for the total remodelling of society.

Popper calls this 'utopian social engineering'. His argument is that this prevents the exercise of freedom and reason in the formulation of policy because implementing such large-scale changes requires a totalitarian state. One should instead adopt 'piecemeal social engineering' aimed at designing and reconstructing particular institutions so as to make society function more efficiently. For Popper the role of the sociologist in matters of policy is thus to be the technician of the state, not the architect of the ideal society.

This view of the sociologist as enlightened reformer rather than revolutionary activist is popular today because it justifies what many sociologists do already. Unlike the nineteenth century when laissez faire was the prevailing political ideology it has today become incumbent upon governments to have a social policy and to be able to make the claim that they can solve social problems. Many sociologists have gone along with this because it seems to prove that sociology could be useful and because it casts them in the role of socially accredited experts.

However, piecemeal reforms suffer from the fundamental weakness that intervention at one point in society triggers changes elsewhere which often frustrate the intentions of the policy. Nowhere is this more evident than in the sociology of education where, inspired by the 'wastage of talent', sociologists have recommended a variety of policies to create greater equality of opportunity. These policies, which include progressive teaching methods, abolition of selection and streaming, compensatory education, curriculum reform, and even sociology training for teachers, have all been singularly ineffective in altering social class gradients in educational achievement. They demonstrate, in the words of the title of Basil Bernstein's article, that 'Education cannot compensate for society' and, in a wider sense, that piecemeal engineering comes up against the fundamental obstacle of social class.

The merging of sociology and social administration in the study of education has other consequences too. It means, as Michael F.D. Young has pointed out, that social practice guides social theory and sociologists come to see 'problems' from the point of view of administrators. This is part of a wider trend towards what C. Wright Mills called 'bureaucratic social science'. Mills was concerned about the employment of sociologists by government agencies and corporations because in these organisations sociologists are used to manipulate pupils, workers, consumers, claimants and others. This kind of piecemeal social engineering is an extension of social control. Although its initial effects may be less spectacular its long term implications may be just as destructive of human freedom as the 'utopian social engineering' so vehemently criticised by the reformers.

All of this suggests that the formulation of social policy is too important to be left to sociologists. This was Weber's point of view and it follows from his insistence that sociology must be value free. This means that an empirical science of social action can contribute only three things to the analysis of policy. It can assess the practical possibility of achieving social goals, it can identify the indispensable means and it can assess the inevitable costs. However, Weber emphasises that an empirical discipline explains only what can be done under certain conditions. Sociologists who attempt to go further, by imposing their own values in the form of recommendations about what should be done, go beyond these bounds irrespective of whether their preference is for large- or small-scale changes.

Commentary

Sir Karl Popper is an internationally renowned philosopher. His early works were written in the 1930s and early 1940s and are imbued with a spirit of anti-totalitarianism.

According to Popper utopian social engineering

> aims at remodelling the 'whole of society' in accordance with a definite plan or blueprint; it aims at 'seizing the key positions' and at extending 'the power of the State . . . until the State becomes nearly identical with society', and it aims, furthermore, at controlling from these 'key positions' the historical forces that mould the future of the developing society.

(The Poverty of Historicism, p.67)

In contrast piecemeal social engineers

> adopt the method of searching for, and fighting against, the greatest and most urgent evils of society, rather than searching for, and fighting for, its greatest ultimate good. This difference is far from being merely verbal. In fact it is most important. It is the difference between a reasonable method of improving the lot of man, and a method which, if really tried, may easily lead to an intolerable increase in human suffering.

(The Open Society and its Enemies, Volume 1, p.158)

Popper believed that piecemeal social engineering was the way to enlarge the exercise of reason and freedom in social affairs and so improve the happiness of humanity. However, writing in the late 1950s C. Wright Mills was not so sure. He argued that

> sociology has lost its reforming push; its tendencies towards fragmentary problems and scattered causation have been conservatively turned to the use of corporation, army, and state. As such bureaucracies have become more dominant in the economic, the political, the military orders, the meaning of 'practical' has shifted: that which is thought to serve the purpose of these great institutions is held to be 'practical'.

(The Sociological Imagination, p.104)

Mills described this as a trend towards 'illiberal practicality' and, far from being a hopeful sign, he interpreted it as a threat.

Question 32
The Welfare State: why has it not led to a significant reduction in inequality?

The Welfare State was set up after the war to provide a minimum standard of living for all, to ensure financial security in times of individual and family crisis, and to make a range of essential services available to all. Many believed that, in conjunction with fiscal policies such as progressive taxation, levies on profits, and death duties, it was creating a more equal society. However, this view was over-optimistic. It confused the effects of economic growth with the goal of social justice and as the postwar economic boom tapered off during the 1960s it became increasingly clear that many of the gains were apparent rather than real. Since then economic recession has shown that far from promoting equality social services are increasingly hard pressed to maintain even a basic level of welfare.

One reason why social services have not brought about a significant reduction in inequality is that benefit levels are too low. In his initial proposals William Beveridge, the architect of the Welfare State, adopted a subsistence definition of poverty derived from Seebohm Rowntree. However, when Beveridge's 1942 report was implemented in 1948 insufficient allowance was made for inflation, and J.C. Kincaid estimates that National Assistance began by paying out only three quarters of the money needed to ensure a standard of living that even Beveridge had regarded as the minimum (*Poverty and Equality in Britain*, p.59). Since then increases in benefits have not closed the gap. For example, Frank Field calculates that between 1948 and 1979 the ordinary rate of social security went up from only 17.6 per cent to 18.6 per cent of the gross average earnings of male manual workers (*Inequality in Britain*, p.63).

In addition economic, demographic and normative changes in British society have combined to increase the number of dependants of the State vastly. When National Assistance was introduced it was regarded as a temporary safety net. However, there has since been a large increase in the number of unemployed, the elderly and one-parent families who claim Supplementary Benefit. For many of these claimants this is not a short-term expedient but a permanent situation brought about by changes in the social structure. These changes include economic recession, increased life expectancy and rising rates of divorce. The result is that today the State supports more people in poverty than ever before.

Despite the massive increase in the number of those who live on the government's poverty line, official statistics disguise the full extent of the problem. In addition to those who register for benefit Peter Townsend estimates there are another two and a half million who are eligible for benefits but are not receiving them (*Poverty in the United Kingdom*, p.829). This is due partly to the sheer complexity of the social services and many claimants are discouraged by broken appointments, long hours of waiting, rude or unhelpful officials, bureaucratic red tape and the secret appeals procedure. Underlying these petty humiliations is the stigma of poverty. This is institutionalised through the means test, reinforced by surveillance, propagated by reports on scroungers by the mass media, and maintained by the relative indifference of governments.

However, hidden poverty is not just a question of those who do not get the benefits to which they are entitled. There is also the problem of low pay. As Brian Abel-Smith and Peter Townsend showed in *The Poor and the Poorest* this is the largest and least recognised cause of poverty. Adopting a poverty line slightly above the government's, their research showed that low wages relative to family size accounted for 40 per cent of those in poverty. For these low wage earners social services do very little.

Meanwhile occupational groups further up the hierarchy have been able to maintain their relative advantage as well as deriving additional benefits from the Welfare State. Although it is widely assumed that social services involve a transfer of resources vertically from rich to poor, much of the redistribution occurs within social strata rather than between them. For example, there is a transfer of resources from adults to the elderly, from the employed to the unemployed, from the healthy to the sick, and from the single to the married. These transfers mean that the main burden of support for social services falls upon the working population, many of whom are themselves low paid. Of course higher income groups contribute through general taxation. However, there are enough loopholes in the law to ensure that this has little effect on the overall pattern of inequality. These loopholes include fringe benefits, 'expenses' claims, non-taxable investments, family trusts and capital transfers. Their effect is to disguise the real extent of economic inequality and to provide access to an even more privileged life style for many who are already in middle and upper income brackets. Some of these tax avoidance schemes verge on tax evasion and though this occurs at all levels those with most to gain are those with the highest tax liability.

In addition to paying less than one might expect to the cost of social services the middle classes also benefit from them. This is particularly so for the army of professionals and administrators who have secure and well paid jobs in social services. However, it is not just as employees but also as clients that the middle classes stand to gain. They are better placed to negotiate with representatives of social services and nowhere is this advantage used to greater effect than in relation to State education. About a quarter of all expenditure on social services goes on education but State schooling benefits children from poor homes the least.

When factors such as this are taken into account it is clear that in Britain's mixed economy the principle of welfare for all remains subordinate to the power of the market. This is nowhere more evident than in the fields of health and education where a higher standard of services is available to those with the ability to pay. These two areas show very clearly why the Welfare State has brought about no general levelling in British society. A significant reduction in inequality would imply forcing the wealthy and the privileged to surrender their advantages. However, the relative absence of complaints from this quarter shows that private property is well able to live with the Welfare State and perhaps even derive strength from it.

Commentary

In *Poverty and Equality in Britain* J.C. Kincaid argues that 'Widespread poverty is a direct consequence of the limited effectiveness of social security provision' (p.10). He goes on to say that

> The whole system is becoming increasingly irrational. Large numbers of people dependent on social security for an income are reduced to desperate poverty. Meanwhile the Government spends larger and larger sums of money on advertising campaigns to guide possible claimants through the maze of schemes, qualifying conditions, exceptions, application forms, means tests, etc., which the attempt to run a Welfare State on the cheap has generated. An increasing array of social workers is employed, one of whose main functions is to offer guidance to citizens lost in the welfare jungle. In many cases the social workers themselves, despite expensive training, have a less than adequate grasp of the complexities of social security entitlement. Increasing amounts of money are devoted to the employment of highly paid administrators to organise the social workers into large, bureaucratic empires. Underlying all these developments is a refusal to see poverty and social equality as issues which are, in reality, quite inseparable. (p.12)

These deficiencies in the Welfare State affect the elderly most of all, and the Department of Health and Social Security estimated that in 1972 there were 980 000 pensioners whose incomes were below the supplementary benefit level. Although a lot of publicity is given to scroungers the greatest problem, seen in terms of the amount of money and number of people involved, is not that of people getting what they are not entitled to, but of people not getting what they are entitled to.

Question 33
The National Health Service: why has it not reduced class inequalities in health and mortality?

Britain's National Health Service came into existence in 1948. The aim was to secure an improvement in the health of the population by making medical care available to all. However, since its inauguration the demands made on the Health Service have increased and today it is still far from meeting the health needs of the nation as a whole. One illustration of this is the evidence on the relationship between social class and infant mortality. This shows that the mortality rate of infants born to mothers from social class V remains approximately twice as high as the rate for infants born to mothers in social class I. However, this is only part of a general social class gradient in mortality. This gradient has got steeper since the 1930s and by 1972 the male mortality rate amongst managers and professionals was 23 per cent below average whereas that of unskilled manual workers was 37 per cent above.

The main cause of these differences in life chances is variations in the incidence of disease. One indicator of such variations is the rate of self-reported illness. This shows a marked increase as one descends the social scale. More specific measures of morbidity confirm this pattern. For example, statistics on specific causes of death amongst adult males show that there are social class gradients in diseases like tuberculosis, various types of cancer, pneumonia, bronchitis and duodenal ulcers. These and other specific causes of death contribute to variations in the overall death rates of particular occupational groups and the report of the working group on inequalities in health (1980) showed that the death rates of adult men in a variety of manual jobs were between two and three times as high as those of men in managerial or professional occupations.

These differences in the health of the adult population are only partly explained by the distribution of occupationally related diseases and variations in the accident rates of different industries. This is because environmental risks to health and life begin to take effect long before one starts work. The most extensive enquiry into these risks is the National Child Development Study, begun in 1958. This longitudinal study took over 10 000 children born in the first week of March that year and followed their development from birth to maturity. In *Born to Fail?* Peter Wedge and Hilary Prosser singled out for special attention the progress of socially disadvantaged children.

The research showed a vast catalogue of differences between the way of life of the disadvantaged children and the rest. These begin to have an effect even before the child is born. For example, mothers of the disadvantaged children were more likely to have had several previous pregnancies or be very young. Also they smoked more frequently during pregnancy and sought less medical attention for themselves and their unborn children. At birth their children were on average smaller and were more likely to be premature. However, this was only the beginning of an accumulation of burdens and by the age of eleven a clear pattern of differences between the health of the disadvantaged children and the rest was emerging. For example, the disadvantaged group had missed more school through illness or emotional disorder. They were more prone to infection, more likely to have had serious accidents and more frequently suffered from hearing impairment and speech difficulties. In addition they were less likely to have been screened for potentially handicapping conditions at an early age or be immunised against serious diseases.

This last point shows that though the disadvantaged children were more in need of preventative medicine they were less likely to receive it. This 'law of inverse care' is the main reason for the apparently widening differences in health and mortality between social classes. To some extent the operation of this law is masked by the fact that the lower classes do use the Health Service more. However, this says nothing about the quality of the care they receive. Furthermore absolute rates are misleading because they do not relate use of the Health Service to the amount of disease in different social classes. However, when one compares visits to doctors with the amount of illness perceived by members of different social classes the gap between medical need and medical treatment is only too apparent. For every visit a man in social class V with a chronic handicapping disease pays to his doctor, a similar man in social class I pays two visits.

Explanations of these variations in willingness to consult a doctor are sometimes sought in the social background of patients themselves. For example, level of intelligence, value orientations and types of family structure have all been cited as possible factors. However, the problem with these explanations is that they take the operation of the Health Service for granted and come dangerously close to blaming the socially disadvantaged for their own poor health. In addition such explanations ignore the fact that good medical care is a scarce resource; a fact which needs to be underlined in view of the expansion of private health schemes, increases in prescription charges and queues for hospital treatment.

On the other hand the problem is not just that the Health Service is underfinanced. Its structure and organisation also need to be questioned. In relation to this it is often argued that higher income groups benefit more from the Health Service because they are better placed to negotiate with medical professionals. However, this ability to work the system is possessed to an even greater degree by medical professionals themselves. They have been very successful in getting their view of health and disease socially accepted and in establishing monopolistic control over the provision of treatment. One result is that the Health Service has become geared to curing diseases rather than preventing them.

All of this seems to imply that a change in policy is needed. This might be achieved by concentrating resources on the environmental risks to health and paying more attention to health education as part of a changeover from a hospital- to a community-based Health Service. Without the introduction of measures such as these it is likely that the Health Service will continue to accentuate rather than reduce class inequalities in health and mortality.

Commentary

One of the problems faced by the health services in Britain and elsewhere is an increased demand for medical care. Amongst the factors which have contributed to this are technical advances in the treatment of disease, an ageing population and a heightened consciousness of sickness and health. However, the medical establishment has itself artificially helped to generate some of the demand. One instance of this is unnecessary operations. Commenting on this, Kenneth and Patricia Jones point out that

> evidence from America suggests that one fifth of the operations performed there are unnecessary, including 50 per cent of tonsillectomies, 30 per cent of hysterectomies and 20 per cent of appendectomies, making a total of 2 000 000 unnecessary operations every year. Apart from factors such as incompetence in surgeons, and a greed for money from the fees, there is a strong pressure for such operations from the patients themselves. Another factor appears to lie in the training of doctors in America. That is, if there is an excess number of surgeons then it is possible that they will perform an excess number of operations. The American system also means that an empty hospital bed costs as much, or almost as much, as a full one, and the tendency is to fill these available beds. The number of appendectomies performed in a given area, for example, does not relate to the number of people in that area that would be liable to have the operation performed but rather to how many surgeons and how many hospital beds there are in the area.

(*Sociology in Medicine*, p.161)

Although in Britain we have a very different system there is also evidence to suggest that unnecessary operations are sometimes performed under the National Health Service. For example, the National Child Development Study found that by the age of seven 16 per cent of children have had their tonsils removed. However,

> The surprising evidence was the variation of the rates throughout the country. In Wales 14 per cent had their tonsils removed, in the North of England 15 per cent, the South 17 per cent, and Scotland 21 per cent. Again, one local area can have fifteen times as many tonsillectomies as an adjoining area. (ibid. pp.161–2)

Question 34
An ageing population: what are the causes? what are the consequences?

An ageing population is a population in which the number and proportion of the elderly is increasing. In Britain the 1901 census figures show that there were then about 1.8 million people of 65 or over whereas in 1982 there were about 8.2 million. Over the same period the proportion of the over 65s has increased from 5 to 15 per cent of the population. In addition the elderly are themselves an ageing population. Whereas in 1979 about one third of the elderly were aged 75 or over Peter Laslett estimates that by 1991 this will rise to more than two fifths.

The causes of Britain's ageing population are bound up with changes in birth and death rates. For example, the decline in the birth rate has slowed population growth and reduced the proportion of the young in the population. Meanwhile the decline in the death rate has extended average life expectancy and increased the chance of living a significant proportion of one's life in retirement. However, changes in birth and death rates have been uneven. This has caused fluctuations in the size of age cohorts and variations within them. Amongst the elderly the most significant of these variations is the imbalance in the sex ratio. In 1982 women outnumbered men by over ten to seven amongst the over 60s and by two to one amongst the over 75s.

These changes in the age structure have had consequences for the social structure of modern Britain. This is not primarily because of the biological process of ageing itself but because of the social significance attributed to it. An example is compulsory retirement. This takes men and women out of the labour force at an arbitrary age and consigns them to an economically unproductive role. Willingly or unwillingly they are forced to adjust to the status of pensioner. This normally involves a sudden and dramatic alteration in daily routine, a disruption of social relationships built around the habits of a lifetime and a reduction in income.

However, concern over the social implications of ageing has been traditionally focused on the social costs rather than the needs of the aged. For example, during the 1940s and 1950s some social scientists were arguing that the growing numbers of the elderly would place an increasing strain on economically productive groups. Since the working population supports dependent groups in society it was argued that the ageing population was increasing the financial burden. With this in mind William Beveridge recommended in his 1942 report that State pensions should be tied to subsistence level.

Although pensions have since risen they remain broadly in line with other benefits. As a result the social policies of successive governments have combined to condemn many elderly people to a life of relative poverty. Figures published by the government show that up to a quarter of the retired receive at least some of their income from supplementary benefit. Furthermore the average income per adult in elderly households is 15 to 20 per cent below households where the head is employed. The elderly are also less likely to possess a range of consumer products such as central heating, telephones and washing machines despite the fact that their need for them is often greatest.

By viewing the social implications of an ageing population in financial terms governments have also contributed to a general insensitivity to the social needs of the elderly. In particular governments have been slow to react to the fact that the elderly are increasingly likely to live alone. Most of these one-person households are female. The main reason is the widening difference between male and female life expectancy coupled with the tendency for women to marry men older than themselves. The result is that many elderly women face social isolation.

This development has been exacerbated by changes in family structure partly caused by trends in geographical and social mobility. In *The Family Life of Old People* Peter Townsend showed that the close-knit traditional working class community is well adapted to the needs of the elderly. Studies of working class extended families have also stressed the importance of the grandmother role. However, when families move to new housing areas it tends to undermine the traditional pattern and encourage a privatised family structure in which the needs of children take precedence over other relationships.

Of course this does not lead to the severing of all relationships with kin and there is evidence that over half the elderly receive visits from relatives at least once a week. Furthermore in *Middle Class Families* Colin Bell describes a pattern of mutual aid between generations and he argues that the telephone often compensates for a lower level of face-to-face interaction. However, Bell also found that even where married children feel a strong obligation towards elderly parents the dependence of one party on the other was not regarded as desirable or even acceptable.

The partial exclusion of the elderly from the nuclear family throws many back on the resources provided by the State. However, problems frequently arise out of the professionalisation of care and its bureaucratic organisation. For many elderly people the stigma of welfare is a powerful disincentive to claim benefits. For those that do claim, the baffling complexity of social services and their own failing health mean that many do not get what they are entitled to. Finally social services have been slow to adapt to the needs of the elderly. For example, hospitals, homes, day centres and the like often impose a routine that denies opportunities for self-expression and encourages dependency. Meanwhile the relationship between social workers and their clients places power over the elderly in the hands of professionals.

All this fosters a feeling of helplessness amongst many old people. Their problems are frequently hidden and very often others speak on their behalf. One consequence of this is the theory of disengagement. According to this society makes fewer demands upon the elderly and they respond by voluntarily reducing their social involvement. However, it is likely that reduced interaction with others by the elderly is more to do with our neglect than their disengagement.

Commentary

According to Dorothy Wedderburn, 'Debate about the adequacy of provision for the elderly has been almost continuous in the post-war period' ('Old People in Britain', reprinted in *Social Problems of Modern Britain*, edited by Eric Butterworth and David Weir, pp.109−21). Richard Titmuss' view of that provision is that

> Viewed historically, it is difficult to understand why the gradual emergence in Britain of a more balanced age structure should be regarded as a 'problem of ageing'. What we have to our credit as humanists and good husbanders is a great reduction in premature death since the nineteenth century; as a result, we have derived many benefits from our growing ability to survive through the working span of life. Much of the inefficiency and waste of early death has been eliminated by an increase in the expectation of life at birth of the working classes to a point that now approaches closer to that achieved by more prosperous classes. This should be a matter for satisfaction.

(*Essays on 'The Welfare State'*, second edition p.56)

Peter Laslett's is that

> Since it is the elderly who lived and worked through the time of educational expansion, it could be said that they have been paying the bill but not sharing the benefits ... Equity suggests that persons of all ages should have equal shares in the social fund, but the young, those between the ages of 15 and 25, have had a monopoly in that very considerable part of it which goes to education. This could only be justified if it could be shown that such a monopoly is for the benefit of everyone at every age. In my view, the historical facts we have examined make such justification impossible today. The elderly, exploited in the past, are being cheated now by the allocation of educational funds as well as by inflation.

('In an ageing world', *New Society*, 27 October 1977)

Chapter 10

Religion

The three theorists who have had the greatest impact on the development of modern sociology are Marx, Durkheim and Weber. Marx's ideas have already been discussed in connection with social stratification. The ideas of Durkheim and Weber have a particular relevance to the sociology of religion.

Durkheim

Emile Durkheim's reputation rests on four major works. They are *The Division of Labour in Society* (1893), *The Rules of Sociological Method* (1895), *Suicide* (1897) and *The Elementary Forms of the Religious Life* (1912).

The Division of Labour in Society is, in Durkheim's own words, 'an attempt to treat the facts of moral life according to the method of the positive sciences' (p.32). For Durkheim that meant relating those facts to changes in the organisation of society. However, moral phenomena are not, in themselves, easily observable. What was therefore needed was to substitute for the direct study of moral life the study of some index which represented it. For Durkheim that index was law.

According to Durkheim 'law reproduces the principal forms of social solidarity' (p.68) and he argues that, by classifying the different types of law, it is possible to discover the types of moral order that they express. He defines law as rules of sanctioned conduct and he classifies these rules in terms of their type of sanction. These are of two kinds. Repressive sanctions exist to inflict some form of suffering upon the transgressor as punishment. This is penal law. Restitutive sanctions exist to restore things to the way they were before the law was violated. This is 'civil law, commercial law, procedural law, administrative law, after abstraction of the penal rules which may be found there' (p.69).

Penal law deals with offences conventionally regarded as crimes. What is and is not a crime varies between societies. However, Durkheim argued that what is common to all crimes is that they consist in 'acts universally disapproved of by members of each society' (p.73). In other words crimes are acts that flout the collective conscience. What then of punishment? According to Durkheim it too has to be seen in relation to the collective conscience. This leads him to reject the common view which sees the main functions of punishment as reforming offenders and deterring others from following their example. On the contrary punishment, says Durkheim, 'is above all designed to act upon upright people . . . it serves to heal the wounds made upon collective sentiments' (p.108). That is to say punishment is mainly an act of vengeance on the part of a community threatened by actions that contradict the deepest feelings of its members.

Restitutive law is different. Here the function is not to inflict suffering upon individuals who violate or disregard a law but simply to make them comply with it. Sanctions are used less as punishments than as means to reinstate what would have been the case if the law had been obeyed, or to compensate those affected by its transgression. Furthermore, the infraction of these rules does not generally arouse strong feelings of repugnance and offenders are not normally disgraced. For Durkheim the reason was that restitutive law is not primarily an expression of sentiments common to the collectivity as a whole. Its main function is to act as a framework for peaceful co-operation between individuals who occupy different positions in the social structure.

Durkheim claimed that the relative preponderance of these two types of law corresponded to stages in the development of an increasingly differentiated society. In primitive societies all law is penal. As society develops a more complex division of labour, penal law is progressively displaced by restitutive law. This process also corresponds to a decline in the power of the collective conscience and the rise of individualism. However, law is also the external manifestation of the moral order of society. Changes in the legal system thus imply corresponding changes in the fundamental principles of social cohesion. Durkheim described this as a change from mechanical to organic solidarity.

Mechanical solidarity is a solidarity of resemblance. The major characteristic of a society in which this prevails is that the individual members are mentally and morally homogeneous. The reason is that they are completely enveloped by the collective conscience. It dominates and suppresses all individuality and the external manifestation of this constraint is repressive law. However, 'It is quite otherwise with the solidarity which the division of labour produces. Whereas the previous type implies that individuals resemble each other, this type presumes their difference' (p.131). In other words in a society in which organic solidarity prevails the individual members are mentally and morally heterogeneous. The reason is that social differentiation creates room for individuals to exercise a degree of personal autonomy. Social order thus comes to depend more and more on the co-operation of members with different qualities and the external manifestation of this is restitutive law.

In general terms Durkheim is saying that individual freedom, and even personality itself, is formed out of an evolutionary process of social differentiation. However, he also believed that the same process posed a potential threat to social solidarity. This was because of the need to bring the socially differentiated elements under normative control. Unless this was achieved anomie would result and social disintegration become a possibility. For Durkheim the symptoms of this were already emerging. Increases in class conflict, suicide, crime and marital breakdown were all signs of an erosion of the sense of moral obligation that cements society together. Thus Durkheim's theory of the progressive disassociation of the individual from the collective type culminates in a diagnosis of the sources of instability in a highly differentiated society.

Durkheim's next major work was *The Rules of Sociological Method*. In it he expounded his views on the nature of social reality and how it should be studied. For Durkheim sociology was the scientific study of social facts. He begins by explaining what a social fact is.

Durkheim notes that every individual is born into a society that is already organised. These forms of organisation are not the creation of any particular individual but they are inherited by us all. On this basis he reasons that there 'are ways of acting, thinking and feeling that present the noteworthy property of existing outside the individual consciousness' (p.2). Moreover, these types of conduct and thought are not only external, they also exercise a coercive power over us. On this basis Durkheim deduces that their source must be society itself. In other words for Durkheim social facts are objective properties of collective life. They constitute a reality in their own right which is quite distinct from their individual manifestations in the conduct of a particular member.

Having established the reality of the phenomena studied by sociology Durkheim goes on to introduce his first and most fundamental rule. It is 'Consider social facts as things' (p.14). However, very often illusions that distort the real nature of things get mistaken for the things themselves. To minimise this danger Durkheim recommends that all preconceptions be eradicated. Only then is the sociologist in a position to define social facts objectively in terms of their inherent properties. For Durkheim that meant classifying social facts in terms of their external characteristics. On this basis he claims that it is possible to classify societies in terms of their level of organisation and, within societies of a particular type, distinguish what is normal from what is pathological (the pathological being that which departs from the standards that prevail in a healthy society of a given species).

However, these rules are only rules for the correct recognition of social facts. The more important task is to discover the laws that govern their occurrence. This involves separating the causes that produce a social fact from the function it performs. As regards the former Durkheim argues that 'The determining cause of a social fact should be sought among the social facts preceding it' (p.110). On the other hand we should look for the function of a social fact in its relation to some social end, a social end being that which corresponds to the general needs of the social organism.

However, Durkheim argues that we shall 'find the function more easily if the cause is already known' (p.96). The most important task is thus to demonstrate that a given phenomenon is the cause of another. According to Durkheim the way to do this is to analyse particular cases in order to see if variations in the occurrence of one social fact are linked with another. In the natural sciences this is generally done by experiments mounted under artificial conditions. However, sociologists are not in a position to produce social facts at will. On the other hand there is a way forward by analysing situations spontaneously produced in different societies at different times. Thus Durkheim was led to advocate the comparative method as the only one suitable for sociology.

Suicide is Durkheim's famous application of his conception of sociological method to the study of a particular social fact. An outline of his arguments is given in Question 30. In general terms Durkheim is saying that for each social group there is a collective inclination to commit suicide and that this inclination comes from suicidogenic currents of egoism, altruism and anomie running through the society under consideration. To many of Durkheim's critics this conclusion appears so strange as to be simply unbelievable. However, an analogy can help. Imagine you have an elastic band. If you stretch it it will eventually break; the exact position of the break will be determined by factors that govern the strength of the material at particular points. However, the overall pressure comes from a different source. Durkheim is saying that it is the same with the relationship between individuals and society. Individuals are like the molecules of the elastic band. Some may have weaknesses in their character which make them more prone to break. However, the pressure that impels them to take their life is the force exerted by society, and Durkheim came to believe that the original manifestation of that force was religion.

In *The Elementary Forms of the Religious Life* Durkheim's purpose was to discover what was fundamental and universal to all religions. This, he argued, would be more readily discoverable by analysing the simplest religions. They lacked the secondary embellishments found in the faiths of more sophisticated people and therefore displayed the essential elements more clearly. This is why he chose to study the religious beliefs and rituals of the Australian aborigines. Their religion is what we call totemism and Durkheim regarded this as the prototype of religious life.

The Australian aborigines were members of clans, a form of social organisation that has two basic characteristics. First, all members of the clan regard themselves as members of one family. Second, the name of the clan is its totem and the totem of the clan is also that of each of its members. Furthermore, the totem is also the name of a particular species of thing, usually a plant or an animal. However, the totem is not just a name. It is also the emblem of the clan and its image adorns everything of significance to the aborigine. It is found on the walls of houses, the sides of canoes, on shields, helmets, utensils and tombs, and is painted, tattooed and even cut or burned into the body of members of the clan.

. The significance of the totem to the tribe stems from its religious character. It is in relation to it that things are classified as sacred or profane. Things that resemble or have contact with the totem partake in its sacred power. Things that are opposed to it are profane. There are also distinctions of degree and some objects, times, places and people are considered more sacred than others. In this way everything that is of interest to the aborigine is classified and brought into determinate relation to other things. On this basis Durkheim was led to argue that the genesis of logical thought lay in religious experience. In other words the sacred and the profane are, in his view, the most fundamental categories of reasoning. They are the original elements of conscious experience or, as Durkheim put it, 'the framework of the intelligence' (p.9).

However, it is a curious fact that the aborigine regards the image of totemic beings as more sacred than the beings themselves. Durkheim argues that the reason for this is that the totem is a symbol. What it symbolises is first the god of the clan and second the clan itself. This invites speculation that if the totem 'is at once the symbol of the god and of the society is that not because the god and the society are only one?' (p.206). According to Durkheim this is the only explanation that fits the facts. Thus he was led to argue that god is society 'personified and represented to the imagination under the visible form of the animal or vegetable which serves as a totem' (p.206).

It is difficult to imagine a more provocative (some would say sacrilegious) point of view. However, Durkheim is quite emphatic about the social origins of religious belief and he goes on to argue that the idea of a soul can also be explained sociologically as the representation of society within us. He claims too that the idea of divinity, first conceived by the aborigine in the form of the totem, is the source of religious ideas concerning the existence of spirits and of a supreme being. Furthermore, Durkheim claims 'there is no reason for not extending the most general results of our researches to other religions' (p.415). Thus in Durkheim's view there would be no reason not to extend his analysis of the aborigine's relation to his totem to the Christian's relation to the cross. Both orientations are claimed by Durkheim to be equally valid, not because of the existence of a deity but because these social facts perform functions that correspond to the general needs of the social organism of which they are a part. (On the functions of religion see Question 35.)

Although virtually everything Durkheim wrote about society and the way it should be studied has come in for constant criticism he articulated positions on fundamental issues which are still at the centre of the debate today. These positions include the view that sociologists should consider social facts as things, that sociology should follow the method of the natural sciences, that it should seek to determine the causes and functions of social facts and that its fundamental task was to explain social order. Although Durkheim was not the first to argue the case for these positions he was their most articulate spokesman and the development of modern functionalism owes more to him than any other thinker.

Weber

Max Weber has, if anything, had an even greater influence on the development of modern sociology. According to Weber sociology is 'a science which attempts the interpretive understanding of social action in order thereby to arrive at a causal explanation of its course and effects' (*The Theory of Social and Economic Organisation*, p.88). The key points on which Weber's conception of sociology differs from Durkheim's are as follows. First, the object of sociological investigation is social action (not 'social facts'). Second, the ultimate unit of analysis is individual action (not collective behaviour). Third, it is necessary to grasp the meaning of action (not just its external characteristics). Fourth, sociology must take into account the subjective point of view of social actors themselves (not treat social facts as things). Whereas Durkheim was a prominent exponent of positivism Weber is conventionally regarded as the founder of interpretive sociology, and the two sides to this are Weber's epistemology (his philosophy of science) and his methodology.

In relation to the former Weber maintains that there is a fundamental difference between the natural and the cultural sciences. The broad outlines of this difference are as follows. Natural events are events that come about of themselves. Culture is the product of what members of society conceive as important. In themselves natural phenomena are devoid of value, and what we scientifically know about them stems from observation of their effects. However, cultural phenomena are relevant to values and in addition to observing their effects one can understand the motives of those whose actions produced them. This is the material basis of a distinction between two types of science. The formal equivalent of this is a difference in their respective points of view. Thus, the natural sciences are generalising sciences. Their aim is to subsume individual phenomena under universal laws, and to this end they abstract from everything that is unique to this or that object or event. However, our interest in cultural phenomena is different. Here it is the unique value-relevant aspects of reality that are the object of explanation. This entails different principles of concept formation.

Weber's methodology deals with the practical implications of this. His principal claims are, first, that sociology can and should be value free. It follows that there is no place for value judgements in an empirical science of social action. Second, such a science must be able to establish demonstrable truths on the basis of the analysis of empirical fact. It follows that intuition and feelings of empathy cannot act as criteria of validity. Third, conceptual tools are required to sift from amongst the multitude of value-facts those that are essential. It follows that what is needed are means for defining what is relevant to a particular point of view. Fourth, this inevitably involves ideal type analysis. An ideal type is formed by the one-sided accentuation of one or more points of view. It is a logically consistent (in Weber's words 'meaningfully adequate') description of the 'idea' of a particular cultural phenomenon and it acts as a limiting concept against which actual situations may be compared. By identifying divergences from and similarities to the rational norm one is able to translate social phenomena into a scientifically explicable form. Thus Weber claims that his methodology establishes the point of departure for causal explanation.

Weber's (unfinished) general sociology is basically a system of ideal types, several of which are discussed in the introductory sections to Chapters 3 and 7. His ideal types of church and sect are dealt with in Question 37. These are but a few of the innumerable conceptual distinctions first introduced by Weber and elaborated by him to varying degrees by empirical illustrations drawn from civilisations ancient and modern. However, Weber did not regard the formulation of definitional concepts as an end in itself. It was only the indispensable means for the empirical analysis of substantive problems in sociology, and for Weber one problem loomed larger than any other. This was the task of comprehending the combination of causal factors that gave rise to the distinctive characteristics of modern western civilisation itself.

For Weber what was distinctive about the modern world was the gradual elimination of magic and superstition from everyday affairs and the progressive rationalisation of all spheres of life. Culturally this was manifest in the growth of scientific knowledge. Economically it was evident in the rational organisation of acquisitive activity under bourgeois capitalism. Other features included the rational calculation of profitability (accountancy), rational means of administration (bureaucracy) and the rational use of technology (modernisation). In all these respects Weber argued that modern society embodied an orientation to experience that was the antithesis of all traditionalism. The problem was to explain why this historically unique form of civilisation had spontaneously emerged only in the west.

Weber's answer to this problem is to be found in his historical and comparative research. The most influential part of this is his famous work *The Protestant Ethic and the Spirit of Capitalism*. In this Weber demonstrated that there was an affinity between Puritan beliefs and capitalist attitudes. However, the meaningful correspondence between the two does not by itself provide conclusive proof of a causal link. Since it is possible that material factors may account for both Weber recognised that other proofs were needed. The most compelling of these is to be found in Weber's comparative analyses of the economic ethics of other world religions. In these studies Weber demonstrated that in China, India and elsewhere material and other conditions favourable to the rationalisation of economic activity existed. However, the crucial difference was that in those societies the economic ethic of the prevailing religions was directly antagonistic to such a development. This confirms Weber's view that ultimate values are not merely a reflecton of material interests. On the contrary they are the crucial elements that differentiate the development of civilisation in the west from developments elsewhere.

Finally, in Weber's analysis of the development of the modern world there are also the elements of a diagnosis of our time. He believed that the religious ideals that had helped form modern civilisation were a spent force. In place of traditional values an attitude of calculation was coming to dominate social relationships and bureaucracy was the institutionalised counterpart of this. It is, he wrote 'the dictatorship of the officials, not of the proletariat, that is marching on' (quoted in Donald G. MacRae, *Weber*, p.87), and Weber's melancholy conclusion was that there was little that could be done to arrest this development.

Question 35
Functionalism and religion: what is the value of functionalist interpretations of the role of religion?

In *The Elementary Forms of the Religious Life* Durkheim set out to refute the views of nineteenth century thinkers who had proposed that religion originated in ignorance and error. For Durkheim it was inconceivable that such a fundamental social fact could be explained away as mere illusion. This was not because he thought that the ideas of religious believers were scientifically true. It was rather that he saw those beliefs as having an underlying objective significance that stemmed from the functional importance of religion to society. As explained by Durkheim, and later taken up by other functionalists, religion promotes social integration and social regulation by furnishing members of society with collective representations and engendering respect for a unified moral order. On this basis functionalists have regarded religion as a conservative force which contributes order and stability to society.

For Durkheim the most fundamental characteristic of religion is the way it classifies things as sacred and profane. Sacred things are things set apart and can include sacred times, places, people, events and objects. The important point about them is not their external characteristics but the reverential attitude that they inspire. The sacred is thus a class of phenomena which always demands the same attitude of respect. For

Durkheim this respect was engendered by the power of society over individuals. Thus he claimed that 'God and society are only one'. The reverence that religion inspires was really evoked and sustained by the power of collective life itself.

However, the vitality of the sentiments enshrined in religion needs to be constantly maintained. For Durkheim this was the significance of ritual. Through it sentiments embodied in beliefs about the sacred are revitalised, or, as Talcott Parsons puts it, 'the function of ritual is to fortify faith' (*The Structure of Social Action*, p.436). It does this in two main ways.

The negative cult consists of abstentions and taboos that surround the human relationship to sacred phenomena. The importance of these rules is clearly revealed by initiation rites in simple societies. These often involve an ordeal and Durkheim claimed that this fosters a willingness to deny selfish impulses and so enhances sentiments favourable to the persistence of the tribe. In contrast the positive cult is the communal ritual behaviour that is expected of the faithful. These religious obligations centre upon the observance of ceremony and Durkheim attached particular importance to sacrificial feasts. These bring members of society together for a common purpose, unite them in a sacred meal and remind them of the faith that binds them to each other. In these ways religious ceremony reaffirms the collective conscience which Durkheim saw as the source of moral unity in tribe and society.

Modern functionalists tend to agree with Durkheim on the integrative effects of religion but the prevailing view is that he overstated his case. For example, Durkheim's treatment of religion as a social fact overstresses the obligatory nature of religion which is far less pronounced in modern industrial societies. It also makes it difficult to account for the rise of new religions and the role of prophets. However, most important of all is Durkheim's view that it is society that sacred symbols symbolise. As Kingsley Davis has pointed out this is not the case. For example, the cross is the most religiously potent symbol of the Christian faith. However, it does not symbolise Christian society so much as redemption from sin and the hope of eternal life.

This last point suggests that it might be more profitable to interpret the role of religion in terms of the needs of individuals rather than those of society. This was Bronislaw Malinowski's view. He argued that a stable society required mechanisms to cope with the emotional problems of its members and that the function of religion is to manage tension and relieve anxiety. To some extent this is similar to Parsons' ideas. He stresses the problem of meaning and argues that one function of religion is to provide answers to questions that lie outside the range of scientific explanation. In particular religion addresses itself to ultimate questions such as the meaning of suffering and death. By providing members of society with explanations of events that might otherwise appear haphazard and contradictory it helps individuals adjust to crises and disappointments and fosters a consensus on questions of ultimate value.

The explanations of more recent functionalists differ from Durkheim's in that they reject the social realism implicit in his idea that society is the cause of religion, whilst agreeing with his view that religion enhances social solidarity. One problem with this is that historical and comparative studies show that the role of religion varies. Whilst in some circumstances religion may perform the integrative role that functionalists suppose there is plenty of evidence to suggest that it does not do so always and everywhere. One obvious example is the Lebanon, where religious differences pose a constant threat of civil war.

Further variations in the role of religion emerge from differences in religious attitudes to the secular order. Functionalists presume that the fundamental role of religion is to conserve and reinforce this order. However, as Max Weber demonstrated in his studies of Protestantism, religion is sometimes a vehicle of change. This is particularly the case with religious sects. Far from legitimating existing values these religious organisations frequently reject them altogether. Furthermore, sects that attract widespread support can develop into powerful political movements. For example, in the US Martin Luther King successfully mobilised religious sentiments in a national crusade for civil rights for blacks. In tribal societies too religious belief can help to focus opposition to the status quo and in his study of cargo cults Peter Worsley showed how the religious beliefs of the indigenous population helped foment political unrest which eventually developed into a movement to end colonial rule.

These examples show that the role of religion in society varies. Although religion can contribute to unity and stability it can just as readily be a source of conflict and change. This was clearly recognised by Weber. He argued that religiously motivated behaviour was so diverse that it could only be empirically studied through an analysis of its subjective meaning and historical effectiveness. Weber's comparative studies of religion confirm the fruitfulness of this approach and in doing so they demonstrate that the attempts by functionalists to construct a general theory of religion are fundamentally misguided.

Commentary

In *Sociologists and Religion* Susan Budd argues that

> The difficulties connected with functionalist explanations have often been noted but the study of religion inside a functionalist framework has perhaps been more successful than that of any other social institution, and the schema is falling from favour less because it is inadequate in explaining religion than because functionalism as a general method has been devalued. (p.47)

Going on to explain the reasons for the decline of functionalism Budd lists

> the impossibility of defining specifically enough the societal needs which must be met . . . logical circularities, such as the explanation of institutions by functions and functions by institutions; the existence of much which can be seen only as entirely dysfunctional, and the failure to look at the causes of this; the implicit conservatism and static nature of the model, which makes it especially difficult to apply to complex societies with internal conflicts and fast rates of growth; the failure to specify causal factors. (p.48)

However, Budd finds none of these arguments conclusive and she goes on to recommend that

> The safest conclusion about the value of the functionalist approach is that it varies; it is more applicable both to aspects of modern America and to simple societies than it is to the older, more openly divided societies of Europe, or to many rapidly modernizing nations. (p.50)

The conclusion drawn by this author is certainly 'safe'. It is doubtful whether it is sound.

Question 36
Marx and Weber: what were their views on the relationship between religion and modern capitalism?

Both Marx and Weber regarded religion as an historical phenomenon which, through its subjective meaning for the faithful, had objective implications for society. However, for Marx religion was part of the superstructure of society and its characteristics were shaped by the mode of production. In contrast Weber considered that in many circumstances religious beliefs direct economic action. He was therefore led to argue that religion was not a dependent variable but a source of stability or change in its own right. This led Weber to develop a very different theory from Marx's as to the relationship between religion and modern capitalism.

Marx interpreted religion as both an escape from reality and an obstacle to social progress. Although he recognised that new religious movements could be the precursor of other social changes his main point was that in the hands of a ruling class religious ideas act as instruments of social control. In particular Marx argued that religious beliefs diverted people's energies from political action designed to change the social conditions that are the primary cause of suffering. Instead of fighting to change their world people are encouraged to mystify it and to believe, for example, that suffering is the consequence of original sin and that the only hope of salvation lies in faith in a supreme being.

Marx argued that religion, by translating historically conditioned social, economic and political relationships into eternal truths, acts as a legitimation of the material distribution of power and reward. In modern capitalist society the established Church was thus seen by Marx as in alliance with the bourgeois State and the clergy as acting in defence of private property. In practice the Church performs this role by disguising the real basis of exploitation under capitalism. Thus, for example, it fosters the view that society is a divine creation and not a human one. It also teaches that the meek and the poor will receive their reward on Judgement Day. The effect of these doctrines is to generate false consciousness amongst the masses. In this way Marx argued that religion acted as an opiate dulling the pain of oppression and preventing the awakening of revolutionary consciousness.

In Marx's explanation the appeal of religion in a capitalist society is seen as lying in the unfulfilled needs of people who are ignorant of the true causes of their suffering. Only in a socialist society would people achieve true liberation and this would include liberation from religious fantasies. However, Weber, who was not a socialist, regarded Marx's philosophy of history as speculative. Although he agreed with Marx on several of the characteristics of modern capitalism Weber considered that modern capitalism's most significant attribute was its historicially unique attitude to economic activity. Weber called that attitude 'the spirit of capitalism'.

The most essential element of the spirit of capitalism is that economic activity is regarded as an end in itself. In all societies people have pursued their material advantage. However, in traditional societies this is always, to some extent, regarded as a necessary evil. What is distinctive about the modern capitalist attitude is that work is regarded as of positive value and the increase of capital as an ethical obligation. However, Weber emphasised that this has nothing to do with mere greed. On the contrary the spirit of capitalism insists upon both a stringent self discipline and an entrepreneurial attitude orientated to the maximisation of business efficiency. Thus it sets up as an ideal the sober, honest, thrifty and hard-working business-owner who employs rational methods in the pursuit of legitimate profits.

Although Weber recognised that once established the modern capitalist system would be able to perpetuate itself, the unique spirit had to come from somewhere. For Weber, the Marxist explanation of it as mere ideology was implausible because of the meaningful correspondence between capitalist values and Protestant ethics. The fact that there existed, prior to the development of modern capitalism, a system of ultimate beliefs congruent with it was reason to investigate whether there might be a causal connection between the two.

Weber examined the possible connection through ideal type analysis of the doctrines of the reformed sects, in particular Calvinism. The most essential belief of the Calvinists was in an absolutely transcendental God who has predestined every individual to either everlasting damnation or perpetual bliss. Only a small minority would be saved and particular individuals could never know for certain whether they were amongst God's elect. Since God's decree stands for eternity it was only human presumption which led to the supposition that human action could influence divine will. In what was for the Calvinists the most important question, namely the fate of their eternal souls, they were deprived of all external comfort and support.

The psychological consequence of Calvinism was an unprecedented inner isolation of the individual. Customary ways of achieving reassurance through friends, family, shared pleasures and good works were regarded as distractions and dangerous self-indulgence. Magical means of salvation such as ritual observance of ceremony and the confession of sins were regarded as useless idolatory. Sincere Calvinists were thus forced back on their own resources. They lived an austere life because they believed in the corruption of everything pertaining to the flesh. They adopted a rational attitude because they believed that God did not continually interfere in nature or society. However, most important of all they believed in the need to work conscientiously and systematically in a calling acceptable to God.

For Weber the theology of Calvinism was the source of a distinctive practical attitude to the world. Although the early Calvinists did not themselves believe in money making for its own sake, the emphasis on rational and continuous labour coupled with an ascetic compulsion to save meant that Calvin's followers were uniquely qualified to succeed in business. Moreover although the performance of good works and a successful career were not regarded as a means of salvation they were interpreted as a sign of God's favour. The incentive to succeed in life was therefore further reinforced by the reassurance that it provided for successful Protestants, and Weber maintained that it was this that fostered the early growth of modern capitalism in Britain and the US.

Commentary

Weber claimed that

> As far as the influence of the Puritan outlook extended . . . it favoured the development of a rational bourgeois economic life; it was the most important, and above all the only consistent, influence in the development of that life. It stood at the cradle of the modern economic man.

(*The Protestant Ethic and the Spirit of Capitalism*, p.174)

In his highly influential treatise on *The Structure of Social Action* Talcott Parsons claims to identify five stages to Weber's proof of this claim. Thus Parsons argues that Weber establishes

1 that modern capitalism has 'empirically associated with it a set of values' (i.e. the spirit of capitalism)
2 that there is a statistical tendency for 'Protestants to outnumber Catholics in the ownership and leadership of capitalistic enterprise'
3 that there is 'a "congruence" on the "meaningful" level between . . . the spirit of capitalism and the ethics of the ascetic branches of Protestantism'
4 that within the Protestant faith 'there is a gradual transition from a religious position . . . to one which yielded direct ethical justification of acquisitive activities'
5 that in other parts of the world where modern capitalism did not spontaneously emerge 'the "economic ethic" of the dominant religious tradition concerned was directly antagonistic to such a development' (from pp.511–13)

Of course whether or not Weber did establish these points is open to dispute. However, if Weber was correct in his assertion that ideal factors shaped the development of modern capitalism it has far reaching implications, and Weber's thesis remains one of the most serious challenges ever mounted against the materialist conception of history.

Question 37
Church, sect and denomination: what are the differences? are sects necessarily short-lived?

A church is a conservative organisation that claims a monopoly of religious truth and seeks to enforce this by dominating the people. It often forms a political alliance with the State and a fully developed church, like the medieval Catholic Church, enforces its authority by the persecution of those regarded as heretics. To maintain their hold over the people churches are organised into a sacred hierarchy. This consists of a series of holy offices, and spiritual power is seen as passing down the hierarchy from the pontiff through the priesthood to the laity.

The priests perpetuate the traditions of the church and regulate religious ritual and belief. They are paid professionals and their status as representatives of a sacred power is emphasised by their separation from the laity and is marked by dress, insignia and restrictions on their conduct. Since the church is regarded as the only route to salvation great emphasis is placed upon observance of its sacraments. These celebrate crucial events occurring in the past and the church teaches that it is the present manifestation of those events.

In contrast to churches, which come to terms with the secular order, sects often turn their backs on it. These are small inward-looking groups which often reject the values of the wider society. In their place sects, like the Jehovah's Witnesses, seek to create a blameless church consisting only of believers personally called by God. Sects, therefore, do not attempt to dominate the world. A common attitude is one of renunciation. This involves intense commitment to the life of the sect and the severing of worldly ties.

The life of a sect depends upon the active involvement of its members. Leaders tend to be those who show the most zeal. Their authority comes from their personal example exhibited through a life devoted to God. This is seen as the way of salvation and religious sacraments, if not rejected altogether, are regarded as relatively unimportant. This is because sects are frequently millenarian movements and for the members the crucial event is seen as happening in the future. Their lives are regarded as a preparation for it.

Denominations normally evolve out of churches and sects. For example, the Church of England, though officially a church, adopts a tolerant attitude towards other faiths that is untypical of the pure church form. Also Methodism, though originally a sect, has relaxed the stringent self-discipline once expected of the members. Although denominations can draw their membership from all social classes their tolerant attitude makes them particularly attractive to the middle classes and it is from these strata that they draw their greatest support.

In most denominations there is some division between the clergy and the laity but there is also an emphasis on democratic participation. Lay preachers are sometimes allowed, the clergy is not always distinguished by special insignia and part-time helpers are encouraged. This spirit of compromise is also carried into the sphere of religious practice. Though the sacraments are regarded as important, emphasis is also placed upon personal devotion. Denominations thus accept that there is more than one route to salvation and individuals should follow their own path.

In *The Social Sources of Denominationalism* H. Richard Niebuhr explains that sects are normally born out of the attachment of disciples to a spiritual leader who opposes the worldly compromises made by existing religious bodies. The commitment of the followers, forged out of conflict and at the risk of martyrdom, manifests itself in an intense upsurge of religious feeling. However, over time the social composition of the sect changes and Niebuhr argued that this leads to a waning of religious enthusiasm and the transformation of the sect's revolutionary message so that it comes increasingly to resemble those institutions that it began by opposing.

According to Niebuhr two main social processes are involved. First, there is the arrival of a second generation of members. Their connection with the sect is primarily based upon family ties and their religious fervour is likely to be less than that of the founding members. Second, there are the effects of economic success. Niebuhr argued that sects normally impose a strict moral code upon their members. One consequence is that the members are more likely to achieve upward mobility. As their social standing increases they find their isolation more difficult to maintain. The extreme teachings are gradually dropped and the sect is reintegrated with mainstream values as a denomination.

There is evidence to suggest that some sects do follow the path outlined by Niebuhr. For example, Methodism began amongst the poor. However, it has evolved into a largely middle class organisation and adapted its teachings to suit the changed social circumstances of its members. There is also some support for Niebuhr's argument in the ideas of Max Weber. He emphasised that many sects are originated by a charismatic founder. Charisma means 'the gift of grace' and followers are bound to charismatic leaders by a belief in their exceptional powers. If the sect is to survive when the prophet who was the original inspiration dies, it must transform the authority once vested in the leader into a permanent routine structure.

However, Weber's argument refers only to the type of legitimate authority within organisations and the mere fact that sects are inevitably forced to develop a permanent structure does not mean that they always compromise on original principles. Religious organisations such as the Plymouth Brethren (founded 1827), the Salvation Army (1878), the Jehovah's Witnesses (1881) and Christian Science (1898) retain an essentially sectarian character. In addition Bryan Wilson has shown that second generation members are in some cases even more committed than the founders.

These exceptions suggest that the social processes involved in the development of sects are more complex than Niebuhr supposed. The main reason is that sects differ in terms of their answer to the question 'What shall we do to be saved?' Sects that stress evangelism will be forced to make contact with non-members and risk the dilution of original principles. However, sects that believe in the imminent end of the world often view the wider society with suspicion and insist upon separating sect members from outsiders. These internal differences help explain why there is no inevitable route from sect to denomination. Whilst some sects have followed the path of religious compromise others have preserved their isolation and retained their intolerant attitudes.

Commentary

The distinction between church and sect stems from the writings of Max Weber and was developed by Weber's contemporary Ernst Troelsch in his book *The Social Teaching of the Christian Church*. According to Weber the basic difference between the two lies in their principles of membership. Thus membership of a church is normally compulsory with infants being admitted at, or soon after, birth and the sacraments being administered to the just and the unjust alike. In contrast membership of a sect is voluntary and the sect consists of a community of personal believers who submit to a self-imposed discipline and reject all those who are regarded as unworthy. Summing up the differences between the two Troelsch wrote

> The church is that type of organisation which is overwhelmingly con-servative, which to a certain extent accepts the secular order and dominates the masses; in principle, therefore, it is universal, that is it desires to cover the whole life of humanity. The sects, on the other hand, are comparatively small groups; they aspire after inward perfection and they aim at a direct personal fellowship between the members of each group. From the very beginning, therefore, they are forced to organise themselves in small groups, and to renounce the idea of dominating the world.

(quoted in G. Hurd, *Human Societies*, pp.189–90)

However, both Weber and Troelsch derived their ideas on types of religious organisation from their studies of Christianity at the time of the Reformation and their model needs extending. This is why H. Richard Niebuhr's work is important. As Michael Hill explains

> Niebuhr broke out of this conceptual framework by arguing that in the more fluid context of American religion it was more typical for sects to develop denominational characteristics.

(*A Sociology of Religion*, p.67)

For Niebuhr denominations were the dominant type of religious organisation in a religiously pluralistic society like the US and, summing up Niebuhr's contribution to sociology, Hill states that

> his major interest was in the origin of denominationalism, and the key observation which has been credited to him by later sociologists is the way it was possible to understand the emergence out of sects of denominations, a process he attributed mainly to the increasing prosperity of sect members.' (ibid. p.59)

Question 38
Secularisation: should the concept be abandoned?

Secularisation is the process whereby religious thinking, practice, and institutions lose social significance. Although on the surface this definition seems clear enough it conceals three kinds of problem. There is first the conceptual problem of defining what religion is, second the methodological problem of comparative measurement of the strength of religious commitment, and third the theoretical problem of interpreting the social significance of religion in advanced industrial societies. In practice those who have accepted the secularisation thesis have failed to resolve these problems.

Before one can even begin to consider whether religion has declined or not one needs to know what it is that is supposed to be undergoing this process of change. This raises the question of whether it is possible to define religion objectively. Certainly there have been many attempts to do so. However, it has been argued that any attempt to define religion objectively is ultimately a value judgement. As long ago as 1905 Georg Simmel pointed out that there was no single concept that, without vagueness, could comprehend the variety of world religions whilst effectively distinguishing religion from magic and superstition on the one hand and from philosophy and pseudo-science on the other.

Although there is no general agreement concerning the nature of religion this has not prevented some sociologists from asserting that it is in decline. In practice these sociologists have frequently adopted a conventional definition of religion. For example, this is Bryan Wilson's approach. In his article 'How religious are we?' (*New Society*, 27 October 1977) he uses statistics to show that regular church attendance, membership of religious denominations, Sunday schools, baptisms and confirmations have all declined. However, as Roland Robertson has pointed out in 'Society Today' No. 23 (*New Society*, 15 December 1977), religion may be studied in at least two ways, firstly as a particular kind of activity (such as going to church) and secondly as a set of cultural attitudes (such as belief in God). In relation to attitudes the evidence is not clear cut and the mere fact that statistics show a decline in participation in organised religion in Britain does not prove secularisation.

This is clarified by David Martin's research. In *A Sociology of English Religion* he argues that those who hold the view that secularisation is a real process have to show that the role of religion today is much less important than in a 'truly' religious society. Evidence on Victorian England, often regarded as a model of religiosity by today's standards, does not always bear out the popular image. As early as 1845 Engels was commenting on the indifference.to religion amongst the urban working class, and the 1851 census confirms this. Despite the fact that attendance at church would for many be obligatory for social rather than religious reasons the census showed an attendance of only 36 per cent.

Just as it is easy to overestimate the importance of religion in the past so also it is easy to underestimate its significance today. Conventional institutional forms of devotion are only one way of expressing religious sentiments and the decline here may be partly due to the growth of a more personal faith. Interview data quoted by David Martin shows that 80 to 90 per cent of Britons admit to a belief in God and 60 per cent have at least some belief in prayer. Meanwhile a growing minority is turning to religious sects. These have proliferated since the 1960s and, if anything, the evidence seems to indicate that it is the authority of the established churches and not the belief in God that is threatened.

In the US the overwhelming majority also claim to believe in God. Furthermore in the US there is no evidence of a decline in participation in organised religion. Nonetheless William Herberg claims to identify secularisation within the main US denominations. These have increasingly compromised with the materialism of US culture and become a virtual celebration of the US way of life. However, in moving the emphasis onto what he sees as the declining religious content of the church's message Herberg seems to be saying that full churches in the US are as much evidence of secularisation as empty ones in Britain.

With so much ambiguity it is not surprising that there is a variety of interpretations of the social significance of religion in modern society. Some early functionalists saw religion as in decline because it had lost its functions. Neo-Marxists like Louis Althusser have interpreted its ideological role in capitalist society as increasingly usurped by education. However, the most important theoretical contribution to our understanding of the changed role of religion is Weber's view that Protestantism led to 'the disenchantment of the world'. Weber argued that one effect of the Protestant's belief in an absolutely transcendental God who did not interfere with either the laws of nature or individual human destinies was to promote a scientific attitude.

A number of sociologists in both Britain and the US have developed Weber's ideas. They have argued that in modern society religious beliefs have declined because they have been overtaken by scientific theories whilst magical attempts to solve human problems have been discredited by modern technology. However, science cannot answer ultimate questions and technology has proved powerless to eliminate human suffering. These problems remain as relevant today as they always were and, as Talcott Parsons emphasises, religious solutions retain their significance. Furthermore, it would be rash to suppose that science has displaced belief in magic. The continued popularity of astrology, palmistry, folk superstitions and faith healing shows that many members of society still feel a need for the reassurance that such beliefs provide.

This evidence on the persistence of the most outlandish faiths is indicative of the continual human quest for certainty. This is the most important fact because absolute certainty transcends the bounds of empirical knowledge. However, it is a matter of opinion which non-empirical beliefs should be designated as religions. This is why the secularisation debate has become bogged down in confusion and, as David Martin has argued in *The Religious and the Secular*, the concept might as well be removed from the sociological vocabulary altogether. This seems like good advice for there is certainly no scientific value in retaining it if the debate is merely going to act as a forum for atheists and Christians to put a pseudo-scientific gloss on their squabbles over ultimate values.

Commentary

The secularisation thesis ultimately hangs on what is meant by religion. According to Durkheim

> A religion is a unified system of beliefs and practices relative to sacred things, that is to say, things set apart and forbidden — beliefs and practices which unite into one single moral community called a church, all those who adhere to them.
>
> (*The Elementary Forms of the Religious Life*, p.47)

However, Roland Robertson criticises this definition for being too vague and for letting in phenomena not conventionally regarded as religion. Instead he proposes that

> Religious culture is that set of beliefs and symbols pertaining to a distinction between an empirical and a super-empirical transcendental reality; the affairs of the empirical being subordinated in significance to the non-empirical.
>
> (*The Sociological Interpretation of Religion*, p.47)

However, this is equally, if not more, vague. It seems also to exclude Confucianism. Although conventionally regarded as a religion its moral teachings do not depend upon belief in a supernatural reality. Peter Worsley argues that

> what distinguishes religious belief from other kinds of social belief is that, in some way or other . . . it refers to, and looks for validation in, a dimension beyond the empirical-technical realm of action.
>
> (*The Trumpet Shall Sound*, p.311)

This differs from Robertson's definition in that whereas Robertson refers to different types of reality Worsley refers to different types of proof. However, this is just as unsatisfactory because the definition does not entitle us to distinguish between religion and philosophy and metaphysics. As Georg Simmel pointed out

> The ambiguity which surrounds the origin and nature of religion will never be removed so long as we insist upon approaching the problem as one for which a single word will be an 'open sesame'.
>
> (quoted in Peter E. Glasner, *The Sociology of Secularisation*, p.12)

Chapter 11

General and theoretical questions

Several of the introductory sections to previous chapters have been given over to an explanation of the basic ideas of various sociological perspectives. Many of the essays go on to apply those perspectives in the analysis of substantive issues, and in the course of the analyses some criticisms of sociological perspectives were made. This chapter will outline the major criticisms in a systematic way.

A useful starting point is Percy S. Cohen's distinction between logical, substantive and ideological criticisms. Logical criticisms are to do with the structure of an explanation. They are criticisms of how an explanation works. Substantive criticisms are to do with the characteristics attributed to the object of explanation. They are criticisms of what an explanation says social phenomena are like. Ideological criticisms are to do with the relationships between explanations and human values or group interests. They are criticisms of the moral and political implications of sociological theories. In the account that follows the major criticisms of functionalism, Marxism, conflict theory, symbolic interactionism and ethnomethodology are organised under these headings.

Criticisms of functionalism

Two logical arguments against functionalism are, first, that functionalist explanations are teleological and, second, that they imply the reification of the social world.

A theory is teleological if it purports to explain the existence of something in terms of its beneficial consequences. An example of a teleological explanation in sociology would be to make the claim that religion exists because it contributes to social order. The objection to explanations like this is that they treat an effect as a cause. As Cohen puts it 'It is as though one were to say: X produces Y, therefore the occurrence of Y, which is desirable, must explain the occurrence of X. Critics rightly argue that this type of explanation defies the laws of logic, for one thing cannot be the cause of another if it succeeds it in time' (*Modern Social Theory*, pp.47−8).

Reification is the attribution of 'reality' to abstractions. Candidates for the charge of reification include the organic analogy and the view that society is a social system. According to Weber 'this functional frame of reference is convenient for the purpose of practical illustration and for provisional orientation. In these respects it is not only useful but indispensable. But at the same time if its cognitive value is overestimated and its concepts illegitimately "reified" it can be highly dangerous' (*The Theory of Social and Economic Organisation*, p.103). The danger that Weber was referring to is the danger of conceiving of society as if it has a life of its own and it is often argued that functionalism succumbs to this error when it subordinates the analysis of individual meaning to the collective point of view.

The principle substantive objection to functionalism is that it presents a very one-sided view of what social reality is like. This criticism has been repeatedly levelled against Talcott Parsons' description of the social system. For example, Parsons emphasises the importance of normative order, the existence of common values and the need for integration of system parts. He neglects enforced constraint, opposing interests and structural sources of conflict. Overall Parsons' account is often criticised for its 'static bias'. It focuses almost entirely on the social processes that are alleged to contribute to social equilibrium and has little to say about the causes of change.

On the other hand the charge that functionalism as a whole ignores conflict, change and coercion is not strictly accurate. For example, functionalists have seen defective socialisation as a cause of deviance, malintegration of system parts as a cause of conflict, dysfunctional consequences of institutionalised behaviour as a cause of instability, and structural differentiation as a cause of change. However, it is one thing to have an explanation, it is quite another to convince others that it is true. The real criticism is thus more to do with the flimsy accounts functionalists give than with what they have neglected altogether.

Ideologically functionalism is often criticised as a conservative point of view. The argument behind this is that since functional analysis proceeds by examining the way various institutions and processes contribute to the survival of society it seems to imply that what exists does so for the good of the whole. The classic example of this is the functionalist theory of stratification. This claims to prove that inequality is indispensable to the functioning of any complex society. Naturally this is attractive to those who stand to gain from the unequal distribution of power and reward because it implies that to change things fundamentally would be harmful to us all. However, critics argue that what the functionalist offers as an explanation of inequality is really a defence of the status quo.

Criticisms of Marxism

Marxism is sometimes alleged to be logically invalid because it rests upon economic determinism. For example, Weber argued that from the point of view of the materialist conception of history the 'need for a causal explanation of an historical event is never satisfied until somewhere or somehow economic causes are shown (or seem) to be operative' (*The Methodology of the Social Sciences*, p.68). To which Weber replies 'The explanation of everything by economic causes alone is never exhaustive in any sense whatsoever in any sphere of cultural phenomena not even in the "economic" sphere itself' (ibid. p.71). However, there is considerable ambiguity about whether Marx was an economic determinist. Certainly there is much in his work to support this point of view. On the other hand Marx himself sometimes attributes causal efficacy to non-economic factors. This has led to all kinds of disputes about what Marx really meant and whether there is one Marx or two.

Another objection to Marxism is the objection aimed against Marx's belief that the laws of capitalist production work 'with iron necessity towards inevitable results' (*Capital*, Volume I, p.8) and that by laying bare those laws it is possible to prophesy the future. Karl Popper calls this method of reasoning historicism and he sums up his logical refutation of it in five simple statements. First, 'The course of human history is strongly influenced by the growth of human knowledge'. Second, 'We cannot predict, by rational or scientific methods, the future growth of our scientific knowledge'. Third, 'We cannot, therefore, predict the future course of human history'. Fourth, 'This means that we must reject the possibility of a theoretical history'. Fifth, 'The fundamental aim of historicist methods . . . is therefore misconceived' (*The Poverty of Historicism*, pp.v–vi).

The principle substantive criticism of Marxism is that Marx's predictions have not come true. Marx predicted the increasing impoverishment of the proletariat, the polarisation of social classes, the spread of class consciousness and the intensification of class conflict. However, societies such as modern Britain have changed in a very different way. According to Dahrendorf what has actually happened is the separation of ownership and control, the growing heterogeneity of labour, the rise of the middle classes, increasing social mobility, the spread of social equality and the institutionalisation of class conflict. For Dahrendorf these developments 'justify speaking of Marx's theory of class as being falsified by empirical observations' (*Class and Class Conflict in an Industrial Society*, p.36).

Finally Marxism is often criticised as left wing ideology. Marxists reply that capitalism is an evil and exploitative system which will inevitably be replaced by 'a higher phase of communist society'. For Marx such a society would be free from class divisions forever and without the need for class control the State would wither away. However, the problem with this is that in practice communist societies have not developed in this way. Furthermore, in these societies there are substantial economic inequalities too. If by communism one means a society which can 'inscribe on its banners: From each according to his ability, to each according to his needs' (Marx, *Critique of the Gotha Programme*, p.18), then there is not and never has been a truly communist society. Of course critics of Marxism doubt whether such a society is possible anyway and they suggest that those who believe otherwise are in pursuit of an illusion.

Criticisms of conflict theory

Conflict theory was popularised by Dahrendorf. In a series of books and articles written in the 1950s and 1960s he proposed a 'conflict model' as an alternative to the prevailing 'consensus model' of the functionalists. In order to give this conflict model an aura of legitimacy it has since been invested with a history and both Marx and Weber are now often retrospectively interpreted as conflict theorists. One logical objection to this is that it involves writing history backwards. Neither Marx nor Weber referred to themselves as conflict theorists and to reinterpret their works selectively in this light is both to distort and to undervalue them.

As to the two models themselves Dahrendorf argues that they can be reduced to four basic assumptions. Thus he argues that the consensus model assumes that every society is a relatively stable structure, that the elements of this structure are integrated with each other, that every element makes a contribution to the system as a whole and that every functioning social structure is based on a consensus of values amongst its members. Dahrendorf's alternative assumptions are that social change is ubiquitous, that social conflict is ubiquitous, that every element in a society makes a contribution to change and disintegration and that every society is based on the coercion of some of its members by others.

To this the following objections have been made. First, that Dahrendorf's statement of the structural functionalist point of view is not just a simplification but a caricature. Second, that it is possible for a society to display in varying degrees some of the characteristics of both models and it is therefore unprofitable to think in terms of either conflict or consensus. Third, that the two models are not mutually exclusive; as Cohen puts it, 'The two models are not genuine alternatives: to say that a room is half-full is not to deny that it is half-empty' (*Modern Social Theory*, p.170).

A further criticism of conflict theory is that whilst it claims to be a radical departure from Marxism and functionalism it is in fact largely built out of a combination of bits of both. From Marx comes the substantive interest in change, conflict and coercion rather than in stability, co-operation and agreement. From functionalism comes a view of sociology as a discipline based on abstract models of what society is like rather than on causal analysis of concrete historical processes. The logical objection to forced amalgamations like this was stated by Weber long ago. He argued that 'we must oppose to the utmost the widespread view that scientific "objectivity" is achieved by weighing the various evaluations against one another and making a "statesman-like" compromise' (*The Methodology of the Social Sciences*, p.10).

Substantive criticisms of conflict theory are often levelled against Dahrendorf's argument that we now live in a post-capitalist society, an argument presented in *Class and Class Conflict in an Industrial Society*. Here Dahrendorf claimed that six major changes have occurred in western industrial nations since Marx was writing and that these changes justify talking of 'the supersedence of capitalism'. These changes (previously mentioned as substantive criticisms of Marx and discussed in detail in a variety of the essays in this book) are regarded by Dahrendorf as 'well known facts of development'. However, the critics have been almost unanimous in their rejection of his 'empirical' refutation of Marx. For example John Rex argues that it is here that 'Dahrendorf's deficiencies and biases become most obvious' and he suggests that 'the most effective criticism which could be made of Dahrendorf would be to write a better book which dealt with the problems which he raises, showing greater respect for empirical evidence' (*New Left Review* No. 2).

Although conflict theory is often confused with Marxism it is ultimately on ideological grounds that one must separate the two. In brief Marxism is a doctrine that preaches the need for revolutionary action, whereas conflict theory is nearer to a social democratic point of view. What this implies is summed up by Ralf Miliband. He argues that 'the hidden assumption' behind a conflict perspective 'is that conflict does not, or need not, run very deep; that it can be "managed" by the exercise of reason and good will, and a readiness to compromise and agree. On this view, politics is not civil war conducted by other means but a constant process of bargaining and accommodation' (*Marxism and Politics*, p.17).

Criticism of symbolic interactionism

Symbolic interactionism manages to avoid some of the logical objections levelled against structural sociologies that start from a consensus or a conflict point of view. To begin with it views society as the construction of its members and avoids the reification of the social world. Second, it focuses on social action and treats it as an object of investigation in its own right, rather than as a product of the social system. Third, it emphasises that in order to explain action one has to understand its meaning. Action is therefore interpreted in its own terms rather than as determined by forces over which the individual has no control. However, although symbolic interactionism recognises the need to interpret action from the subjective point of view there is still the problem of judging whether the interpretation is true.

The interactionist response to this problem has been to recommend that sociologists immerse themselves in the experience of others and by empathetic intuition seek to reconstruct their point of view. This means that in practice the psychological process whereby knowledge is discovered also acts as the main guarantee of its theoretical value. However, logicians allege that this is unsatisfactory. For example, it is one thing to say 'I know what you mean' and to feel genuinely that it is so. It is quite another to be able to demonstrate the empirical adequacy of our conceptualisation of another's point of view. Intuitionist theories of knowledge confound the two. As Weber put it 'They confuse the question of the psychological conditions responsible for the genesis of knowledge with the completely different question concerning the logical "content" of knowledge and its empirical "validity"' (*Roscher and Knies*, p.170).

Take, for example, Erving Goffman's book *Asylums*. It purports to be an account from the patient's point of view of what it is like to enter a mental institution. However, the appeal of Goffman's study of how the patient feels lies in the sympathy he is able to evoke in the reader rather than in the comparative empirical analysis of alternative points of view. In fact his study has more in common with a dramatised documentary than a scientific investigation. It can seem plausible. It may even be true. But critics complain that what Goffman offers us is essentially an artistic reconstruction of what it possibly means to be a patient and that the relationship between this aesthetic construct and the actual causal processes operative in any particular context remains unknown.

Substantive objections to symbolic interactionism centre on the allegation that it is at best only a partial explanation. In general terms this objection has been made by Merton in his criticism of Thomas's 'subjectivism'. Thomas asserted that 'If men define situations as real, they are real in their consequences'. Merton accepts that this is true. However, he claims that there is more to social life than actors' definitions and that the Thomas Theorem 'leads us astray by neglecting social, demographic, economic, technological, ecological, and other objective constraints upon human beings' (*Contemporary Social Problems*, p.22).

More specifically interactionists are often accused of failing to examine the relationships between meaningful action and the social structure. This boils down to three questions to which the interactionists are alleged to provide no proper answer. First, why do social actors make the decisions that they do? Second, where do meanings come from? Third, how is interaction shaped by the nature and distribution of power in society as a whole? In relation to the sociological study of crime the corresponding specific substantive criticisms are as follows. First, that interactionists ignore the initial motivation to commit a crime. Second, that they neglect to analyse possible relationships between types of crime and types of social environment. Third, that they fail to relate the role of agencies of social control to the class structure as a whole. As Anthony Giddens explains, the interpretive sociologies (amongst which he counts symbolic interactionism) recognise that society is 'a skilled accomplishment of its members' but have 'not managed successfully to reconcile such an emphasis with the equally essential thesis . . . that if men make society, they do not do so merely under conditions of their own choosing' (*New Rules of Sociological Method*, p.126).

Ideologically Howard Becker claims that 'interactionist theories look (and are) rather left'. Becker outlines this point of view in his paper 'Whose Side are We On?' Here he argues that it is impossible for social scientists to conduct research 'uncontaminated by personal and political sympathies' and that all sociological work must be written from either the standpoint of superiors or that of subordinates. The standpoint Becker adopts is what Alvin Gouldner calls an 'underdog identification' (*For Sociology*, p.29). That is to say Becker's sympathies lie with the deviant who is labelled by the agencies of social control.

However, critics have expressed doubts as to whether this is as radical as it appears to be. For example, Alvin Gouldner argues that although 'Becker seems to be adopting the position of the outcast . . . he is also embracing the position of "enlightened" but no less respectable liberalism toward the outcast. Becker appears to be taking up arms against society on behalf of the underdog. Actually he is taking up arms against the ineffectuality, callousness, or capriciousness of the caretakers that society has appointed to administer the mess it has created' (ibid. p.40). In other words labelling theory (and to some extent this applies to other brands of interactionism) is mainly a critique of the professions and the organisations they work for. It stops short of a critique of society as a whole.

Criticisms of ethnomethodology

The major logical objection to ethnomethodology is that carried to extremes it implies that nothing is ever knowable at all. This criticism has been made by Anthony Giddens. He argues that 'the aim of ethnomethodology is to make the accountability of social practices itself accountable'. However, 'ethnomethodology is itself an artful practice that is made accountable by its practitioners' (ibid. pp.38, 41). Hence it should be possible to take the same attitude towards ethnomethodology as ethnomethodology takes towards accounts and so on ad infinitum. This is known as an infinite regress and ultimately it is self-defeating.

Even some ethnomethodologists seem to acknowledge that this is so and they sometimes adopt a completely relativistic position from which it is alleged that no accounts, not even the accounts of natural science, have a special claim to validity. However, if ethnomethodology (which of course is an account) cannot have, or even claim, intellectual value one is entitled to ask 'What value does it have?' To this ethnomethodology gives no clear reply.

Substantive criticisms of ethnomethodology are similar to the criticisms of symbolic interactionism but, if anything, they apply more forcefully. To begin with, ethnomethodology is mainly to do with how members construct their social world. It does not tell us why they act the way they do. In Giddens' words, ethnomethodology 'cuts off the description of acts and communications from any analysis of purposive or motivated conduct' (ibid. p.40). Second, the social structure (which has a shadowy existence in symbolic interactionism) is utterly dissolved. It is now no more than an appearance of order. Third, ethnomethodology is often accused of failing to recognise the centrality of power. As Giddens puts it 'The production of an "orderly" or "accountable" world cannot merely be understood as collaborative work carried out by peers: meanings that are made to count express asymmetries of power' (ibid. p.53).

Ideologically ethnomethodology appears at first sight to have no point of view. However, commenting on the implications of Garfinkel's sociology C. Robert Freeman argues that 'the implicit nihilism of his position encourages other ethnomethodologists to abandon all notion of truth and falsity' (Jack Douglas, editor, *Introduction to the Sociologies of Everyday Life*, p.144). In philosophy nihilism is the doctrine that nothing is real and nothing is true. However, it has another meaning too. It is the name of a branch of anarchism and this also seems to connect with the ethnomethodologists' point of view. Thus, as regards ideas, there is anarchy because we have no valid grounds for deciding what is true. As regards research, there is anarchy because Garfinkel creates disruption in order to study the ways members of society produce accounts that create an appearance of order. Critics have expressed doubts as to whether this is a fruitful approach or a responsible thing to do.

This section only outlines some possible points of departure from which to criticise sociological perspectives. Beyond these points of departure are further arguments and counter-arguments and other ways of both attacking and defending a point of view. In practice this means that one can use sociological reasoning to justify adopting any one of a variety of positions on major issues in sociology and that ultimately deciding on the value of different perspectives is up to you.

Question 39
The organic analogy: what are its implications for sociology?

Comparisons between society and an organism involve conceiving of society as having the same kind of unity as a living being and as being subject to similar laws of change. Elements of this view go back at least as far as classical Greek philosophy but in its modern form the organic analogy stems from the nineteenth-century English sociologist Herbert Spencer. He was amongst the more extreme of modern organicists and his views influenced a variety of sociologists and anthropologists including Emile Durkheim and A.R. Radcliffe-Brown.

The point of view of the organicists is best explained through the specific similarities they see between societies and living beings. For example, Spencer pointed out that both organisms and societies develop over time and as they evolve they increase in complexity. Furthermore, just as complex life forms are made up of millions of individual cells specialising in and adapted to specific activities so societies are made up of individuals who as role players have a similar relationship to the social whole. Spencer made much of this comparison between cells and individuals pointing out that whilst they both die the organisms and the societies of which they are a part persist because each contains a mechanism for producing new cells or people.

Radcliffe-Brown developed this analogy by arguing that societies, like life forms, depend on necessary conditions of existence which must be met if they are to survive. He saw the internal organisation of both as a reflection of the way these needs are catered for and claimed that the life of society should be conceived of as the functioning of the structure. This implies that there must be some degree of functional integration between the parts of society, and Radcliffe-Brown saw this as the basic premise of any systematic sociology.

Functionalists apply this point of view when describing how the social structure works. The basic principle that they follow is to interpret the characteristics of social institutions in terms of their contribution to the continuity of society as a whole. These institutions are sometimes even compared to the organs of a living body and are seen as adapted to perform specific functions just as the heart, liver and lungs are. In line with this, functionalists have interpreted stratification as a mechanism for ensuring that important positions are occupied by the most able, education as a means of providing a trained achievement orientated workforce and the family as a 'factory' socialising the young into the norms and values of society. However, just as in a living body the organs must be compatible with each other so in society the various subsystems need to be integrated. For example, the structural isolation of the family is often interpreted by functionalists as beneficial to society. It fits the needs of a complex social organism in which schools act as the proving ground for ability and meritocratic principles govern role allocation.

However, one disadvantage of this analogy is that it is all too easy to take it too far and from arguing correctly that there are certain similarities between societies and organisms go on to claim that there is an identity between the two. This was Spencer's mistake and in his *Principles of Sociology* he announced that 'society *is* an organism'. However, even Spencer was forced to recognise differences. These include the fact that organisms have clearly defined physical boundaries whereas societies do not. For example, it is impossible to say precisely where the influence of a society's culture ends. It certainly cannot be assumed to be coextensive with its political frontier. Also the relative positions of cells in a living body are mostly fixed, but in society individuals are mostly free to move from place to place and to adopt a variety of statuses and roles.

In addition to the specific differences there are fundamental objections too. For example, the normal state of an organism is that the parts work together to maintain the life of the whole. Applying this in sociology would mean assuming that the normal state of society is equilibrium and that whatever disrupts peaceful co-operation is pathological. However, this implies a preference for social order and functionalism is often regarded as a conservative perspective which tends to justify existing institutional arrangements implicitly by assuming that the various parts of society function for the common good. Furthermore, there are also objections to the functionalist theory of change. By analogy with change in biological species functionalists have often been led to conceive of change in society as a gradual evolutionary process. However, this is inadequate because it neglects structural contradictions between the parts of society and fails to account for the fact that social change is often sudden, violent and revolutionary.

The organic analogy also has serious implications for individual freedom since this tends to disappear in the works of those who adopt this point of view. Just as cells in a living organism are genetically programmed to perform specific activities so functionalists see role players as programmed to behave in ways that correspond to the needs of society. In this scheme of things society takes precedence over individual actors. They are pictured as robots or as puppets whose own reasons for acting are regarded as unimportant in comparison to the collective or holistic point of view.

This determinist perspective on social action involves the reification of the social world. Reification occurs whenever an idea is given the characteristics of a thing and social facts, which are ultimately aggregates of individual events, are reified when they are treated as if they were distinct and separate entities in their own right. By relying on the organic analogy this is precisely the trap into which some functionalists fall. They convert society into a real system which is interpreted as if it has a life of its own and is able to think and act for itself. The result is a distorted image of both social reality and individual action, an image that overemphasises the integration of parts and neglects the subjective point of view.

Commentary

Spencer argued that

> So completely is society organised on the same system as an individual being that we may perceive something more than mere analogy between them; the same definition of life applies to both. Only when one sees that the transformation passed through during the growth, maturity, and decay of a society conforms to the same principles as do the transformations passed through by aggregates of all orders, inorganic and organic, is there reached the concept of sociology as a science.

(quoted in N. Timasheff, *Sociological Theory*, revised edition, p.356)

Durkheim was influenced by Spencer and he equates 'function' with 'the general needs of the social organism'. However, Durkheim did not make direct use of the organic analogy.

Radcliffe-Brown was influenced by both Spencer and Durkheim. In relation to biology he claimed that

> As the word function is here being used the life of an organism is conceived as the functioning of its structure. It is through and by the continuity of the functioning of an organism that the continuity of the structure is preserved. If we consider any recurrent part of the life process, such as respiration, digestion, etc., its function is the part it plays in, the contribution it makes to, the life of the organism as a whole.

In a similar way Radcliffe-Brown argued that in sociology

> The social life of the community is here defined as the functioning of the social structure. The function of any recurrent activity, such as the punishment of a crime, or a funeral ceremony, is the part it plays in the social life as a whole and therefore the contribution it makes to the maintenance of the structural continuity.

(quoted in L.A. Coser and B. Rosenberg, *Sociological Theory*, third edition, pp.624–5)

Finally, notice how Radcliffe-Brown relates the concepts of 'structure' and 'function'. From here it is but a short step to Talcott Parsons' version of 'structural functionalism'.

Question 40
The definition of the situation: what are its implications for sociology?

So far as we know the behaviour of animals is governed by genetic or environmental stimuli. From a natural scientific point of view it is explained in stimulus-response terms. This involves seeing behaviour as determined by forces over which the individual organism has no control. Scientific knowledge of what those forces are is inferred from the scientific study of their effects. In this way the naturalist seeks to establish causal laws and by these means account for behaviour which is not intrinsically meaningful. However, in the words of Thomas 'If men define situations as real, they are real in their consequences'. This implies that human action is different and that in order to infer its causes one first needs to understand why people choose to act the way they do.

The important point is that members of society are both conscious and self-conscious beings, and, to a large extent, their actions are a product of the will. For the most part they do not therefore simply react automatically to physiological stimuli. They act because they have a point of view. This implies that the premise of any meaningfully valid orientation to experience is the individual's belief about what constitutes appropriate conduct in that particular context. This definition of the situation will, from the actor's standpoint, be normatively correct. However, it need not be empirically true. It thus follows that the real consequences of action are not necessarily those anticipated by the acting participants. Therefore, in order to explain the relationship between motive and behaviour one needs to analyse action from the subjective point of view.

A classic piece of research which illustrates these points is Weber's *The Protestant Ethic and the Spirit of Capitalism*. In this study Weber explained how the early Calvinists believed in an absolutely transcendental and all powerful God whose wisdom surpassed human understanding. They also thought that God had predestined all human souls to either eternal damnation or salvation. Although things pertaining to the flesh were regarded as irretrievably lost in sin and deserving only of death, the Calvinists believed that an elect few, amongst whom they hoped to be counted, would be saved through God's divine grace.

This system of ideas embraced a definition of the situation with practical implications for conduct. Since direct communion with God was regarded as impossible Calvinists were opposed to all forms of mysticism. This was reinforced by their belief that people should labour to perform God's will. So monasticism was rejected in favour of an active ethic aimed at achieving success in their chosen callings. However, this was not without dangers and temptations and Calvinists condemned all worldly indulgences and idle pleasures that might distract people from their duty to work for the increase of God's glory.

The result was that sincere Calvinists led an austere life, and their belief that God had ordered the world for all eternity led to their rejecting superstition, magic and idolatry. In addition Calvinists believed that labour was not a punishment for sin but the epitome of positive value. Their faith in rationality, hard work and frugality helped many Calvinists to accumulate wealth and Weber demonstrated that as their social circumstances changed it fostered the growth of a practical ethic which made a virtue out of making money. This unanticipated yet real consequence was the spirit of capitalism.

Both Thomas and Weber emphasised the subjectivity of social phenomena. However, social reality is intersubjective too. That is to say the definitions of the situation adopted in particular contexts are not created or sustained by isolated and self-sufficient individuals but arise out of social relationships with others. Thus socially valid meanings are always shared and the freedom of individuals to sustain a private world view is limited by public orders of meaning that impose typical expectations concerning conduct and belief. Furthermore, in relation to those expectations the distribution of power is crucial because some individuals and groups are in a stronger position to get their definition of the situation accepted as valid.

A piece of research that illustrates this is Erving Goffman's study *Stigma*. Goffman explains that stigma refers to a class of attributes that are regarded as discrediting. The blemish can be physical, as in the case of the handicapped, or moral, as in the case of those who have a criminal record. However, in both cases what is distinctive is that those who do not possess the stigma tend to regard the stigmatised as less than fully human. This practical attitude is also likely to be rationalised in various ways and the beliefs combined to form a stereotype that acts as a framework for interaction.

Goffman argues that the central feature of stigma is the acceptance by the stigmatised of many of the beliefs that others have about them. This is because in practice it is very difficult to resist psychologically the effects of labelling. Unable to get themselves accepted as normal in the wider society, the stigmatised are reduced to techniques of stigma management and this can set in motion a self-fulfilling prophecy in which the stigmatised become more like the kind of people they were originally thought to be.

If anything the power dimension is even more noticeable in total institutions. These are organisations in which individuals are cut off from the wider society and for an appreciable period of time are required to live under an enforced regime. Prisons and mental hospitals are examples of such institutions. Deprived of the conventional props that served to sustain their former self-image inmates are forced to conform outwardly to the official definition of themselves as criminal or insane and sometimes end up accepting this as their true identity.

Goffman's research illustrates the need to study the meaningfulness of individual action in relation to patterns of normative constraint. In total institutions that constraint is at its most repressive and inmates may be physically compelled to submit to the prevailing order. However, to some extent all social relationships impose an obligation upon participants to act in ways that others regard as socially acceptable. Thus, in the words of A.L. Stinchcombe, 'People define situations, but do not define them as they please'. This implies that though action is not determined as the behaviour of organisms is, the scope for individual freedom is in practice limited by social control.

Commentary

In the Introduction to *Contemporary Social Problems* Merton criticises what he sees as the subjectivism of Weber and Thomas. There he argues that

> To correct the inbalance that comes with total subjectivism and to restore the objective component of social situations to their indispensable place we plainly need this counterpart to the Thomas Theorem:
>   And if people do not define real situations as real, they are nevertheless real in their consequences.

(fourth edition, p.22)

Merton goes on to argue that though we often say that what we do not know about cannot hurt us, this is in fact not the case. As an example Merton mentions the diseases of tuberculosis and Asiatic cholera and points out that they decimated many populations (i.e. a real consequence) before the microbiologist Robert Koch isolated the bacteria which cause them and laid the basis of subsequent treatment and control.

Merton feels that there is a lesson in this for sociology. He argues that social problems should be defined by their consequences and that these are real. However, he claims that people do not always recognise social problems for what they are. On this basis he asserts that

> It is therefore a function of sociologists to study not only manifest social problems – those widely identified in the society – but also latent social problems – those that are also at odds with current interests and values but are not generally recognised as being so. (ibid. p.13)

The difficulty with this is that though Merton claims that 'sociologists do not impose their own values upon others', in claiming to be able to recognise latent social problems objectively he already does so. The reason why this is not immediately noticeable is because it is disguised by the comparison Merton draws between sociology and biology. However, as has already been seen, there are all sorts of problems in modelling sociology on the natural sciences.

Question 41
Social system and social action: one sociology or two?

The essential difference between the sociology of the social system and the sociology of social action lies in the contrasting ways they conceptualise the relationship between individual and society. Systems theory interprets human behaviour as a reaction to external forces and sees the individual as controlled and manipulated by society. In contrast the action frame of reference stresses that action has an internal logic and sees individuals as imposing their own meaning upon experience. Today these two perspectives are realised in structural functionalism, which sees society as the cause of action, and symbolic interactionism, which sees society as the outcome.

Functionalist explanations are holistic. This means that functionalists consider that a valid explanation of individual acts and social regularities depends upon understanding how they are related as parts of a wider system. Just as the biologist claims that the parts of an organism can only be explained in terms of the functions they perform for a living being, so the functionalist interprets the parts of society in terms of their contribution to the stability and presistence of the whole. This means explanations tend to be positivist. Biology acts as a model for sociology, which is viewed as the science of the life of society.

Characteristically functionalism begins with the assumption that society has needs. The various institutions of a particular society must be adapted to meet its needs as well as being integrated with each other so that the system remains in equilibrium. This is achieved mainly by socialisation, a process through which members of society come to internalise society's values. With their personalities moulded to conform to the needs of society they willingly act out the predetermined roles that society demands. The individual is thus conceived of not merely as living in society but as created by and existing for it.

For functionalists the objective consequences of action for society (its latent function) are more important than the subjective meaning of action to actors themselves (its manifest function). This is because the actors' choices and decisions are regarded as being moulded by socialisation. Their real significance lies not in the actors' own intentions but in the functional importance of action for society. This provides the functionalists with their solution to the problem of order. Beginning from a view of human nature as basically selfish, egotistical and antisocial, functionalism views the powerful moral force of society as necessary to prevent social disorganisation and anomie. However, in the process of explaining society as a coercive and external force determining human action functionalists are inclined to picture individuals as 'cheerful robots', 'puppets', or 'cultural dopes'. It is what Dennis Wrong describes as this 'oversocialised conception of man' that is rejected by symbolic interactionism.

Interactionism is part of the humanist tradition within sociology and it emphasises that society is created out of the social relationships formed by its members. The task of sociology is not therefore seen to be to explain how action serves the needs of a pre-existing system but to explain how social structures emerge out of shared definitions of roles and concepts of personal identity. The point of view of interactionism is that people construct a social world by imposing meaning in the face of chaos. To regard society as a real system and to attribute to it needs is thus seen as reification. This is because social facts are not things, for the interactionist, but shared ideas and beliefs. Should these definitions of the situation change then the social world itself would change. The existence of society at any particular time is therefore precarious, fluid and dependent upon the values of its members.

Interactionist explanations are atomistic. This means that a valid explanation of individual action is regarded as dependent upon understanding the subjective point of view of social actors. Unlike natural scientists who work with matter that obeys natural laws, sociologists study people who are, for the most part, conscious of their own actions and the actions of others. This means that explanations of social action must be aimed at interpreting meaning by describing how actors define a situation and explaining what their motives are.

The emphasis upon explaining the motives of individuals rather than the functions of institutions means that socialisation is interpreted in a very different way. For the functionalist, individuals conform to cultural norms because they have been programmed to do so. However, interactionism views socialisation as a creative process in which the self emerges out of social relationships with others. Personal identity is learned through face-to-face contact in which individuals come to see themselves as others see them while roles are negotiated in a never ending process of self-reflection in which individuals continually improvise and adjust their behaviour to meet social expectations.

For interactionism the crucial problems are posed by the need to understand interpersonal relationships. Unlike functionalists who, in their concern with the problem of order, have been led to construct abstract models of how society works, interactionists are more concerned with the day-to-day problems of typical actors and the strategies they adopt. In the sociology of everyday life this can lead to studies of the ways in which individuals seek to project and sustain a favourable self-image. However, in practice, interactionists have been more concerned with the social construction of deviant identities and psychological consequences of labelling. These studies have included studies of mental hospital patients, drug takers and deviance in classrooms, and in all these areas the interactionist research reveals a sympathy for the underdog that contrasts with the functionalists' support for the views of the establishment.

This difference in values is one reason why the two perspectives are not complementary as some functionalists have claimed. According to Merton social reality can be explained from many points of view and he argues that various perspectives need to be combined to produce a comprehensive view. However, closer inspection of the system and action approaches reveals that in their value attitude, their views on human nature, their choice of methods and their ideas about the fundamental problems of sociology the two perspectives adopt very different and even contradictory positions.

Commentary

In his influential article 'The Two Sociologies' (*British Journal of Sociology*, Volume 21, 1970, pp.207–18), Alan Dawe argues that 'if the problem of order is the central problem for sociology, then the social-system perspective must be the sociological perspective'. However,

> Throughout the history of sociology, there has also been a manifest conflict between two types of social analysis: namely the conflict variously labelled as being between the mechanistic and organismic approaches, between atomism and holism, methodological individualism and collectivism and so on.

On this basis Dawe argues that 'sociology has been concerned not with one central problem but with two'.

David Silverman tends to agree with this. He sums up the central issues as follows:

> The systems approach tends to regard behaviour as a reflection of the characteristics of a social system containing a series of impersonal processes which are external to actors and constrain them. In emphasising that action derives from the meanings that men attach to their own and each other's acts, the action frame of reference argues that man is constrained by the way in which he socially constructs his reality. On the one hand, it seems, Society makes man, on the other, Man makes society.

(*The Theory of Organisations*, p.141)

However, the distinction between system and action is not the only distinction that could be drawn. Marxism, for example, has every right to claim that it should be regarded as a separate perspective and, more recently, conflict theory, feminism and ethnomethodology have staked a claim. Although it is not possible to give a definitive list of perspectives you should treat with caution any textbook that refers to *the* sociological perspective. The construction should be plural and not singular.

Question 42
Sociology as a whole: should it apply the logic and methods of the natural sciences?

The logic and methods of the natural sciences rest upon the assumption that natural phenomena obey universal laws which it is the task of the natural scientist to investigate. From this perspective discoveries are made by demonstrating causal relationships between objects of perception. This has meant, in practice, that scientists have had to develop a scientific language of concepts and theories. In this language concepts are the ideas used by scientists to define and measure the existence and attributes of categories of fact. Theories are the empirically confirmed relationships between the conceptually defined facts or variables. However, for scientists the important point about theories is the way they are validated. This is because through their connection with empirical data scientific theories lay claim to objectivity. In the natural sciences this claim usually rests upon systematic observation and experiments set up to determine whether the hypothetical result expected in accordance with the theory can in practice be observed or replicated. Normally experiments are carried out under controlled conditions in a laboratory and it is possible to quantify relationships more precisely and predict under what conditions or to what extent they will occur in the future. This has important practical implications because the ability to predict offers the hope of controlling natural processes and applying the results of science in the pursuit of human values.

It was because sociologists in the nineteenth century saw natural science as both a model of how to achieve valid knowledge and a means of bringing about change that they were inspired to imitate its procedures. The lead in this was taken by Auguste Comte and he is often regarded as the founder of positivism in sociology. However, ultimately the view that the logic and methods of the natural sciences can be applied to the study of human society implies that social facts and natural phenomena have the same kind of reality. This is because, from a positivist point of view, the behaviour of social actors, like that of natural events, is seen as determined by forces that can be discovered using the same objective techniques of systematic observation and controlled experiments. In practice this has come to be seen as involving, first, the objective recognition of social facts through quantitative methods and, second, the testing of hypotheses through statistical measurements of their association with other variables. Although positivists have always recognised that there were problems in ever finally proving a causal relationship by these means, they have generally attributed the failure of sociology to develop a system of laws, analogous to the laws of nature, to contingent factors such as the complexity of social reality or the ethical limitations on experimenting with humans. Further research, they believe, will enable sociology to develop into a more mature science which, through its ability to make scientific generalisations, will help society devise, agree on and implement beneficial social changes.

The clearest example of the application of positivist principles is in the work of Durkheim. His most fundamental assumption was that the sociologist should consider social facts as things. By this Durkheim meant that the sociologist should regard the general characteristics of society as the objective properties of a distinct and independent reality external to and exerting a coercive power over individuals. This reality was what Durkheim called the collective conscience and he argued that social facts such as the suicide rate or the religion of a society are as definite and substantial as natural phenomena like rocks, plants or animals. It was therefore possible to define social facts objectively, measure them empirically and, most important of all, demonstrate that there were laws of social change and cohesion which, like laws of nature, were external and waiting to be discovered by scientific means.

Although there have been various theories about how such discoveries are made the most influential of modern positivist thinkers has been Popper. He argues that the logic of scientific discovery conforms to a hypothetico-deductive model of explanation. Science does not advance by accumulating more and more facts (as was widely believed in the nineteenth century) but is, to use Popper's words, 'theory impregnated' from the beginning. By this he means that what all scientists do is test hypotheses and Popper argues that theories, both natural and social, can be provisionally accepted as scientific in so far as they survive attempts at falsification. Sociology is therefore seen by Popper as sharing essentially the same method with the natural sciences even though in practice its conclusions usually take the form of trends or probability statements rather than invariable laws.

However, Popper's argument that science advances through a process of conjecture and refutation has come in for considerable criticism. Although he correctly emphasises that facts do not speak for themselves and that all scientific research involves the scientist in taking a perspective, it is precisely the question of the point of view of the natural and social sciences that is at the heart of the problem of whether a natural scientific approach is applicable in sociology. This is because in the study of nature there is only one point of view that scientists can take. They are logically bound to accept the principle of determinism since it is only in terms of this assumption that they have a criterion for recognising which facts are relevant to the testing of any particular hypothesis. However, in the study of social action there is the possibility of changing points of view. For, in addition to observing action from the outside in terms of its consequences or effects, the sociologist can seek to understand it from the inside in terms of the meanings and motives of the social actors involved.

It is this fundamental difference between natural and cultural phenomena which is at the root of all criticisms of positivism. For example, in relation to Durkheim critics have argued that social facts cannot be treated as things because unlike natural events, which are governed by universal laws, social action depends upon the conscious choices and decisions of individuals. Giddens has pointed out that this means we reify society if, along with Durkheim, we regard it as a 'pre-given universe of objects'. This is because, unlike the natural world, human society is a reality that is created and sustained by the shared meanings of social actors. This is important for explanation because it means that the cause of social events cannot be directly attributed to external factors but must instead be sought in the values of social actors committed to a particular course of action.

It is because meaningful action is orientated in terms of values that sociologists must begin by analysing it not as a cause-effect but as a means-end relationship. However, this difference in the logical structure of explanation in the natural and the social sciences also has implications for methodology. This is because unlike natural phenomena which can be directly or indirectly observed social facts have a subjective element which can only be understood. For example, a death only becomes a suicide when others attribute this meaning to it and a belief is only of genuine religious significance from the point of view of the faithful. In both cases, therefore, what is essential about such phenomena is not their external characteristics but the particular values upon which their subjective significance depends. Any attempt to define social phenomena such as suicide or religion objectively is thus simply irrelevant to the task of making sense of social and historical action.

The realisation that sociology had to develop new tools of analysis as a means to comprehend the point of view of social actors led Weber to propose the analysis of social phenomena in terms of ideal types. An ideal type is a very different kind of concept from that found in the natural sciences because its role is not to define and measure the extent of a social fact objectively but to make explicit its subjective and historical meaning. In contrast to natural scientific concepts that describe what various individual phenomena have in common as a means of formulating general laws, Weber argued that sociology required individual constructs in order to analyse unique historical relationships such as that between Protestantism and modern capitalism.

Although Weber's attempt to construct for sociology a determinate qualitative methodology founded upon the value relevance of cultural phenomena raises many problems, his work is still the basis of the interpretive critique of positivism. In practice one of the most important consequences of Weber's influence is that many sociologists have abandoned quantitative methods like the use of official statistics and questionnaires. They argue that such techniques distort social reality by imposing an arbitrary definition that rests upon the point of view of officials or sociologists when what is needed is an authentic definition that takes the point of view of the social actors themselves. This is often taken to mean that sociologists should develop strategies to help them empathise with those they study and phenomenologists in particular have stressed the usefulness of qualitative methods like informal interviews and participant observation. Whether these methods can be called scientific is still an open question. However, what is clear is that sociologists face different kinds of problems from the natural sciences and are not therefore bound to follow their example.

Commentary

Many of the commentaries to previous essays develop points that you could use to go beyond my account and produce a more sophisticated answer. However, in this essay additional points of this sort are included in the answer itself.

Bibliography

Abel-Smith, B. and Townsend, P. *The Poor and the Poorest* (G. Bell and Sons, London, 1965)

Althusser, L. *Lenin and Philosophy and other essays*, second edition (New Left Books, London, 1977)

Anderson, M. (ed.) *Sociology of the Family* (Penguin Books, Harmondsworth, 1971)

Atkinson, J.M. 'Societal Reactions to Suicide: the Role of Coroners' Definitions' in Cohen (1971)

Atkinson, J.M. *Discovering Suicide* (Macmillan, London, 1978)

Ball, S. *Beachside Comprehensive* (Cambridge University Press, Cambridge, 1981)

Banks, J.A. *Prosperity and Parenthood: a Study of Family Planning among the Victorian Middle Classes* (Routledge and Kegan Paul, London, 1954)

Banks, O. *The Sociology of Education*, third edition (Batsford, London, 1976)

Baran, P.A. and Sweezy, P.M. *Monopoly Capital* (Penguin Books, Harmondsworth, 1968)

Barber, B. 'Some Problems in the Sociology of Professions', *Daedalus*, volume 92, no. 4 (1963)

Barrett, M. and McIntosh, M. *The Anti-Social Family* (Verso, London, 1982)

Becker, H. 'Whose side are we on?', *Social Problems*, volume 14 (Winter, 1967)

Becker, H. *Outsiders*, enlarged edition (The Free Press, New York, 1973)

Becker, H. 'Social class variations in the teacher-pupil relationship' in *School and Society*, second edition, edited by Cosin, B.R., Dale, I.R., Esland, G.M., Mackinnon, D. and Swift, D.F. (Routledge and Kegan Paul, London, 1977)

Bell, C.R. *Middle Class Families* (Routledge and Kegan Paul, London, 1968)

Bell, C.R. and Newby, H. *Doing Sociological Research* (Allen and Unwin, London, 1977)

Benyon, H. *Working for Ford* (E.P. Publishing Ltd, Wakefield, 1975)

Bernard, J. *The Future of Marriage* (Penguin Books, Harmondsworth, 1976)

Bernstein, B. *Class, Codes and Control*, volume 1, *Theoretical Studies towards a Sociology of Language*, second edition (Routledge and Kegan Paul, London, 1974)

Bernstein, B. 'Education cannot Compensate for Society' in Cosin et al. (1977)

Blau, P.M. and Meyer, M.W. *Bureaucracy in Modern Society*, second edition (Random House, New York, 1971)

Blauner, R. *Alienation and Freedom* (University of Chicago Press, Chicago, 1963)

Blumer, H. *Symbolic Interaction: Perspective and Method* (Prentice Hall, Englewood Cliffs, 1969)

Bott, E. *Family and Social Network*, second edition (Tavistock, London, 1971)

Bourdieu, P. and Passeron, J. *Reproduction in Education, Society and Culture* (Sage Publications, London, 1977)

Bowlby, J. *Child Care and the Growth of Love*, second edition (Penguin Books, Harmondsworth, 1965)

Bowles, S and Gintis, H. *Schooling in Capitalist America* (Routledge and Kegan Paul, London, 1976)

Braverman, H. *Labour and Monopoly Capital* (Monthly Review Press, New York, 1974)

Budd, S. *Sociologists and Religion* (Collier-Macmillan, London, 1973)

Bukharin, N. and Preobrazhensky, E. *The ABC of Communism* (Penguin Books, Harmondsworth, 1969)

Burns, T. and Stalker, G.M. *The Management of Innovation,* second edition (Tavistock, London, 1966)

Byrne, E. *Women and Education* (Tavistock, London, 1978)

Central Policy Review Staff and Central Statistical Office, *People and their Families* (HMSO, London, 1980)

Chinoy, E. *Sociological Perspective: Basic Concepts and their Application* (Random House, New York, 1954)

Cloward, R.A. and Ohlin, L.E. *Delinquency and Opportunity* (The Free Press, New York, 1961)

Cohen, P.S. *Modern Social Theory* (Heinemann, London, 1968)

Cohen, S. (ed.) *Images of Deviance* (Penguin Books, Harmondsworth, 1971)

Cohen, S. *Folk Devils and Moral Panics* (MacGibbon and Kee, London, 1972)

Cohen, S. and Taylor, L. *Psychological Survival: the Experience of Long-Term Imprisonment* (Penguin Books, Harmondsworth, 1972)

Cohen, S. and Young, J. (eds) *The Manufacture of News* (Constable, London, 1973)

Cooper, D. *The Death of the Family* (Penguin Books, Harmondsworth, 1972)

Coser, L.A. and Rosenberg, B. (eds) *Sociological Theory: a Book of Readings,* third edition (Macmillan, New York, 1969)

Dahrendorf, R. 'Out of Utopia', *American Journal of Sociology,* volume 64, no. 2 (1957)

Dahrendorf, R. *Class and Class Conflict in an Industrial Society* (Routledge and Kegan Paul, London, 1959)

Davis, K. *Human Society* (Macmillan, New York, 1948)

Davis, K. 'The Myth of Functional Analysis as a Special Method in Sociology and Anthropology', *American Sociological Review,* volume 24 (December, 1959)

Davis, K. and Moore, W.E. 'Some Principles of Stratification', *American Sociological Review,* volume 10, no. 2 (1945)

Dawe, A. 'The Two Sociologies', *British Journal of Sociology,* volume 21 (1970)

Deem, R. *Women and Schooling* (Routledge and Kegan Paul, London, 1978)

Delamont, S. *The Sociology of Women* (Allen and Unwin, London, 1980)

Demerath, N.J. III, and Peterson, R.A. (eds) *System, Change and Conflict* (The Free Press, New York, 1967)

Douglas, J.D. *The Social Meanings of Suicide* (Princeton University Press, Princeton, 1967)

Douglas, J.D. 'The Meaning we give to Suicide' in *Society Today,* no. 4, *New Society* (19 November, 1976)

Douglas, J.D. (ed) *Introduction to the Sociologies of Everyday Life* (Allyn and Bacon, Boston, 1980)

Douglas, J.W.B. *The Home and the School* (MacGibbon and Kee, London, 1964)

Durkheim, E. *The Division of Labour in Society* (The Free Press, New York, 1964)

Durkheim, E. *The Rules of Sociological Method* (The Free Press, New York, 1964)

Durkheim, E. *Suicide: a Study in Sociology* (Routledge and Kegan Paul, London, 1970)

Durkheim, E. *The Elementary Forms of the Religious Life* (Allen and Unwin, London, 1976)

Edgell, S. *Middle Class Couples: a Study of Segregation, Domination and Inequality in Marriage* (Allen and Unwin, London, 1980)

Engels, F. *The Condition of the Working Class in England* (Panther Books, St Albans, 1969)

Field, F. *Inequality in Britain: Freedom, Welfare and the State* (Fontana, Glasgow, 1981)
Fletcher, R. *The Family and Marriage in Britain*, revised edition (Penguin Books, Harmondsworth, 1966)
Forcese, D.P. and Richer, S. *Social Research Methods* (Prentice-Hall, Englewood Cliffs, 1973)
Ford, J. *Social Class and the Comprehensive School* (Routledge and Kegan Paul, London, 1969)

Gallie, D. *In Search of the New Working Class* (Cambridge University Press, Cambridge, 1978)
Garfinkel, H. *Studies in Ethnomethodology* (Prentice-Hall, Englewood Cliffs, 1967)
Gavron, H. *The Captive Wife: Conflicts of Housebound Mothers* (Penguin Books, Harmondsworth, 1968)
Gerth, H.H. and Mills, C.W. (eds) *From Max Weber: Essays in Sociology* (Routledge and Kegan Paul, London, 1948)
Giddens, A. *New Rules of Sociological Method: a Positive Critique of Interpretative Sociologies* (Hutchinson, London, 1976)
Glasgow University Media Group, *Bad News* (Routledge and Kegan Paul, London, 1976)
Glasner, P. *The Sociology of Secularisation* (Routledge and Kegan Paul, London, 1977)
Glass, D.V. *Social Mobility in Britain* (Routledge and Kegan Paul, London, 1954)
Goffman, E. *Stigma: Notes on the Management of Spoiled Identity* (Penguin Books, Harmondsworth, 1968)
Goffman, E. *The Presentation of Self in Everyday Life* (Penguin Books, Harmondsworth, 1969)
Goffman, E. *Asylums* (Penguin Books, Harmondsworth, 1970)
Goldthorpe, J.H., Lockwood, D., Bechhofer, F. and Platt, J. *The Affluent Worker: Industrial Attitudes and Behaviour* (Cambridge University Press, Cambridge, 1968)
Goldthorpe, J.H., et al. *The Affluent Worker: Political Attitudes and Behaviour* (Cambridge University Press, Cambridge, 1968)
Goldthorpe, J.H., et al. *The Affluent Worker in the Class Structure* (Cambridge University Press, Cambridge, 1969)
Gouldner, A.W. *Patterns of Industrial Bureaucracy* (The Free Press, New York, 1954)
Gouldner, A.W. *Wildcat Strike* (Routledge and Kegan Paul, London, 1957)
Gouldner, A.W. *For Sociology* (Penguin Books, Harmondsworth, 1975)

Halsey, A.H. *Change in British Society* (Oxford University Press, Oxford, 1978)
Hargreaves, D. *Social Relations in a Secondary School* (Routledge and Kegan Paul, London, 1967)
Hawthorn, G. *The Sociology of Fertility* (Collier-Macmillan, London, 1970)
Heath, A. *Social Mobility* (Fontana, Glasgow, 1981)
Hebdige, D. *Subculture: the Meaning of Style* (Methuen, London, 1979)
Herberg, W. *Protestant-Catholic-Jew*, revised edition (Anchor Books, New York, 1960)
Hill, M. *A Sociology of Religion* (Heinemann, London, 1973)
Hindess, B. *The Use of Official Statistics in Sociology: a Critique of Positivism and Ethnomethodology* (Macmillan, London, 1973)
Hurd, G., et al. *Human Societies: an Introduction to Sociology* (Routledge and Kegan Paul, London, 1973)
Hyman, R. *Strikes*, revised edition (Fontana/Collins, Glasgow, 1977)

Illich, I. *Medical Nemesis* (Calder and Boyars, London, 1975)

Inkeles, A. *What is Sociology? an Introduction to the Discipline and Profession* (Prentice-Hall, Englewood Cliffs, 1964)

Jackson, B. and Marsden, D. *Education and the Working Class* (Penguin Books, Harmondsworth, 1969)

Johnson, T.J. *Professions and Power* (Macmillan, London, 1972)

Jones, R.K. and Jones, P.A. *Sociology in Medicine* (The English Universities Press, London, 1975)

Katz, E. and Lazarsfield, P.F. *Personal Influence* (The Free Press, New York, 1955)

Kelsall, R.K., Poole, A., Kuhn, A. *Graduates: the Sociology of an Elite* (Methuen, London, 1972)

Kerr, C. and Siegel, A. 'The Inter-Industry Propensity to Strike' in *Industrial Conflict* edited by Kornhauser, A., Dubin, R. and Ross, A.M. (McGraw-Hill, New York, 1954)

Kincaid, J.C. *Poverty and Equality in Britain: a Study of Social Security and Taxation*, revised edition (Penguin Books, Harmondsworth, 1975)

Kuhn, J.W. *Bargaining in Grievance Settlement* (Columbia University Press, New York, 1961)

Labov, W. 'The Logic of Nonstandard English' in *Tinker, Tailor . . . the Myth of Cultural Deprivation* edited by N. Keddie (Penguin Books, Harmondsworth, 1973)

Lacey, C. *Hightown Grammar* (Manchester University Press, Manchester, 1970)

Laing, R.D. *The Politics of Experience and the Bird of Paradise* (Penguin Books, Harmondsworth, 1967)

Lambert, J. 'The Police Can Choose' in *Society Today*, no. 5, *New Society* (3 December, 1976)

Lane, D. *The Socialist Industrial State: towards a Political Sociology of State Socialism* (Allen and Unwin, London, 1976)

La Piere, R. 'Attitudes vs. Actions' in 1. Deutscher, *What We Say/What We Do* (Scott, Foresman, Glenview, 1973)

Laslett, P. 'In an ageing world', *New Society* (27 October, 1977)

Lazarsfield, P.F., Berelson, G. and Gaudet, H., *The People's Choice* (Duell, Sloan and Pearce, New York, 1944

Leach, E.R. *A Runaway World?* (BBC Publications, London, 1967)

Lemert, E.M. *Human Deviance, Social Problems and Social Control*, second edition (Prentice-Hall, Englewood Cliffs, 1972)

Lewis, O. *La Vida* (Panther Books, London, 1968)

Liebow, E. *Tally's Corner* (Little Brown, Boston, 1967)

Lockwood, D. *The Blackcoated Worker* (Allen and Unwin, London, 1958)

Lockwood, D. 'Some Remarks on *The Social System*' in Demerath and Peterson (1967)

Lorenz, K. *On Aggression* (Methuen, London, 1966)

MacIver, R.M. and Page, C.H. *Society: an Introductory Analysis* (Macmillan, London, 1950)

MacRae, D.G. *Weber* (Fontana/Collins, London, 1974)

Malinowski, B. *Magic, Science and Religion and Other Essays* (Anchor Books, New York, 1954)

Martin, D. *A Sociology of English Religion* (Heinemann, London, 1967)

Martin, D. *The Religious and the Secular* (Routledge and Kegan Paul, London, 1969)

Marx, K. *The Holy Family, or Critique of Critical Criticism* (Lawrence and Wishart, London, 1957)

Marx, K. *Critique of the Gotha Programme*, second revised edition (Progress Publishers, Moscow, 1960)

Marx, K. *Capital* (Progress Publishers, Moscow, 1965)

Marx, K. *Economic and Philosophical Manuscripts of 1844* edited by Struik, D.J. (Lawrence and Wishart, London, 1970)

Marx, K. *Early Writings* (Penguin Books, Harmondsworth, 1975)

Marx, K. and Engels, F. *Manifesto of the Communist Party* (Progress Publishers, Moscow, 1969)

Marx, K. and Engels, F. *The German Ideology* edited by Arthur, C.J. (Lawrence and Wishart, London, 1970)

Mead, M. *Male and Female* (Penguin Books, Harmondsworth, 1962)

Merton, R.K. 'Manifest and Latent Functions' in Demerath and Peterson (1967)

Merton, R.K. 'Social Structure and Anomie' in Coser and Rosenberg (1969)

Merton, R.K. 'Bureaucratic Structure and Personality' in Coser and Rosenberg (1969)

Merton, R.K. and Nisbet, R. (eds) *Contemporary Social Problems*, fourth edition (Harcourt Brace Jovanovich, New York, 1976)

Michels, R. *Political Parties* (The Free Press, New York, 1949)

Miliband, R. *The State in Capitalist Society* (Weidenfeld and Nicolson, London, 1969)

Miliband, R. *Marxism and Politics* (Oxford University Press, Oxford, 1977)

Mills, C.W. *The Sociological Imagination* (Penguin Books, Harmondsworth, 1970)

Morgan, D.H.J. *Social Theory and the Family* (Routledge and Kegan Paul, London, 1975)

Newson, J. and Newson E. *Patterns of Infant Care in an Urban Community* (Penguin Books, Harmondsworth, 1965)

Newson, J. and Newson, E. *Seven Years Old in the Home Environment* (Allen and Unwin, London, 1976)

Niebuhr, H.R. *The Social Sources of Denominationalism* (The World Publishing Company, New York, 1929)

Oakley, A. *Housewife*, (Penguin Books, Harmondsworth, 1976)

Oakley, A 'What makes girls differ from boys?', *New Society* (21 December, 1978)

Ortner, S.B. 'Is Female to Male as Nature is to Culture?' in *Woman, Culture and Society* edited by Rosaldo, M.Z. and Lamphere, L. (Stanford University Press, Stanford, 1974)

Parkin, F. *Class Inequality and Political Order: Social Stratification in Capitalist and Communist Societies* (Paladin, St Albans, 1972)

Parsons, T. *Essays in Sociological Theory* (The Free Press, New York, 1949)

Parsons, T. *The Social System* (The Free Press, New York, 1951)

Parsons, T. *The Structure of Social Action* (The Free Press, New York, 1968)

Phillips, D. *Abandoning Method* (Jossey-Bass, San Francisco, 1973)

Plant, M. *Drugtakers in an English Town* (Tavistock, London, 1975)

Popper, K.R. *The Poverty of Historicism* (Routledge and Kegan Paul, London, 1961)

Popper, K.R. *The Open Society and its Enemies*, fifth edition (Routledge and Kegan Paul, London, 1966)

Popper, K.R. *Conjectures and Refutations* (Routledge and Kegan Paul, London, 1972)

Pryce, K. *Endless Pressure* (Penguin Books, Harmondsworth, 1979)

Rex, J. 'Review of *Class and Class Conflict in an Industrial Society*', *New Left Review*, no. 2 (1960)

Rex, J. *Key Problems in Sociological Theory* (Routledge and Kegan Paul, London, 1961)

Rex, J. and Moore, R. *Race, Community, and Conflict: a Study of Sparkbrook* (Oxford University Press, London, 1967)

Roberts, K., Cook, F.G., Clark, S.C. and Semeonoff, E. *The Fragmentary Class Structure* (Heinemann, London, 1977)

Robertson, R. *The Sociological Interpretation of Religion* (Blackwell, Oxford, 1970)

Robertson, R. 'Religion' in *Society Today*, no. 23, *New Society* (16 December, 1977)

Rosenfeld, E. 'Social Stratification in a "Classless" Society' in *Social Stratification: a Reader*, edited by Lopreato, J. and Lewis, L.S. (Harper and Row, New York, 1974)

Rosenthal, R. and Jacobson, L. *Pygmalion in the Classroom* (Holt, Rinehart and Winston, New York, 1968)

Rosser, R. and Harris, C. *The Family and Social Change* (Routledge and Kegan Paul, London, 1965)

Russell, B. *Marriage and Morals* (Allen and Unwin, London, 1932)

Schofield, M. *The Sexual Behaviour of Young People* (Penguin Books, Harmondsworth, 1968)

Sharpe, S. *Just Like a Girl: how Girls Learn to be Women* (Penguin Books, Harmondsworth, 1976)

Silverman, D. *The Theory of Organisations* (Heinemann, London, 1970)

Stacey, M. *Tradition and Change: a Study of Banbury* (Oxford University Press, Oxford, 1960)

Taylor, F.W. *Scientific Management* (Harper and Row, New York, 1947)

Taylor, I. *Soccer Consciousness and Soccer Hooliganism* in Cohen (1971)

Taylor, I., Walton, P. and Young, J. *The New Criminology* (Routledge and Kegan Paul, London, 1973)

Taylor, L. *Deviance and Society* (Michael Joseph, London, 1971)

Tiger, L. and Fox, R. *The Imperial Animal* (Secker and Warburg, London, 1972)

Timasheff, N.S. *Sociological Theory: its Nature and Growth*, revised edition (Random House, New York, 1957)

Titmuss, R.M. *Essays on 'The Welfare State'*, second edition (Allen and Unwin, London, 1963)

Townsend, P. *The Family Life of Old People* (Penguin Books, Harmondsworth, 1963)

Townsend, P. *Poverty in the United Kingdom* (Penguin Books, Harmondsworth, 1979)

Troeltsch, E. *The Social Teaching of the Christian Churches* (Allen and Unwin, London, 1931)

Tumin, M.M. *Some Principles of Stratification: a Critical Analysis* in Coser and Rosenberg (1969)

Tunstall, J. *The Fishermen* (MacGibbon and Kee, London, 1962)

Tyler, W. *The Sociology of Educational Inequality* (Methuen, London, 1977)

Warner, M. 'Decision Making in Network TV News' in *Media Sociology* edited by J. Tunstall (Constable, London, 1970)

Weber, M. *The Protestant Ethic and the Spirit of Capitalism* (Allen and Unwin, London, 1930)

Weber, M. *The Methodology of the Social Sciences* (The Free Press, New York, 1949)

Weber, M. *The Theory of Social and Economic Organisation* (The Free Press, New York, 1964)

Weber, M. *Roscher and Knies: the Logical Problem of Historical Economics* (The Free Press, New York, 1975)

Wedderburn, D. 'Workplace Inequality', *New Society* (9 April, 1970)

Wedderburn, D. 'Old People in Britain' in *Social Problems of Modern Britain*, edited by E. Butterworth and D. Weir (Fontana/Collins, Glasgow, 1972)

Wedderburn, D. and Crompton, R. *Workers' Attitudes and Technology* (Cambridge University

Press, Cambridge, 1972)

Wedge, P. and Prosser, H. *Born to Fail?* (Arrow Books, London, 1973)

Westergaard, J. and Resler, H. *Class in a Capitalist Society* (Penguin Books, Harmondsworth, 1976)

Whyte, W.F. *Street Corner Society*, second edition (University of Chicago Press, Chicago, 1955)

Willmott, P. and Young, M. *Family and Class in a London Suburb* (Nel Mentor, London, 1967)

Wilson, B. 'How Religious Are We?', *New Society* (27 October, 1977)

Winston, B. *Dangling Conversations*, Book 1, *The Image of the Media* (Davis-Poynter, London, 1973)

Worsley, P. *The Trumpet Shall Sound*, second edition (MacGibbon and Kee, London, 1968)

Wrong, D. 'The Oversocialised Conception of Man in Modern Sociology,' *American Sociological Review*, volume 26 (1961)

Yablonsky, L. *The Violent Gang* (Penguin Books, Harmondsworth, 1967)

Young, J. *The Drugtakers: the Social Meaning of Drug Use* (Paladin, St Albans, 1971)

Young, J. *The Role of the Police as Amplifiers of Deviancy* in Cohen (1971)

Young, M. and Willmott, P. *Family and Kinship in East London* (Penguin Books, Harmondsworth, 1962)

Young, M. and Willmott, P. *The Symmetrical Family* (Penguin Books, Harmondsworth, 1975)

Young, M.F.D. *Knowledge and Control* (Collier-Macmillan, London, 1971)

Zweig, F. *The Worker in an Affluent Society* (Heinemann, London, 1961)

Name index

Subject index